France since 1800

France since 1800

Squaring the Hexagon

D. L. L. Parry
Pierre Girard

OXFORD
UNIVERSITY PRESS

Great Clarendon Street, Oxford OX2 6DP

Oxford University Press is a department of the University of Oxford.
It furthers the University's objective of excellence in research, scholarship,
and education by publishing worldwide in

Oxford New York

Auckland Bangkok Buenos Aires Cape Town Chennai
Dar es Salaam Delhi Hong Kong Istanbul Karachi Kolkata
Kuala Lumpur Madrid Melbourne Mexico City Mumbai Nairobi
São Paulo Shanghai Taipei Tokyo Toronto

Oxford is a registered trade mark of Oxford University Press
in the UK and in certain other countries

Published in the United States
by Oxford University Press Inc., New York

British Library Cataloguing in Publication Data
Data available

Library of Congress Cataloging in Publication Data
Data available

ISBN 0–19–925229–7

1 3 5 7 9 10 8 6 4 2

Typeset in Minion
by RefineCatch Limited, Bungay, Suffolk
Printed in Great Britain by
Biddles Ltd., Guildford and King's Lynn

For Jane, John, and Anna
D. L. L. P.

A Sophie Combes
Pour Alexandre, Simon, et Maxime
P. G.

Acknowledgements

One of the pleasures of completing this book is to be able to thank family, friends, and colleagues who have made it possible. My parents, Christopher and Margaret Parry, come first, for everything they have done. A great many professional colleagues have contributed their ideas and enthusiasm, for which I have been grateful. I should like to thank Robert Tombs and Geoffrey Ellis in particular, for all their support and for reading the chapters on the nineteenth century with their exemplary attention to detail—any remaining errors are of course mine. I am most grateful for the encouragement and generosity that I have received over the years from Christopher Andrew, Jonathan Steinberg, Roy Foster, and Toby Barnard. My visits to France have been made all the more enjoyable by the hospitality I have received there, especially from Fabrice and Isabelle Hugot, Lynn Goodfellow, and all the Girard family. Back in Britain, this book could certainly not have been completed without the help of Robin, Jean, and Kate Catchpole. Above all, my thanks go to Jane, for her patience, advice, and encouragement.

D. L. L. P.

Thanks to my mother, Babette, and to my father, who introduced me to history; to my mentors, Serge Berstein and Antoine Prost; to my colleagues and friends Philippe Levallois, Yves Souteyrand, Bernadette Vinatier, Jean-Christophe Haglund, Jean-Paul Huvelin, Gilles Martin, and Eric Nadaud for the interest they take in my work; to Nathalie Leca and Gerard Buret for their advice on translation; to the Moynihan family for introducing me to England decades ago; special thanks to my students of the Orléans Khâgne: Nicolas, Marion, Clémence, Madeleine, Erwan, Elodie, Cécile, Thomas, Matthieu, Kevin, Fanny, Claire, Stéphane, Emilie, Lucie, Nina, Sylvain, Olivier, and to Sophie for her daily interest, reading, and sound advice.

P. G.

Contents

List of illustrations   xi
List of abbreviations   xii

Introduction   1

1   The new regime: 1800–1824   7
    'Domination personified'   7
    Return of the Bourbons   24
    The legacy of revolution and empire   27

2   Charles X to Marshal MacMahon: 1824–1877   34
    Social and economic life in the nineteenth century   35
    Revolutions, constitutions, and political life   52

3   Republic, state, and nation confront the Father, Son,
    and Holy Ghost: 1877–1914   73
    The triumph of the republic, 1879–1885   74
    The new democracy   79
    'How beautiful the republic was under the empire'   82
    The new empire   86
    Protectionism and the *Ralliement*, 1890–1898   89
    The Dreyfus Affair: citizenship and nationality   92
    The limits of republican solidarity, 1905–1914   101
    Women and feminism   106
    The bicycle and the cobbler   110
    The outbreak of the Great War   113

4   The stranglehold of the Great Patriotic War: 1914–1926   116
    The *Union sacrée*   116

From the *Union sacrée* to the *Union nationale*   128
The return of the left: the *Cartel des gauches*   135
Mourning   140
The war veterans   142
Economic progress and social anxiety   144
Conclusion   151

5   **Disaster and renewal: 1926–1958**   152

The economic crisis of the 1920s and 1930s   153
The crisis of the political system, 1926–1935   159
The Popular Front   163
The fall of France   171
Vichy: the French State in a spa town   174
The Fourth Republic, 1944–1958   185
The crisis of French power   194
Conclusion   200

6   **A new republic, a new France: 1958–2002**   202

A new regime   203
The many faces of the Fifth Republic   207
Economic modernization and social transformation   225
The politics of grandeur   238

Conclusion   246

The normalization of France?   246
Today . . . and tomorrow?   253

Chronology   262
Guide to further reading   273
Index   277

List of illustrations

Figures

1.1 Population, births, and deaths, 1790–1913   29

1.2 Birth and death rates, 1790–1913   29

Tables

2.1 The industrialization of France and its peers   47

2.2 The compound annual growth rates of the major
     European economies   48

C.1 Distribution of the workforce by size of enterprise, 1996/7   251

Maps

3.1 Catholic observance in France, 1877   100

5.1 The occupation and liberation of France   175

6.1 Changes in the social geography of France since the 1960s   229

List of abbreviations

ARAC	Association Républicaine des Anciens Combattants
CFDT	Confédération Française Démocratique du Travail
CFLN	Comité Français de Libération Nationale
CFTC	Confédération Française des Travailleurs Chrétiens
CGPF	Confédération Générale de la Production Française
CGT	Confédération Générale du Travail
CNPF	Conseil National du Patronat Français
CNR	Conseil National de la Résistance
DATAR	Délégation à l'Aménagement du Territoire
EDC	European Defence Community
ENA	École Nationale d'Administration
EMS	European Monetary System
ERM	Exchange Rate Mechanism
FLN	Front de Libération Nationale
MRP	Mouvement Républicain Populaire
OAS	Organisation Armée Secrète
PACS	Pacte Civil de Solidarité
PC	Parti Communiste
PMF	Pierre Mendès France
PS	Parti Socialiste
PSF	Parti Social Français
PSU	Parti Socialiste Unifié
RPF	Rassemblement du Peuple Français
RPR	Rassemblement pour la République
SFIO	Section Française de l'Internationale Ouvrière
SNCF	Société Nationale des Chemins de Fer Français
UDF	Union pour la Démocratie Française
UDR	Union des Démocrates pour la République
UDSR	Union Démocratique et Socialiste de la Résistance
UMP	Union pour la Majorité Présidentielle
UNEF	Union Nationale des Étudiants de France
UNR	Union pour la Nouvelle République

Introduction

Squaring the Hexagon

It took France just over a thousand years to take its present shape, from the end of Charlemagne's empire to the heyday of Napoleon III. Its boundaries gave it the shape of a hexagon, which has since become a nickname for the country. Yet creating the Hexagon was only half the battle: the other half is uniting it. A thousand years of history laid on top of geographical variety has produced tremendous diversity within the Hexagon, with the result that it can be cut up in myriad ways, from the ancient north/south divide between the France of butter and the France of olive oil to the present east/west divide between supporters of Jean-Marie Le Pen and of his opponents. Since the French Revolution began in 1789, no fewer than a dozen regimes have tried to rule the country before being swept away by war, revolution, or *coup d'état*: the Convention, Directory, Consulate, First Empire, Bourbon monarchy, Orléanist monarchy, Second Republic, Second Empire, Third Republic, Fourth Republic, French State, and Fifth Republic (not counting provisional governments). Each political regime was tangled up with a mass of other divisions, social, religious, economic, and anthropological. Squaring the Hexagon—getting France to live in peace with itself—may be as impossible as squaring the circle.

Asterix and the Big Mac

Even when an event rallies the country around a common cause, it can hide a mass of contradictions. One of the most popular icons of France, both at home and abroad, is Asterix the Gaul. This plucky little man with a big moustache defended his village against invasion by the most powerful state in the world with courage, humour, and plenty of good food. A little more than two thousand years later, the French press hailed a new Asterix in the shape of José Bové, a moustachioed farmer from the Larzac plateau in the south-west of the country who took on today's superpower by attacking one of its best-known symbols, a McDonald's restaurant. For many of Bové's supporters, this was simultaneously an attack on American power and on junk food, because it was triggered by a trade dispute between the European Union and the USA. The EU had blocked imports of hormonally treated beef from America on health grounds, and when it refused to change its policy after the World Trade Organization rejected this complaint, the USA imposed punitive tariffs on selected EU goods including Roquefort, one of the finest of French cheeses. In protest, Bové and some friends ransacked the building site of a new McDonald's restaurant in August 1999.

Yet this is not a simple story of Roquefort against the cheeseburger. For a start, this defence of the countryside is being led by ecologists rather than farmers. Bové himself is not fighting for the traditions of his native village, for he is the son of a professor of biology who moved to the Larzac plateau in the 1970s during one of France's first 'green' protests. This was sparked by plans to extend a military base there, pitting sheep against cannons (the sheep won). Bové has also destroyed genetically modified crops to protect the environment, whereas the main farming union supports GM crops. This union represents large farmers primarily, who have turned farming into one of France's most valuable export industries. Bové is a leader of the opposing Confédération Paysanne union that represents small farmers. The term *paysan* is now so laden with nostalgic values that Jacques Chirac has even claimed that 'we are all *paysans*' in France. In fact, only 2 per cent of the population now works on the land, none of whom subsists in the poverty of the nineteenth-century peasant. (In his autobiography, one small farmer from the first half of the twentieth century was happy to call himself a *paysan* but carefully termed his son, a farmer of the second half, a *cultivateur*.)[1] The reality of rural France is depopulation and even abandonment.

Responses to Bové's protest throw up contradictions in France's

---

[1] E. Grenadou and A. Prévost, *Grenadou, paysan français* (Paris, 1966). *Paysan* translates as 'peasant' in the strict context of a small, family-owned farm not far from subsistence farming; its broader meaning is 'countryman'. *Cultivateur* means a small farmer—large farms are run by *fermiers*.

attitudes to the rest of the world as well as to its own countryside. McDonald's is attacked by commentators for making mass-produced, industrialized food eaten on the move, the antithesis of traditional French cooking, which uses local recipes and ingredients and which is eaten among family or friends. Yet if McDonald's is building new restaurants in France it is because plenty of people buy its food—and they are not all American tourists. This is one of the many ways that France is simultaneously pro- and anti-American: condemning American culture while tens of millions watch its films; keeping at arm's length from NATO while sheltering under its protection; criticizing globalization while benefiting massively from trade in agriculture and industry. Any debate around farming also raises contradictions around the EU. The EU has been a tremendous boon to France by funding its farmers through the Common Agricultural Policy (CAP), by tying West Germany into partnership instead of conflict, and by amplifying French policy as European policy. These gains are being overshadowed as France's voice has become one among many in the expanding EU, and as regulations constrain it. The true test will come when thorough reforms to the CAP are finally made, though Chirac has successfully removed these from the EU's agenda till 2006.

The case also highlights two distinctive features of French social and political life. One is the use of violence in political protests. Bové's attacks on McDonald's and on GM crops have been extremely mild in comparison either to the mass demonstrations that are commonly organized or to the threats of damage made by specific groups. The last time a massive wave of strikes and protests brought much of the country to a halt was in 1995, against reforms proposed by the government of Alain Juppé; since then specific groups have often taken to the streets in demonstration, even the police and gendarmerie. The most outrageous protests are no more than blackmail: in 2000, 150 workers made redundant from a factory in Givet in the Ardennes occupied their factory and threatened to blow it up. The incentive for such protesters is that they nearly always succeed in extorting concessions from the government. The nineteenth century's cycle of revolutions may be over, but the strikes of 1968 and 1995 showed that the French state may not be so robust. Revolutions in France have often occurred when there was a political crisis on top of a disjuncture between society and the political regime in force, and the elections of 2002 have shown that France may once again be entering such a condition. Fragility of the central state matters because it holds more power in France than in most other western countries, and much more than in federal states such as Germany and the USA.

The second distinctive feature is that of French attitudes to foreigners and immigration. France has long been a haven and an inspiration to foreigners, whether as tourists, artists, students, or political refugees. Its need for labour sucked in millions of foreign workers over the past two centuries, mostly from elsewhere in Europe but also from across the world, especially from its empire and now ex-empire. As part of the European Union, its borders are today completely open to fellow citizens of the EU. Immigration has also been met by suspicion, xenophobia, and racism, none of which is unique to France. Where it differs is in the state's attitude towards the behaviour of its immigrants. The French Revolution based its new regime on the notion of citizenship, which could be acquired by immigrants who adopted its principles and duties. The French state was thus blind to ethnic origins, and this was reinforced in 1889 when nationality became based on residence (as in the USA), not parentage (as in Germany). The new republic described itself as *une et indivisible*, one and indivisible. This principle underlay the development of the centralized state—and it also put an obligation on its citizens to become uniform. If immigrants were to become citizens, they must assimilate and dissolve within the French community; multiculturalism was not an option. The sensitivity of this became even more acute through another legacy of the Revolution, its rift with the Catholic church. This was settled for a hundred years by Napoleon, until the formal separation of church and state took place in 1905, when religious practices were excluded from the public sphere. Since the French nation is not defined by blood or birth, it is not inherently racist, but the French state is most certainly secular, and this principle has produced conflicts between the state and the Muslim population. In practice, the ideal of assimilation is no longer adequate, and multiculturalism is the reality in many major cities. Some aspects of this have been happily accepted either by the mass of the population (such as couscous) or by the state itself (sponsor of the gleaming Institut du Monde Arabe in Paris). Muslims worship without difficulty in the same way as Catholics, Protestants, and Jews, keeping religious practice within the private sphere. Other aspects have not been accepted, producing resentment amongst French people who want immigrants to return home, and amongst immigrants who are excluded from mainstream society through unemployment and racial discrimination.

A history of France since 1800

This book explores the historical context of these themes by tracing the history of France over the past two hundred years. The framework of the book is provided by chronological political history, which then branches off to discuss France's society and economy, its regimes and institutions, the role of religion in politics, and its relations with the rest of the world. These themes are explored as they rise to the fore, rather than being covered in each chapter. Given the limitations of space, some aspects of French history are not analysed here, notably military history and artistic, musical, or literary culture.

The chronological divisions of the book require some explanation. The first chapter discusses the new regime that was built in the wake of the French Revolution. The Revolution of 1789 successfully tore down the old regime, including the monarchy, the aristocracy, feudal rights and dues; it abolished the old regions, the old weights and measures, and even the old calendar. The chaos produced by this was brought to order by Napoleon Bonaparte, whose rule laid much of the institutional framework for the country for the next two centuries. What he did not do was establish a durable constitutional or political settlement, and his empire fell with him. Louis XVIII returned to the throne after Waterloo and continued to build the new regime, accepting most of the Napoleonic settlement whilst developing a constitutional monarchy. Chapter 2 is bounded by two attempts to break Louis XVIII's constitutional settlement by asserting the authority of the head of state against an elected parliament, by Louis's brother Charles X and by the first President of the Third Republic, Marshal MacMahon. This chapter examines the economic and social changes of the middle decades of the nineteenth century, before turning to the turbulent political events of the period and its three revolutions. Chapter 3 begins with the fall of MacMahon in 1877, the definitive victory of the parliamentary democratic regime in the nineteenth century. It was also the climax of the conflict between the state and the Catholic church, which gives the chapter its title.

The outbreak of the First World War marks a profound divide in the history of modern France. Chapter 4 examines both the war and the stranglehold that it held over the postwar years. It was not until 1926 that the grip of the war on French life loosened, when the country realized that the price of victory had been so high that France too had lost the war. This realization was formalized by the return of the franc to the gold standard at just one-fifth of its prewar value. The first steps towards recovery taken under Poincaré were followed by a thirty years' crisis that lasted until 1958, and which is the subject of Chapter 5. The country was destabilized by a series of disasters that came from outside: the Great Depression, the Spanish Civil War, the Second World War, the Occupation, the Cold War, and decolonization. At the same time, changes in economic and social structures had produced a disjuncture between society and the parliamentary regimes of the Third and Fourth Republics, leading to a sustained crisis of institutions and regimes. Chapter 6 covers France from the foundation of the Fifth Republic to 2002. Initially this constituted another new regime similar to that of 1800, with de Gaulle in the role played by Napoleon: an authoritative leader able to resolve many of the problems that had defeated his predecessors, notably by settling the Algerian war, restoring French power, and creating a regime in keeping with the new organization of society. Yet changes since then have undermined this settlement, and the Fifth Republic itself now needs reform.

1

The new regime: 1800–1824

'Domination personified'

The rise to power of Napoleon Bonaparte

Napoleon Bonaparte was only just born a Frenchman. Though the island of Corsica had been held by many different Mediterranean powers over the centuries, it had never been French until 1768, when Louis XV bought it from the Republic of Genoa. An expedition sent later that year finally defeated the last Corsican resistance on 8 May 1769. Neither Corsica's harbours nor its rocky soil offered much reward for its conquerors—but its children were to remake France, Europe, and even the world. On 15 August that same year, Napoleone Buonaparte was born into a family of minor Corsican nobles who had rallied to the French cause. As a result, he received a military education at royal expense from 1779 and became an officer in the army of Louis XVI in 1785. A few years later, the French Revolution and its wars overturned the old order in France and Europe, and enabled Napoleon to fulfil what he believed to be his destiny.

Napoleon's personality combined elements of the old regime, the Revolution, and military discipline, and he stamped these three features on the new regime in France. He grew up under the old regime, was educated in schools for the sons of noblemen, and was confirmed as a Catholic. Like many youths of the period, he was entranced by Enlightenment philosophy, and wrote romantic fiction badly ('Napoleon began a life of action because of his failure in literature,' observed Goethe). His conquests created an empire for himself and kingdoms for his family in the manner of old regime dynasties and Corsican clans, not in accordance with the Revolution's nationalism. But if the old regime raised him, it was the Revolution that made him. In 1789 he was just a lieutenant in the king's army. He sided with the Revolution in 1791 by joining the Corsican National Guard, and then with France in 1792, when he returned as a captain in the regular army. War provided him with a chance to show his abilities as a commander, beginning with the capture of Toulon from the British in 1793. He demonstrated his loyalty to the Revolution in 1795, when he helped suppress a royalist rising with a 'whiff of grapeshot', in Carlyle's phrase, and was repaid by the patronage of Revolutionary politicians, notably his brother Lucien and Paul Barras (whose mistress, Josephine de Beauharnais, Napoleon married in 1796). Trained as an artillery officer, Napoleon applied the principles of military discipline to the civil administration of France: one of his ministers said that Napoleon claimed to be able to manoeuvre French trade 'like a battalion', while an enemy, Chateaubriand, described him as 'domination personified'.

This combination of military success and political support won Napoleon a great promotion in 1796, when he was made supreme commander of the Army of Italy. He led this army of 50,000 men to a string of victories in 1796–7, which was followed by a much more ambitious campaign in Egypt in 1798–9. Although Napoleon won his battles on land, Nelson destroyed the French fleet on the Nile, thus isolating the land forces, and in August 1799 Napoleon abandoned his troops in Egypt to return to France. The fruits of this expedition were scientific, artistic, and above all political, for Napoleon returned just as a coup was being prepared against the Directory, the regime that had ruled France since 1795. By 1799, the Directory had proved no more capable of building a lasting settlement or of ending the wars that began in 1792 than had the previous revolutionary regimes, and some of the Directors themselves planned to give power to three consuls instead, led by the army's most successful general. The coup nearly misfired, but Lucien Bonaparte managed to rescue it through his influence as president of the lower legislative chamber, on 18 Brumaire of the Year VIII by the Revolutionary calendar (9 November 1799). It was the last time Napoleon needed political protection, for he outmanoeuvred the politicians immediately afterwards, rewriting their draft constitution to concentrate power in the hands of the First Consul—Napoleon himself.

The Napoleonic regime

Napoleon's lasting creations were the new regime, a new political formula, and a legend of martial glory. The first has endured constantly while the other two have waxed and waned over the decades, haunting the nation's memory. His new political formula changed over the years of his rule as it became increasingly dynastic. The original formula of 1799–1804 was that of rule by one man, who healed past divides by standing above party factions and who created a united nation. Such a man was chosen because of his personal authority and genius, and his rule was subsequently legitimized by the voice of the people. Since the French Revolution had both established the sovereignty of the people and discredited representative democracy, this sovereignty was expressed by plebiscites, not by parliaments. This mantle has since been claimed by Napoleon III, General Boulanger, Paul Déroulède, Philippe Pétain, and Charles de Gaulle, amongst others. René Rémond identified Bonapartism as one of the main variants of the right wing in France, and many Bonapartists were indeed men of the right; but Maurice Duverger has argued that as a system, it was one of the two ways in which France has been ruled by the centre, because Bonapartism stood above parties and stopped either extreme from persecuting the other.[1]

The rule of Napoleon himself was certainly authoritarian, even dictatorial, but it can be seen as rule from the centre: he eliminated the extremes of both left and right then sought to reconcile the country behind him. This strategy of repression and reconciliation continued throughout his rule, but it was profoundly changed by his coronation as emperor in 1804. Though there was a plebiscite to approve the change to a hereditary system, the coronation left no doubt that France had returned to dynastic rule, and that its people were once again subjects, not citizens. Napoleon completed the transition when he dissolved his marriage with Josephine (who had not produced an heir, and at the age of 46 looked unlikely to do so) in December 1809 and married Marie-Louise, the daughter of the emperor of Austria, less than four months later. An heir, the king of Rome, was born in 1811. By this time, the Bonaparte family held

[1] R. Rémond, *The Right-wing in France*, 2nd edn. (Philadelphia, 1969); M. Duverger, *La Démocratie sans le peuple* (Paris, 1967).

thrones spread across Europe: where the Revolutionary armies had established 'sister republics', Napoleon created duchies, principalities, and kingdoms for his brothers and sisters. The legacy of this version of his political formula proved much less successful than the previous formula; neither republicans nor royalists could easily accept Napoleon's coronation, and support for the dynasty vanished with defeat in 1814–15.

From 1789, the Revolutionaries had begun the process of building a new regime, a process which extended into the Bourbon Restoration, as Isser Woloch has shown.[2] The Napoleonic period did most to found the new regime, by giving France a period of stability, by preserving or rejecting the work of the Revolution, and by adding its own distinctive elements. The Revolutionaries sought to create equality and uniformity. Before 1789 there were hundreds of law codes in France, innumerable systems of weights and measures, and a mass of legal and fiscal privileges. On 4 August 1789, the National Assembly began the process of abolishing these privileges and establishing civic equality for all. The Revolutionaries emancipated Protestants and Jews, established the metric system by a law of 1795, and began work on creating a single law code. They introduced a decimal calendar in 1793 to complete this break with the past (abandoned at the end of 1805), and abolished the historic provinces of France, replacing them with eighty-three departments of a roughly similar size. However, they did not reorder the basic unit of old regime life, and recognized every town, parish, or village which had some legal status under the old regime as a commune—some 44,000 in all, often with fewer than 100 inhabitants. The turmoil of 1792–9 put many of these developments in jeopardy: for example, conscription and the de-Christianization campaigns of 1793–4 led to a religious war with the Catholic regions of the west, the Vendée and Brittany; the costs of war took precedence over reform; draft dodgers filled the rebel armies or turned to brigandage. Napoleon's first contribution to the new regime was to restore order: nothing else could happen until this was done.

Authority began with Napoleon in person, aided by a civil service that grew constantly (there had been fewer than 1,000 officials in the Parisian bureaucracy in the 1780s, compared with 25,000 in 1810).

---

[2] I. Woloch, *The New Regime* (New York, 1994).

The first major innovation was the creation of the prefects on 17 February 1800; these were officials in charge of each department, appointed by the government and answerable only to it. Below the prefects were sub-prefects, also appointed by the government, who supervised the three or four *arrondissements* that made up a department; below them lay the communes, whose independence of action was henceforth severely limited. Mayors and justices of the peace were also appointed, not elected as they had been during the Revolution. Municipal police kept order in towns, and rural policemen (*gardes champêtres*) protected villages; both had the support of the gendarmerie, a branch of the ministry of war. In 1812, the ministry of the interior proposed that the dubiously effective *gardes* be incorporated into the gendarmerie, bringing the state into every village; although the military defeats of 1813 prevented this, this system of 'administrative tutelage' appeared to hold all France in its web. However, the practicalities of distance, bad roads, uncooperative mayors, or local customs all acted against the prefects. Shortly after the Restoration, an official at the ministry of the interior lamented: 'Out of the 500 mayors to whom a prefect writes on any kind of measure at all, 200 execute it, 150 answer that they are executing it without actually doing so, and 150 do not respond at all.'[3]

Order was also secured by the church authorities. In the course of the nineteenth century, bishops become known as 'prefects in purple', while the parish priest acted as a mayor in black, a schoolteacher, 'a gendarme for the rogues and a soothsayer for the idiots'. The Revolution had introduced a civil constitution of the clergy in 1790 which the pope had rejected, splitting the Catholic church in France; on top of this, Jacobin de-Christianization had turned the majority of Catholics against the Revolution. This division between Catholics and the Revolution remained one of the fundamental divides in French society and politics until well after the Second World War (and in some ways is still present), and presents us with the paradox of a country where attitudes to religion and the churches were vastly important even though the majority of the adult male population was at best lukewarm in its own faith. Although the philosopher Fouillée exaggerated when he observed that nineteenth-century France 'offers the almost unique example of a people which, in sum

[3] Ibid. 131.

and in mass, is atheist', it was true for large parts of the country. Napoleon wished to reunite the Catholic church in France and gain the acceptance of the Catholic population. A new pope, Pius VII, was elected in March 1800, and Napoleon rapidly opened negotiations with him. The result was a Concordat signed on 16 July 1801, which regulated the church in France until 1905 and restored the freedom of public worship. The Catholic church gave up any claims to its land, which had been seized by the Revolution and sold as 'national property' (*biens nationaux*), in return for which clergymen were to be paid stipends by the state instead. Bishops were nominated by the state and invested by the pope, while parish priests were appointed by bishops with the approval of the state. Napoleon reorganized the Protestant and Jewish communities too, although only Protestant clergy were paid by the state. His treatment of the Jewish community was typical of the Napoleonic spirit. In 1790–1, the Revolution emancipated Jews and made them full citizens. In 1808, Napoleon centralized the administration of Jewish communities by creating consistories, whose members were elected by Jewish notables; he also reimposed restrictions on the largest (and poorest) Jewish community, in Alsace-Lorraine. These restrictions were intended to accelerate Jewish assimilation, thus furthering the ideals of the Revolution by coercion.

The Concordat with the Catholic church was a realistic and fair agreement, if a little vague in places. Unfortunately, Napoleon did not leave it alone. He had a detailed code of seventy-seven articles drawn up and added to the Concordat (under the name of the 'Organic Articles') without the consent of Pius VII, which put the Catholic church under much stricter control by the government in Paris. An imperial catechism was published in 1806, to ensure uniformity across the empire. Although pay for bishops was generous (10,000 francs a year), only a fifth of parish clergy had the status of curé, which gave them tenure and a reasonable income (at least 1,000 francs); the rest were ill-paid and liable to be moved at their bishop's will. In 1814 there were just 36,000 parish clergy in France, compared to 60,000 before the Revolution, and the monastic orders abolished by the Revolution were not officially restored. In the short term, the Concordat settled the religious crisis that had riven France since 1790. However, Napoleon's continuing abuse of the Concordat and of the pope undermined Catholic support for him as the years progressed:

after he seized the Papal States in 1808 and annexed them to his empire the following year, Pius VII excommunicated him, was taken prisoner in revenge, and was only freed in 1814.

One of the Revolution's aims in education had been to release primary schooling from the Catholic church. Laws of 1793 and 1794 laid down provision for free primary schooling for the first time, although the availability of qualified teachers was limited and was made worse by conscription. Napoleon had little interest in boys' primary schools and left them to local initiatives, be they municipal, private, or religious. Primary school teachers were monitored by curés, who sent reports to their bishops, who in turn gave them to the educational authorities. As for girls, Napoleon regarded them as 'mere machines to make children' who only needed to learn a senti-mental and submissive piety. Although both of the main laws on education were largely drafted by Fourcroy, who had been active in educational reform since the 1790s, Napoleon's military attitudes prevailed. The main creations, which were little changed until 1968, were the lycées, the baccalaureate, and the Imperial University. Legislation to create the lycée, or secondary school, was passed in 1802, and forty-five of them were founded during the empire. They ressembled barracks more than schools, and were run by government-appointed officials with minimal independence. The University was created in 1808 as a hierarchical body to oversee all institutions of secondary and higher education, and the baccalaureate was established the next year. Napoleon held that there would 'be no settled political state so long as there is not a teaching body with settled principles. So long as one does not learn from childhood whether to be republican or monarchist, Catholic or nonreligious, etc., the State will not form a nation.'[4] Although subsequent regimes disagreed about which principles to teach, they all agreed that education made loyal Frenchmen.

Fiscal and monetary policies were areas where stability and lasting achievements were produced without much innovation. Two previ-ous regimes had been broken by their problems in these matters: Louis XVI had called the Estates-General because he was buried in debt, while the Convention of 1792–5 had drowned in its own paper money, the *assignats*. By the end of the Directory the *assignats* had

---

[4] Cited in L. Bergeron, *France under Napoleon* (Princeton, NJ, 1981), pp. 32–3.

been eliminated, and Napoleon further stabilized the currency by introducing the *franc de germinal* in 1803, gold and silver coins whose intrinsic value equalled their face value. The Banque de France was founded in 1800, but since its bank notes were valued at 500 francs or more, they were used by businesses only; nor did the Banque raise great loans to finance war as the Bank of England did, in order to avoid recreating the debts of Louis XVI. Tax collection was centralized and made more efficient. Napoleon kept the direct taxes used by the Revolution, revived the old regime's indirect taxes on drinks and salt (1804 and 1806), and restored the state monopoly on tobacco (1810). This taxation system lasted for over a century, until an income tax was belatedly introduced in the First World War, while the *franc de germinal* survived a little longer.

Another enduring Napoleonic creation is the Legion of Honour. When it was founded in 1802, it seemed in keeping with the Revolution because it rewarded merit regardless of birth. Rewards became more generous but less revolutionary in 1806 when Napoleon created the *majorats*, hereditary estates carved out of conquered territories and given to his most prominent followers. The creation of an imperial nobility in 1808 went still further against Revolutionary principles to pursue two of Napoleon's other aims: the creation of an elite loyal to him, and a merger of the old aristocracy with the new elite. He succeeded in the second better than in the first because imperial nobles abandoned the emperor rather than lose their titles in 1814–15, and they became part of Parisian high society in the following decades. Imperial titles were primarily rewards for service to the state and so were dominated by soldiers, administrators, and local notables; just 1.5 per cent went to artistic or scholarly talents, and 0.5 per cent to businessmen.

Perhaps Napoleon's greatest domestic achievement was the Civil Code; his worst was conscription. Before 1789, French laws were a combination of Roman, canon, feudal, and customary law, with over 360 versions of the latter. Work to unify French laws began in 1790; this produced a Criminal Code in 1791, legalized divorce, and secularized the registers of births, deaths, and marriages in 1792. But no final Civil Code was produced until Napoleon pushed it to a conclusion; it was promulgated in 1804. Though the Code became known as the *Code Napoléon*, his main contribution was to provide conditions of stability and the political will to complete it; Cambacérès, the Second

Consul in 1799, deserves particular recognition because he had worked on the Code since the early 1790s. The Civil Code reconciled customary traditions, written law, and Revolutionary laws. The Revolutionary legacy was protected because civil equality and liberty were guaranteed, feudal land tenure was rejected, and the rights of those who had bought *biens nationaux* (land confiscated from émigrés and from the Catholic church) were protected. The recording of births, deaths, and marriages remained secular, as a responsibility of mayors. Though divorce was still legal, it was made more difficult to obtain. Because the Code secured the rights of property and the freedom of contract, it has been seen as a capitalist document, though it had little to say about liquid assets and concentrated on land. One of the reasons for the Code's success is that it did not impose a single system on the whole of France. In inheritance, the general principle of the equal division of property was established among male heirs, but it was possible to privilege one heir, within limits, in order to avoid breaking farms up too much, thus satisfying custom in areas which already practised equal division and in those which did not (in such places the law was often bent to favour one heir even more). Not only was the Civil Code exported with some success by Napoleon's empire, but a number of other countries imitated it voluntarily. It was followed by further legal reforms: the Code of Civil Procedure (1806), the Commercial Code (1807), the Criminal Code and Code of Criminal Procedure (1808), and the Penal Code (1810). However, the diversity of French village life resisted such uniformity, and attempts to produce a Rural Code failed.

The losers from the Civil Code were undoubtedly the women of France, especially wives. The Civil Code asserted the superiority of fathers over their children and of husbands over their wives: the equality of husband and wife established by law in 1796 was overturned. Henceforth women could not sell their own property nor manage joint property without their husbands' permission; they owed obedience to their husbands, and had inferior rights regarding divorce and the penalties for infidelity. These provisions were not altered until the end of the nineteenth century. Other losers under legal reform included the rural poor and urban workers. Because the Civil Code gave landowners full rights over their estates, the rural poor lost some rights of grazing, and common land was slowly sold off. Urban workers had lost the right of association by Le Chapelier's

law of 1791, and this was confirmed by the Penal Code. The movement of workers was regulated by the introduction of workers'
identity cards (the *livret*) in 1803. This was primarily intended to
control the vast floating population of these troubled times, but
it also gave employers leverage over their workforce. Industrial
tribunals were established in 1806 to solve labour disputes without
strikes or legal action—but for many decades they were run by
employers and workshop masters, with no place for workers on the
tribunal. Such constraints were relatively minor compared to those
reimposed in the colonies: the Convention had abolished slavery in
1794, only for Napoleon to re-establish it in the Antilles and French
Guiana in 1802 and 1803 respectively.

The biggest impact on families' lives and on society in general
came from conscription. Before 1789, taxation had formed the central
relationship between state and society, which Napoleon replaced with
this 'blood tax'. Conscription under the Directory was formalized by
Jourdan's law of 1798. It had two main weaknesses: first, mayors were
in charge of conscription, and they were too willing to discharge men
they knew (one-third were deemed unfit or too short for service—the
minimum height was just 4 feet 9 inches), and secondly there were
vast numbers of evaders or deserters in France, who survived by
brigandage. Napoleon corrected these by giving sub-prefects
responsibility for conscription and by declaring an amnesty for fugitives in 1802, which yielded up 155,000 men. Over the next decade, the
routine of conscription became increasingly accepted while mobile
columns searched out evaders. The system reached its peak in 1811,
when 100,000 more fugitives were caught and just 6,500 evaded that
year's draft. In one sense, the system had become too successful,
because Napoleon was able to raise army after army by it, until extra
conscription in November 1813 led to riots and mass desertions once
again. Though Louis XVIII initially abolished conscription, relying
on a volunteer army of 150,000, it was restored in 1818. The annual
lottery for recruits became a rite of passage for young men,
when each year-group marched off rowdily from their village in
mock-military order, to draw their number and learn their fate.

The Napoleonic regime was held together by reconciliation and
repression. It was not so difficult to reconcile republicans to the Consulate, since the republic had discredited itself by the Jacobin Terror
of 1793–4 and by the Directory's manipulation of elections, although

they found the empire harder to accept. But by 1804 diehard republicans were few in number and were rarely influential. Napoleon anchored his regime on the 'notables': men of influence and landed wealth, regardless of whether they were royalist or republican. He won over those who had gained power under the Revolution by appointing them to national and local offices, and those who had bought *biens nationaux* by guaranteeing their ownership. The Concordat reconciled the Catholic church and its flock to the regime (at least temporarily), and early amnesties were arranged for émigrés. Some 48,000 of these were allowed to return in 1800, and to recover any unsold land that had been taken from them; after 1802, only about 1,000 émigrés remained proscribed. Increasing numbers of nobles entered the imperial service: of 281 prefects appointed between 1800 and 1814, 171 were of bourgeois origin while 110 were from old regime noble families.

Napoleon built 'notability' on wealth, not merit (the Revolutionaries' option) because he knew that the rich prefer order while talent produces change. He knew that social status depended on landed wealth, so he fixed high salaries for marshals, judges, and bishops, and membership of legislative or representative bodies was limited to the rich. Elements of universal male suffrage survived in the use of plebiscites, held in 1800 (on the new constitution), 1802 (on the life consulate), and 1804 (on the hereditary empire), although there were no further plebiscites until 1815, when Napoleon attempted to reinvent the empire by introducing liberal measures into the constitution. In contrast to the wide suffrage of the plebiscites, lists of departmental notables were drawn up by a series of electoral colleges that steadily erased any popular influence—especially after 1802, when notables had to be chosen from the 600 highest tax-payers in each department. The constitution of 1799 created an appointed senate, which chose members of a tribunate and a legislative body from the departmental lists. These bodies had little power and Napoleon could dismiss their complaints or purge them as he wished (the tribunate was abolished in 1807). On 29 December 1813, the legislative body did find the courage to vote against continuation of the war, but to no effect; the empire rested on military power, and it was the marshals who eventually toppled Napoleon.

Repression took many forms. Press censorship had begun as early as January 1800, when the number of Parisian newspapers was cut from seventy-three to thirteen; by 1811 there were just four in Paris and one per department, all controlled by the government. Theatres were censored too, and in 1807 the number of theatres in Paris was cut from thirty-three to eight. Exile removed unwelcome critics of the government, notably Madame de Staël. The counterpart to censorship was propaganda on behalf of the regime. This took the form of epic paintings, festivals, monumental architecture, the *Bulletins of the Grand Army*, dazzling uniforms, and military reviews. Napoleon's greatness was inescapable—as long as he did not lose too many battles. Active opposition to the regime was rooted out by Joseph Fouché. Fouché was elected to the Convention in 1792, where he voted for the execution of Louis XVI. He was one of the most extreme members of the Convention, a violent atheist (despite or because of his training as a priest) and a leading figure in the Terror: he suppressed the federalist revolt in Lyon bloodily. Expelled from the Convention in 1794, he returned to power in 1799 as minister of police for the Directory. Napoleon employed him in this post until 1802, and then from 1804 to 1810, where he developed a network of police agents and informers that suppressed underground opposition effectively. Although the police could not prevent all attempts to assassinate Napoleon, the latter knew how to take advantage of them. After the failure of a royalist attempt to kill him on 24 December 1800, he had 130 Jacobins deported, which ended any serious opposition to him from the far left. The royalist rebels in the west were pacified by the end of 1800 by a combination of amnesties and force, though this did not end their conspiracies. A plot by Georges Cadoudal to kidnap Napoleon, invade France, and restore Louis XVIII was exposed by Fouché in 1804, and the ringleaders were shot or exiled. Controversially, Napoleon ordered the kidnapping of the duc d'Enghien, one of the Bourbon family, from the neutral state of Baden in the belief that he had been part of Cadoudal's plot; d'Enghien was shot at Vincennes in March 1804. This action shocked the royal families of Europe, especially Tsar Alexander I . . . whose own record on such matters was not spotless since he had murdered his own father.

Not content to protect the empire, Fouché also intrigued with its enemies, to arrange a successor to Napoleon should he fall. His rewards were to be made duke of Otranto in 1809 and to be sacked in 1810. For a quarter of a century, Fouché had only one rival for intrigue and deceit: Charles Maurice de Talleyrand-Périgord. Talleyrand came from one of the grandest families in France, but his family had shown him little love as a child and in return he had little love for the aristocracy. A limp prevented him from entering the army, so he became a priest and rose to become bishop of Autun. He was elected to the Estates-General in 1789, where he sided with the reformists, helping to write the Declaration of the Rights of Man and of the Citizen, and voting for the confiscation of church property (which led to his excommunication); after exile in 1792–6, he served as foreign minister from 1799 to 1807, when he resigned from a combination of opposition to Napoleon's ever-growing ambition and the offence he caused the emperor by collaborating with Fouché in making arrangements for Napoleon's succession. The uneasy partnership of Talleyrand and Fouché (of vice and crime, thought Chateaubriand) had to wait a few years more before they could finally achieve this.

The Napoleonic conquest of Europe

Napoleon fought about sixty battles in his career and won all but a few of them; he rose to power because of his victories and fell because of his defeats. Two questions arise from this: how did he win so many battles, and why did he keep on fighting?

Mobility was the essence of Napoleon's success, in both strategic and tactical terms. Eighteenth-century armies tended to be rigid: they were under one command, were composed of distinct infantry, artillery, and cavalry regiments, and moved slowly because they depended on their supply train. Napoleon used changes introduced by the old regime and Revolutionary line armies, dividing his forces into independent army corps. Each corps had its own commander, contained infantry, artillery, and cavalry units, and lived off the land when on campaign. Once a large army had been broken up into several smaller corps, it could move much faster and be far more flexible; victory depended on bringing the scattered corps together again in time for a battle. Here bureaucracy was as important as flair: Napoleon's strategic genius was complemented by the efficiency of his chief of staff, Berthier, in coordinating manoeuvres. Tactical flexibility was achieved by combining infantry, cavalry, and artillery, and by the use of light troops. Light infantry and cavalry were used to reconnoitre, to screen the advance of the main body of men, to create feint attacks, and to pursue a defeated opponent.

The purpose of this mobility was to fight decisive battles, to destroy the enemy's armies, and to dictate peace terms to the enemy's ruler. Napoleon's aim was not to occupy territory as such: although great areas of Europe were annexed either to France or to new satellite states, control of them was passed to civil administrators in due course. This strategy won Napoleon a series of famous victories, most notably crushing Austria at Marengo (1800), Austria and Russia at Austerlitz (1805), Prussia at the double battle of Jena and Auerstädt (1806), Russia at Friedland (1807), and Austria again at Wagram (1809). Though Napoleon did lose some major battles, at Aspern-Essling (1809), Leipzig (1813), and Waterloo (1815), his worst military failures came from situations where he was unable to engage in a decisive battle, in Spain and in Russia. The Peninsular war of 1807–14 slowly drained French strength because the main enemies were Spanish guerrillas, who did not fight pitched battles, and British forces, who stayed behind defensive positions for long periods of time. The French army was forced to act as an army of occupation for once, in a country whose infertile land prevented them from foraging successfully. The Russian campaign of 1812 destroyed a vast army of over 600,000 (most of whom were not French) in a matter of months. Napoleon's plan had been to engage the Russians in battle in the summer of 1812, but their forces evaded him until the tsar felt he had to defend Moscow. The two armies met in the inconclusive but bloody battle of Borodino on 7 September, after which Napoleon was able to enter Moscow with 95,000 men just as its governor set the city alight. Whatever mistakes Napoleon might have made up till then, he certainly erred by staying in Moscow too long, waiting vainly for the Tsar to negotiate. The retreat began on 19 October, and within three weeks the first snows had fallen. Cold, starvation, disease, and the pursuing Russian army reduced the Grand Army with every step, despite the valiant efforts of the rearguard under Marshal Ney; just 25,000 men completed the retreat. 65,000 remained in other bases in the east, meaning that half a million men had died or been captured, and 200,000 horses and 1,000 cannon had been lost.

The victories of the Revolutionary and imperial armies reshaped the European order. France's own borders were expanded by the Revolutionaries to include Savoy, Nice, Belgium, the German left bank of the Rhine, and Geneva with its environs. Ideas of national unity and the 'natural frontiers' of France underlay these conquests, since they took over mostly francophone territories or pushed out to geographical boundaries such as the Rhine. Napoleon's annexations paid no attention to these criteria. By 1812 there were 130 departments in the empire, which stretched one arm along the North Sea coast to Hamburg and another along the Mediterranean to Rome. Myriad German and Italian states were consolidated into a few large territories, and the west German states were then gathered into the Confederation of the Rhine. In 1806, Francis of Austria abandoned the title of Holy Roman Emperor and offered it to Napoleon—who rejected it. Poland's hopes for rebirth were partially satisfied by the creation of the duchy of Warsaw, but it was never given real independence. Such was the shock of Napoleon's victories that his defeated enemies in Austria, Prussia, and Russia were forced into reforms which they would never have considered otherwise, and which sometimes outlasted the reforms introduced by Napoleon into his own satellites.

Several of these new states were given to Napoleon's brothers and sisters to rule. His brothers Louis, Jérôme, and Joseph all became kings: Louis was king of Holland from 1806 to 1810 (when Napoleon deposed him for favouring the Dutch and annexed Holland to France), Jérôme became king of Westphalia (1807–13), and Joseph was first made king of Naples and Sicily (1806–8) and then king of Spain (1808–13). He was succeeded in Naples from 1808 to 1815 by his sister Caroline and her husband, Marshal Joachim Murat, Napoleon's finest cavalry commander. Another sister, Élisa, was made princess of Piombino in 1805 and of Lucca in 1806, then grand duchess of Tuscany in 1809 because of her success in governing these territories. Eugène Beauharnais, Josephine's son by her first marriage, became viceroy of Italy in 1805. Lucien Bonaparte was offered Italy and Spain on condition that he divorce his second wife; he refused, and lived in semi-exile in Italy until 1810, when he left for the USA (he was captured en route and held prisoner in England until 1814). Pauline Bonaparte married Prince Camillo Borghese, who became one of Napoleon's governors; Pauline's talents were for love not government, and her gift to posterity was to model for Canova's sculpture of *Venus victrix* (1808).

Defeat and exile

Before his invasion of Russia in 1812, Napoleon ruled the largest European empire since Charles V, more than 250 years earlier. Why then did he keep fighting, and ultimately lose everything? The precise causes of the Russian campaign lay in Napoleon's attempt to extend the continental system (his blockade of British trade) and in the tsar's desire to overthrow French superiority. But these causes were just symptoms of Napoleon's desire for ever-greater power, where each victory opened up new possibilities. The Russian campaign was modest compared to a plan of 1807 that included expeditions through Gibraltar to conquer North Africa and through Constantinople to threaten India. If Napoleon had been content with compromise, he would never have become emperor in the first place. Defeat in Russia was the signal for the major European powers and their allies to form a sixth coalition against him. After victory at Leipzig, the combined allied armies entered France in 1814 while Wellington's army crossed the Pyrenees from Spain. Although Napoleon fought and won a series of battles in France, his own marshals rebelled and insisted that he abdicate. He did so on 6 April 1814, and was sent in exile to the Mediterranean island of Elba.

The Bourbon family, in the person of Louis XVIII, returned to the throne in 1814 partly by edict of the allies and partly because of support organized for them inside France by the ultra-royalist conspirators known as the *Chevaliers de la foi* and (more importantly) by Talleyrand. Unlike his ultra-royalist supporters, Louis XVIII did not intend to erase the whole legacy of Revolution and empire, nor did he purge the administration of Napoleonic officials. However, he took two symbolic steps back towards the old regime by replacing the Revolution's tricolour flag with the white of the Bourbons (the tricolour was formed by this white plus the red and blue of Paris), and by ruling as the eighteenth Louis, not the seventeenth, maintaining that he had been king since the death of Louis XVI's uncrowned son in captivity in 1795. Some of his practical measures had an even worse effect on his popularity: he alienated much of the army by dismissing many officers and replacing them with former émigrés, and angered the general population with an increase in taxes. This was enough to provide Napoleon with an opportunity to recover his lost empire. He escaped from Elba and landed in France on 1 March

1815, still unsure whether he would be cheered or lynched. He avoided the royalist Rhône valley by marching north through the Alps, on a road now known as the *Route Napoléon*, and reached Paris in triumph on 20 March. The Allied powers did not believe Napoleon's promise that this time the empire would be peaceful and liberal, and led their armies against him. On 18 June Napoleon fought them at Waterloo, with little of the sophistication of his earlier campaigns, and was routed by the Allied forces under Wellington and Blücher. Exile was replaced by captivity on the Atlantic island of St Helena, where Napoleon made his last contribution to history by recording his version of events, before his death on 5 May 1821.

It is impossible to deliver any final judgement on Napoleon. Pieter Geyl studied the many conflicting interpretations of him in *Napoleon: For and Against*, first published in Dutch in 1947, and many more interpretations have been offered since then. The following verdict comes from a contemporary of Napoleon, the writer and royalist politician Chateaubriand. Chateaubriand detested Napoleon as ambitious, jealous, and domineering, as an enemy of liberty and equality, and as a bad statesman. Yet one could not escape from Napoleon even after his death, such were his achievements.

Bonaparte was not great by his words, his speeches, his writings, by a love of liberty which he never had and never pretended to establish; he is great because he created a powerful and orderly government, a legal code adopted in several countries, law courts, schools, an intelligent, active and strong administration by which we still live; he is great because he revived, enlightened, and skilfully governed Italy; he is great because he re-created order from the heart of chaos in France, because he stood altars upright again, because he laid low the furious demagogues, arrogant philosophers, anarchic writers, Voltairean atheists, street-corner orators, prison cut-throats, and chatterboxes of platforms, clubs and scaffolds, because he forced them to serve him; he is great because he put chains on a whirlwind of anarchy; he is great because he put a stop to the familiarities of a common fortune, making soldiers who were his equals or officers who were his superiors and rivals bend to his will; he is great above all because he was his own creation, because—with no other authority than his own genius—he knew how to make himself obeyed by thirty-six million subjects in an era when no illusions surrounded a throne; he is great because he overcame all the kings who opposed him, because he defeated all armies regardless of their discipline or their value, because he made his name known to savage and civilized peoples alike, because he surpassed all the conquerors who came before him, because he filled ten years with such prodigies that they can scarcely be understood today.[5]

The last of Napoleon's achievements was the creation of his legend. Like the French Revolution, Napoleon has cast a long shadow over France, which has not always been welcome. The history of his statue in the place Vendôme in Paris itself reflects this ambivalence. This column was erected after Austerlitz, made from the bronze of captured cannons; Napoleon stands on a modern version of Trajan's column in imperial Roman clothing, at a site where a statue of Louis XIV had once been. But the present version is not the original. In 1814 the statue was removed, melted down, and recast as Henri IV, whose statue on the Pont-Neuf had been taken away in the Revolution. Louis-Philippe was prepared to rehabilitate Napoleon the general but not the emperor, so he put a statue of Napoleon wearing his famous greatcoat and hat on the Vendôme column in 1833. Louis-Napoleon reclaimed the imperial title, and duly swapped Napoleon in a greatcoat for a toga-clad one in 1863, only for the Paris Commune to topple both statue and column eight years later, under the direction of the artist Gustave Courbet. However, the Third Republic restored an imperial Napoleon with his column in 1875 (nominally at Courbet's expense—he fled to Switzerland), and it is this version which stands today.

Return of the Bourbons

The Bourbon Restoration of 1814 turned into an embarrassing false start. Louis XVIII was rescued once again by the allies and by Talleyrand, whom he had made foreign minister in 1814. This time he also had the support of Fouché, recalled by Napoleon as minister of police during his 'Hundred Days' reign in 1815. This time, Louis did purge Napoleonic officials, and a 'White Terror' erupted in royalist and counter-revolutionary areas of the country. Bourgeois Protestants in Languedoc, who had backed the Revolution because it emancipated them, suffered most of all: the White Terror there combined political reaction with class conflict and a religious vendetta. Marshal

[5] Chateaubriand, *Mémoires d'outre-tombe* (Paris, 1992 edn., 2 vols.), ii. 680–1.

Ney was another victim, shot because he had rallied to the emperor's cause when sent to arrest him. Yet in most practical ways, Louis XVIII accepted the new regime and consolidated it. The legal codes were kept (although divorce was eliminated from the Civil Code in 1816), and a Forest Code was added in 1827. The Concordat, the prefectoral system, a reduced version of the gendarmerie and financial reforms remained, though central authorities loosened their grip on local government a little from 1818. Owners of *biens nationaux* had their rights to this land recognized, and alternative compensation was arranged for the émigrés. The Bourbons extended some of the work of the empire, for example in opening more primary schools (in 1816, 17,000 communes had a school; in 1821, 24,000 had one), in making use of the metre general, and in continuing the land survey begun in 1807 (it was only finished in 1851).

One major aspect of the new regime which fell with Napoleon was the idea of a popularly elected and authoritarian head of state. What system would the Bourbons use in its stead? There were two options for royalism after 1814: to attempt to revive absolutism or to accept constitutional monarchy—in other words, royal Bonapartism or royal parliamentarianism. Their major contribution to the creation of a new regime was the installation of a parliamentary system despite themselves. In 1814 Louis XVIII accepted a charter which was the basis for a constitutional monarchy, even though he insisted that its preamble said that *he* granted the charter to the French people, not vice versa. The French Revolution had proclaimed the doctrine of popular sovereignty, but had not known what to do with it. The Revolutionaries had wanted to keep the people's will as pure as possible, so they had had one chamber and opposed the formation of parties as being divisive. This had culminated in the Convention and the Terror. The Directory put a check on the executive's power by having two chambers to the legislature and separating them from the executive, but the Directors themselves opposed the development of parties by purging the legislative councils after elections that returned too many royalists or Jacobins. Louis XVIII's two chambers were hardly democratic, since the House of Peers contained appointed members and the electorate for the Chamber of Deputies was limited to 90,000 in 1817. Electors were limited to men over 30 who paid over 300 francs in direct tax (*cens*) per year, and deputies to men over 40 who paid over 1,000 francs in tax. What mattered most was that a parliamentary system began to emerge; over the next 150 years this was the rival to the Bonapartist system, until the Fifth Republic tried to marry them together in 1958.

Ironically, it was the ultra-royalists, who were the most opposed to constitutional monarchy, who did the most to develop the parliamentary system. The restricted franchise returned a chamber full of ultras in August 1815; Fouché and Talleyrand resigned from office soon afterwards. Although Louis XVIII called this the 'incomparable chamber', he found it a nuisance since his own views and the necessities of government dictated a more moderate position; frustrated by this, the ultras demanded that the king govern in accordance with the elected majority, one of the basic rules for a parliamentary system. Elections in October 1816 gave victory to the moderates, after which the ultras voted in concert, in the first exhibition of 'party' discipline. The moderates held office from 1816 to 1820 under the duke of Richelieu and Élie Decazes, while the liberal faction (who favoured a constitutional monarchy as long as the legacies of the Revolution and empire were preserved) made ground in elections from 1817 to 1819. France's international standing rose in 1818 when it was able to participate in the Congress of Aix-la-Chapelle as a great power, its war indemnities were settled, and the last foreign troops had quit the country. Internal stability was also improved by a good harvest in 1818, after a severe grain crisis in 1816–17 had provoked widespread rioting. This encouraging position was overturned in 1820 when the king's nephew, the duke of Berry, was assassinated—his wife bore him a son a few months later, who became the heir to the Bourbon line. Decazes was forced to resign, and elections later that year gave the ultras a majority.

From here on, reaction stiffened, although checked by the ministry of Villèle for some years. Villèle was an ultra preoccupied with finance instead of religion, and he moderated reaction for several years while making the third ultra contribution to the parliamentary tradition: he took the title President of the Council of Ministers. The Catholic church had been regaining its strength since 1814 (a law to ban work on Sundays had been passed as early as November 1814), and it had opened many private schools since then, before gaining control over the whole system of secondary and higher education in 1822, when a bishop was appointed grand master of the University. When liberals in Spain overthrew their king, the ultras pressed the reluctant government for action. Villèle hoped to control this by appointing the more moderate Chateaubriand as foreign minister, only for Chateaubriand to outflank both Villèle and the ultras by ordering a successful intervention in April 1823. The ultras made further electoral gains in 1824, then secured the throne in September when Louis XVIII died. Louis had secured the new regime by making the work of the empire acceptable to royalists; when he died, the Restoration was poised between a continuation of constitutional monarchy and royal Bonapartism. Since Louis XVIII had never been crowned in the traditional setting of Reims cathedral, the splendid coronation there of his brother Charles X in May 1825 left no doubt that Charles intended to pursue the latter course.

The legacy of revolution and empire

How much had France been changed by the Revolution and empire? Karl Marx believed that France had moved from feudalism to capitalism during this period, so the change could hardly have been more profound. On the other hand, Alexis de Tocqueville found continuity too: Napoleon had merely completed the work of the old regime monarchy by centralizing the state. Certainly the economy and society were to be much more profoundly changed during the rest of the nineteenth century, as the following chapters will show; but many characteristic features of the next century (or two) were shaped by the events of 1789–1815.

Politics had been transformed in meaning and in form. The Revolutionaries of 1789 had proclaimed the doctrines of popular sovereignty and of citizenship, and these concepts remain at the heart of French constitutional politics. The rival forms of French constitutions were set by the opposing models of Bonapartism and parliamentarianism. The Revolution had declared that the nation was sovereign, and that this nation was much more than a simple collection of its citizens: it was their homeland, their *patrie*. This nationality was far from being an exclusive identity in two ways. First, it was not exclusive, in that foreigners could become French by acquiring citizenship; secondly, it was not exclusive, in that one could be both French and Breton, or Occitan, or Corsican, or Limousin. The French 'nation' existed in 1815 as a weaker and more diverse identity than in 1914.

Apart from subjective questions of identity, one of the most important and distinctive characteristics of the French nation was already in place by 1815: the slowest population growth rate in Europe. In international terms, France was a populous country in 1800, yet by 1914 it had fallen behind its rivals: in 1789, there were 27.5 million souls in France, compared to 28.5 million in the German territories and 14 million in the UK. By 1911, France had 39 million inhabitants, Germany had 65 million, and the UK had 36 million. This weakened its military position because mass armies were created in the late nineteenth century by mobilizing millions of reservists: the most important limit on an army's size was that of its country's population. Emigration from France was low, and totally out of proportion to the size of its empire; except for Algeria, French colonies did not become lands of settlement nor did many Frenchmen colonize the New World. Although per capita economic growth was respectable, the slow increase in population meant that total output rose more slowly in France than elsewhere. Because families were smaller, parents were able to tend their children better and infant mortality fell from 200 per 1,000 births in 1800 to 144 per 1,000 in 1845. Fewer children meant fewer inheritors, enabling peasants to keep their land together and businessmen to keep their firms in the family. The use of contraceptive methods may even have contributed to the low participation rate of men at Mass: they preferred to skip Mass rather than have to confess their intimate sins beforehand.

The main cause of this slow growth was that the birth rate fell in France decades before it did so anywhere else. It is possible that compared to other European countries the French rate had been low since the 1760s, and it was certainly low from 1800 on. It declined from about 33 per 1000 in 1816–20 to about 26 per 1000 between 1846–80, then fell again to below 20 per 1000 by 1914. To explain how the rate was kept low is not easy: late marriage, abstinence, prostitution, abortion, and infanticide were elements; contraception probably played the biggest part, which usually meant coitus interruptus. Explaining why the rate fell is even harder. Socio-economic explanations include rural overpopulation and the effects of equal inheritance. Cultural explanations include the idea that children were valued more as individuals, so fewer were born in order to concentrate care

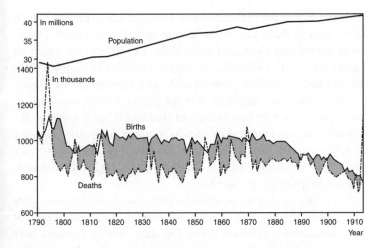

Figure 1.1 Population, births, and deaths from 1790 to 1913.

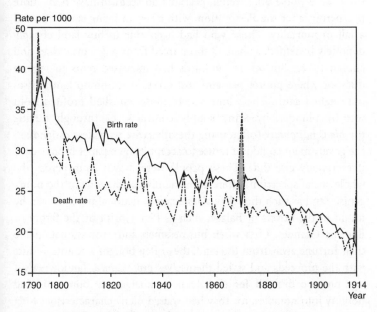

Figure 1.2 Birth and death rates from 1790 to 1913.

Source: J. Dupâquier *et al.*, *Histoire de la population française* (Paris, 1988), iii. 125

on them; or that the Catholic church lost its ability to prevent the use of contraception; or that the Revolution and empire uprooted traditions, spread new ideas, and killed about 1.4 million Frenchmen on battlefields and in civil strife. No single explanation is adequate: there are marked variations geographically and between social classes. Hervé Le Bras has suggested that the geography can be explained by mapping together four factors, each of which had a different distribution across France: low fertility resulted from low mortality (notably around Paris), high population density (the north-west), high levels of literacy (the north-east), and a high proportion of peasant proprietors (the south).

Since the next chapter sketches the general outlines of the economy and society in 1830, this chapter will only consider the impact of Revolution and empire on them. The daily lives of peasants were most affected by taxation, the conscription of men, and requisitioning of food; after the turmoil of war was over, some were better and some were worse off. Overall, peasants do seem to have been more prosperous after the Restoration, with a rise in living standards and a fall in mortality. Those who had been able to buy land cheaply definitely benefited, as had all those freed from seigneurial dues and church tithes. But where landlords had increased rents to replace dues, or where poorer peasants lost access to common land, losses outweighed gains. The winners were those who had profited from war by plunder, by army supply contracts, or through buying the *biens nationaux* (often using the otherwise worthless *assignats*— the government could not refuse to accept its own paper money even if everybody else did). These people were drawn from across the whole social spectrum, often from the diverse factions of the bourgeoisie, and as such they defy classification; fictional portraits can be found in the novels of Balzac, such as Père Goriot or the father of Eugénie Grandet. Even when businessmen and professionals made their fortune away from the land, they often bought a country estate with the proceeds and styled themselves *propriétaire*, 'landowner'. It was not too difficult for Napoleon to amalgamate bourgeois and nobility into notables, for they had shared many characteristics long before the Revolution swept away the artificial distinctions of privilege. The nineteenth-century French nobility almost defined itself by its dual life, spending the winters in town and summers on country estates; the difference between a noble and a bourgeois was that individual members of the bourgeoisie tended to be limited to either town or country. Poor nobles who could not afford two properties melted into the mass of landowners, while the richest bourgeois bought both a town-house and château, and joined the nobility on Napoleon's departmental lists and on Louis XVIII's electoral rolls. These notables comprised landowners, professionals, merchants, bankers, and industrialists, and although it was far from homogeneous (social snobbery could cut a thousand lines across it), wealth, prestige, and political power had merged into a single elite.

The period 1789–1815 had a paradoxical effect on the development of the French economy. It became more of a market economy because guilds were abolished and workers' associations were banned, the Bank of France regulated credit effectively, the Civil Code protected freedom of contract, standardized weights and measures aided trade, and the Commercial Code consolidated the law. But the impact of war and of the Continental system damaged many parts of the economy. The Continental system banned trade between Britain and Europe in an attempt to ruin British business and government finance, so that Britain would be unable to subsidize its allies and would be forced to make peace. The damage done by the system hurt France's allies more than Britain, and Napoleon's attempts to enforce it across Europe hurt him most of all because it drew him into Spain and Russia. War with Britain and loss of the colonies closed down the main business of Nantes, Bordeaux, and Marseille and of their hinterlands (Marseille's industrial output fell from 50 million francs in 1789 to 12 million in 1813). Industries like linen and iron either shrank or stagnated. There were beneficiaries too, especially the cotton and chemicals industries, and the north-east of France flourished with the help of the highly protectionist tariffs imposed in 1806. Napoleon took a detailed interest in the economy, and boasted of many advances made under his guidance. Industrial growth was indeed strong from 1802–10, but a crisis in 1810–11 broke this growth, and a period of stagnation was followed by more bankruptcies in 1813–14. It took until 1817 for the economy to recover from the costs of war and the transition to peace. Economic policy in France has mixed state direction (*dirigisme*) and liberalism for several centuries, following one course then another, or even both at the same time. Napoleon's efforts to direct the economy were followed by indifference and suspicion from the Bourbons: to them, the movement of peddlers spelt subversion, not trade. Their one active measure was to continue to protect the economy—swamped by cheap British goods after the end of the Continental system—with high tariffs from 1816. Lobbies of producers demanded tariffs even where there had been none before or where France was an exporter, as with grain; the Continental system had left too few merchants to lobby for free trade.

The Catholic church had been endowed with new structures by Napoleon and was then left to stagnate. The Bourbons and the old nobility rediscovered a religious faith that had often been missing in their youth, especially in the case of Charles X himself. There are no statistics to say how many people attended church regularly before the Revolution, but by 1815 it was a minority in many districts (97.2 per cent of the adult population took Easter communion in Clermont-Ferrand, 1807–13, against 40.5 per cent in Soissons, 1807–10).[6] Traditions were broken, millions left their native villages, churches were desecrated or left empty because there were simply too few priests. The Restoration saw a massive recruitment into the parish clergy, mostly from humble rural or urban families (though seventy out of ninety bishops appointed during the Restoration were noblemen). The church offered an avenue for social and intellectual promotion for these classes, though seminaries' training was so arduous that few can have remained there for long without faith. Seminaries encouraged piety and a rejection of worldly things more than intellectual abilities, and French Catholicism in the nineteenth century became increasingly sentimental. The emblematic figure of the Restoration was Jean-Marie Vianney (1786–1859, canonized in 1925), sent to the long-neglected parish of Ars in 1818. With the help of the peasant elite and of the local noble family, and by his great success in the confessional, he brought the whole village back to church by 1830. Vianney was an enthusiatic collector of relics, amassing over 500 items in his lifetime before his own vestments and bones became relics after his death. Religious orders expanded in great numbers, especially female ones: the number of nuns rose from 12,300 in 1808 to 135,000 in 1878. Although geography was the most important factor, gender and social class mattered too. Women consistently outnumbered men in counts of church attendance or in

---

[6] See R. Gibson, *A Social History of French Catholicism, 1789–1914* (London, 1989) on this subject, and pp. 174–6 for the statistics.

taking communion; the Revolution had shocked most of the nobility back into its faith and the revolution of 1848 did something similar for many bourgeois. However, attendance in church is an inadequate guide to religious belief: some noble households resembled convents in their piety, in stark contrast to the viscount of Landeronde in the diocese of Angers. Known as 'Sacré-Maudit', he attended services only to fall asleep, named his hounds after local republicans, and kennelled them in a disused chapel without thinking it any harm.

France's position in the world was transformed during the Napoleonic wars. Before 1789, France had a distinctive position as both a European and a world power; only Russia had a similar role. At the height of his power, Napoleon was the master of Europe but had lost France's overseas empire, for its colonies fell away after 1789, to slave revolts (Santo Domingo gained independence as Haiti in 1803) or British conquest. No sooner had France regained land around the Mississippi from Spain than Napoleon sold it to the USA, as the Louisiana Purchase of 1803. By the time Napoleon fell, France had no colonies left. The allies returned most of its possessions to Louis XVIII: Martinique and Guadeloupe in the Caribbean, French Guiana in South America, St Pierre and Miquelon off Newfoundland, Réunion in the Indian Ocean, plus some outposts in India and Senegal. In Europe, Napoleon's conquests did not outlast him. The 1814 Treaty of Paris undid his work by pushing France back from its supposed 'natural frontiers' on the Rhine to the borders of 1792, which still left Louis XVIII a larger state than Louis XVI had had. Napoleon then undid even this by his campaign of 1815, because the second Treaty of Paris pushed France back to its borders of 1790. The net result of his campaigns was negative, losing territories of the old regime overseas and some of the Revolution's gains on the Continent. What had been changed utterly in France and abroad was the image of France as a liberator, conqueror, or invader. At least Corsica had not been lost—and thanks to the deeds of its most famous son, it was now proud to be part of France.

2

Charles X to Marshal MacMahon: 1824–1877

Every French head of state from 1824 to 1877—king, emperor, or president—was either overthrown by revolution or forced out of office. Was France trapped in a cycle of monarchy, republic, and empire, or did it advance stumblingly towards stability, finally achieved by the Third Republic? Two sets of revolutionary tensions were in play: a political conflict between governments and parliamentary assemblies, and a social conflict between the haves and have-nots. François Furet has called the Third Republic the 'harbour' reached by France after a century of revolutionary turmoil,[1] establishing the victory of parliament and universal male suffrage. A course can be charted towards this port from 1830, when Charles X fell for refusing to accept the verdict of elections, through February 1848, when the July Monarchy of Louis-Philippe fell for refusing to extend the franchise, to 1877, when President MacMahon repeated Charles's action by calling elections to dispose of a chamber he did not like. However, Louis-Napoleon Bonaparte (Napoleon's nephew) demonstrated that this parliamentary victory was not inevitable when he revived Bonapartism as both a political and a dynastic formula. His *coup d'état* of December 1851 finished the Second Republic and replaced it with an empire underpinned by elections; though he tacked back towards parliamentarianism in the 1860s, defeat in the Franco-Prussian war finished his experiment before it had been tested. Throughout the century, there were also eruptions of social revolution, which made the political revolutions of 1830 and 1848 possible, and which turned into civil war in June 1848 and in the Paris Commune of 1871.

[1] F. Furet, *Revolutionary France 1770–1880* (Oxford, 1992; 1st edn. Paris, 1988).

Social and economic life in the nineteenth century

Le pain de Monsieur: white bread and class formation

The upheavals of these political revolutions appeared out of keeping with France's slow-moving society and economy. However, the social and economic transformations driven by the development of a national market were ultimately more profound than all the political turbulence, even if they were slow to happen. Because the railways played such a large role in creating this market, the dates of this chapter could have been set as 1832–78: in 1832, the first railway line using steam locomotives was opened between Saint-Étienne and Lyon; a few more lines were built to serve specific industrial areas before a government plan of 1842 established a national network, radiating from Paris. A new phase began in 1878, when Charles de Freycinet guided a law through parliament that drove railway lines into the heart of the countryside, bringing economic and social change to the depths of France.

What was French society and its economy like in the mid-nineteenth century? A person's condition in life was marked most of all by their age, gender, and social class. Age was the dominant factor only during infancy and old age; social class and gender predominated during the rest of an individual's life. For example, nearly all bourgeois and noble children learnt to read, but over half the children of peasants and industrial workers did not. This social divide was lessened by Guizot's law of 1833, which obliged every commune of more than 500 souls to have a primary school, every department to have a teacher training college, and every teacher to have a state qualification. Even as it closed class divides, this law opened up the gender divide, since it only concerned boys' education. This divide widened as one advanced through the school system, for there were no state lycées for girls until 1867 and although relatively few boys from outside the elites reached university, virtually no girl did: until 1876, no more than five women obtained a degree each year, thus closing the liberal professions to them. Education, and childhood itself, stopped early in peasants' and workers' families. Even if they could only mind some animals on a farm and earned a quarter of a man's wage in industry, these contributions were vital to their families. Textile industries in particular employed children as unskilled labour, for long hours and pitifully low pay; the first law on child labour was introduced in 1841. This was largely the result of a survey of factories made by Dr Louis Villermé, but it only applied to factories with twenty or more hands and these were a minority. A stricter law in 1874 improved conditions, though enforcement was erratic. After childhood came youth; there was no such category as adolescence in the modern sense, although youths did have distinct codes of behaviour and a degree of excess was tolerated in both bourgeois students and apprentices. This period of youth ended with marriage, on average at the age of 27 to 28 for men and 24 to 26 for women.

Most women's work was directed by their husbands or fathers on a farm, in household crafts or in a shop, or they worked for themselves in the needle trades, domestic service, and as unskilled labour. Their pay was usually half that of a man because these trades were inherently badly paid, and they had little prospect for advancement. Many women became full- or part-time prostitutes (there were an estimated 34,000 prostitutes in Paris in mid-century), whence a few ascended to the glory of courtesans like Cora Pearl, dressed by the same couturier as the Empress Eugénie, while tens of thousands succumbed to venereal diseases. Membership of a religious order offered a very different life. Most orders (called congregations) were not enclosed and contemplative; instead they looked after children, taught girls, and nursed the sick. One of the most important orders was the Petites Sœurs des Pauvres, founded in 1840 by Jeanne Jurgan to enable the aged to die within the church. By 1878 it had 2,700 sisters, and was the main provider of housing for the old outside hospitals and poorhouses. Instead of being a retreat from the world, orders like this were one of the main ways in which a woman could have a career.

The worlds of men and women were not two separate spheres, for four main reasons. First, social class mattered more than gender. To be sure, there was a gender division of labour: for example, in agriculture women worked in the farmyard and sold produce at the local market, while men ploughed the fields and dealt in livestock at fairs. Yet such differences between the lives of male and female peasants were minor when the lives of peasants of both sexes are compared to those of artisans, bourgeois, and nobles. Secondly, many divisions between the male and female worlds were more apparent than real. Certainly men represented the family in public matters and took part in political life, but as Martine Segalen notes, from an anthropological view, men's gossip about politics in bars served the same sociable purpose as women's gossip about neighbours in the washhouse.[2] Women were not absent from high politics because of the importance of salons in French political life, where hostesses like Juliette Adam played the central role. Nor were women absent from popular politics: protests about food prices often began among women in market squares. One revolutionary in a novel about the Commune was less afraid of the bourgeoisie than he was of *la bourgeoise* (slang for 'the wife'): 'If the *bourgeoise* turns against us . . . the Revolution is lost.'[3] Thirdly, Segalen describes wives as the 'pivot' of the family, seen as a unit of production, consumption, and reproduction. Most of the nineteenth-century economy was based on household production in peasant farms, artisanal workshops, and retail shops, where a wife's work was essential. In bourgeois family businesses, although it was not necessary for women to take an active part, many did. Wives controlled the family budget—an important task that became central when the family became a unit of consumption more than of production, when members of the household went out to work, returning to pool their earnings. This change has been described by Louise Tilly and Joan Scott as a shift from the pre-industrial family economy, to a family wage economy, and then to a family consumer economy by the late nineteenth century.[4] Bourgeois consumption was centred on the home, and both bourgeois and noble wives played a greater part than their husbands in the creation of the family's social network. As for reproduction, obviously women bore children and cared for them, helped by elder children, grandparents, other relations, and neighbours. Fourthly, women had as great a part to play in class formation as men, for classes were primarily formed by social not economic activity; while

[2] M. Segalen, *Historical Anthropology of the Family* (Cambridge, 1986), pp. 205–6.
[3] J. Vallès, *L'Insurgé* (Paris, 1970 edn.; 1st edn. 1886), p. 231.
[4] L. A. Tilly and Joan W. Scott, *Women, Work and Family* (New York, 1978), esp. pp. 227–9.

men played the greater role in production, women played at least as great a role in organizing consumption, lifestyle, and social solidarity.

What made a 'class'? Jürgen Kocka identified three elements in class formation. First came an economic class, a group of people with common economic interests. These then formed a social class, where the group became conscious of itself and formed a common social identity. Finally this became a class in action, when its members acted together in their joint interests.[5] Socialists long fought to instil class consciousness in industrial workers and encouraged them to action, though without much success. Recent historiography has emphasized that workers did not form a coherent economic class (nor indeed did peasants, bourgeois, or nobles), with the implication that class action failed because it lacked this essential foundation. However, Kocka emphasized that there was no causal, linear connection between these three elements: that there was a complex relationship between economic class, social class, and 'class in action'.

In France, classes were primarily social not economic entities, for what distinguished one class from another, and gave it internal solidarity, was lifestyle. As mentioned in Chapter 1, nobles were distinguished by their mobility between town and country, province and Paris. Noble families unable to afford this slipped into the lifestyle of the bourgeoisie, while bourgeois families rich enough to adopt it joined the elite of notables. The 1830 revolution sealed this by abolishing the last privileges of aristocracy restored by the Bourbons, and henceforth the elites either merged or stayed apart by their chosen 'art of living'. In Paris, the old nobility maintained its distance by remaining in Saint-Germain on the left bank of the Seine even when the new boulevards of the right bank and the west of Paris were developed during the Second Empire. Conversely, they merged with the bourgeoisie at fashionable resorts. Deauville was founded as a high-society resort in 1859, with seaside promenades, bathing, yachting, luxury hotels, restaurants, races, and a casino. There were no social distinctions between bourgeois and noble at Deauville because the whole resort acted like a single club—you could even settle a bill in the racing club's restaurant with chips from the casino.

This elite dominated administration and politics unchallenged

---

[5] J. Kocka, 'The Study of Social Mobility and the Formation of the Working Class in the Nineteenth Century', *Mouvement social*, 111 (1980), pp. 97–117.

until 1877. The civil service was a self-perpetuating elite because recruitment was by appointment and because these appointments went to those with political and family connections. The *grandes écoles* (specialist institutions of higher education) provided another source of recruits, selected by meritocratic examinations (known as *concours*). However, the threat of meritocracy was still only latent by 1872, when Émile Boutmy pre-empted it, founding the École Libre des Sciences Politiques (*Sciences-Po*) to train sons of the old elite in the supposedly democratic arts of passing exams. Parliament too was filled by different segments of the elite. Restoration assemblies were replete with nobles, while landowners and civil servants dominated July Monarchy parliaments; in both cases, only those paying a large amount of personal tax were eligible for election. The doors of parliament were opened wide in 1848 when civil servants were banned from sitting in parliament, the tax qualification was removed, and deputies were paid 9,000 francs a year (until 1852): yet this only changed the balance within the elites, and men from the liberal professions joined landowners as deputies. Because most Second Empire deputies were official candidates, a third were former civil servants and officers; a quarter were industrialists, merchants and bankers, one-fifth liberal professionals, and another fifth landowners or *rentiers*. Even democratic elections like those of 1848 and 1871 returned notables simply because they were the dominant figures in their locality: a great many shopkeepers, peasants, and artisans had the same sceptical view of lesser men who stood for election as the duke of Castries had of d'Alembert and Rousseau: 'He wants to reason about everything yet doesn't have a thousand *écus!*'

The bourgeoisie cannot be called an economic class because it received its income in diverse ways—with the one common feature that these did not include manual labour. Those who lived on the income from their investments were named *rentiers* (after government bonds, *rentes*). Others lived off the income from their land and styled themselves *propriétaires*, 'landowners'. Since land values tripled and rents doubled between 1815 and 1881, buying land was a sound investment as well as a prestigious one. Businessmen formed another tranche of the bourgeoisie, subdivided amongst themselves. Different industries had conflicting interests, for example over free trade, while firms within the same industry competed with each other. A third tranche was the bourgeoisie of talent. This world contained both independent liberal professionals and careerists employed in a hierarchy; careerists subdivided further between the private and public sectors, and within these sectors, for state employment covered such diverse creatures as bureaucrats, lycée professors, and army officers. In his study of Rouen, Jean-Pierre Chaline calculated that 10 per cent of its inhabitants were bourgeois, measured by their wealth (over 50,000 francs), their lifestyle (they employed at least one servant and paid an annual rent above 500 francs), and their social standing.[6] Members of this group were fully aware that they formed a distinct social class and behaved according to its values. Its men were respectfully addressed as *Monsieur*, dressed in black coats, and ate white bread (*le pain de Monsieur*). Bourgeois households were identified by the presence of a salon, furnished with a piano as a mark of education, culture, and leisure, especially among women. There were no hard distinctions between the bourgeoisie and the other classes. They mingled with them in public events, shaded (and married) into the nobility above and into the petty bourgeoisie below, while social mobility kept individuals and families in circulation between these strata.

The petty bourgeoisie, estimated in 1866 as a third of the non-agricultural workforce, were typically shopkeepers, tradesmen, and master craftsmen. During the nineteenth century the *classes moyennes* made their appearance, more like the English middle and lower middle classes than the bourgeoisie, who were upper middle class. They were typified by white-collar workers, travelling salesmen, and clerks. Over the century, it became harder to move directly from the 'popular classes', manual workers and peasants, into the bourgeoisie, and the *classes moyennes* formed an intermediate step. Notaries, medical officers, and innkeepers formed the elite of small towns and villages. The petty bourgeoisie and middle classes remained close to workers and peasants, and many socialist leaders emerged from them when they were excluded from political life, when their careers withered because they lacked patronage, or when economic crises ruined them. Increasingly, they moved towards republican politics and anti-clericalism for the same reasons as workers and peasants: to win the independence, respect, and dignity denied to them by the established elites.

---

[6] J.-P. Chaline, *Les Bourgeois de Rouen* (Paris, 1982), p. 41.

Just as nobles and bourgeois were defined by their lifestyle, so too were workers, with the common economic feature that they all worked with their hands. What did the workers of mid-nineteenth-century France do? About a quarter of the active population worked in industry, of whom 30 per cent were women. A survey of 1866 found that just over half of industrial workers were employed in textile production, with 13 to 14 per cent in metallurgical industries and the same again in construction. The other quarter did everything from mining coal to making paper flowers; they worked as tanners and carpenters, typesetters and bookbinders, bakers and pastry-cooks. The tertiary sector (transport and services) was even more diverse, including street hawkers, hairdressers, railwaymen, domestic servants, and water carriers (there were about 20,000 of the latter in Paris alone, around 1850). Relatively few worked in large factories: the 1866 survey recorded 1.3 million employers for just 2.8 million employees. Even in a new textile town like Roubaix, three-quarters of its 50,000 employees worked in the surrounding countryside by the 'collective factory' system (*fabrique collective*), where manufacturing took place in a mass of small workshops and households scattered across a district, coordinated by merchants. The dispersal of industry was greatest between the 1830s and 1860s, after which concentration began to prevail. The textile industry was centred in Alsace, Normandy, and the Nord, while coal was mostly mined in Saint-Étienne, Le Creusot, and the Pas-de-Calais. These regions boomed because of access to raw materials and labour, though even more workers were employed in old cities like Paris, Lyon, and Marseille, where firms had direct access to capital, labour, and consumer markets, and good communications brought raw materials to them. Le Bras also suggests that labour was more available in the north than the south because the nuclear family that predominated there gave up its labour to production outside the household more easily than the complex families of the south.[7] This diversity was increased still further by occupational mobility over time. Although craftsmen who learnt their trade in a long apprenticeship tended to stay in that business, others changed trade several times during their lifetime, moved between town and countryside seasonally, or combined agricultural and industrial labour. Workers did not form a single

---

[7] H. Le Bras, *Les Trois France* (Paris, 1986), pp. 220–39.

economic class because they had very different occupations, incomes, skills, prospects, and ambitions. There were stark contrasts in factories between skilled male workers and unskilled women and children, and between independent male artisans and sweated female domestic labour. Skilled men were able to defend themselves or find another job, while unskilled women and children were at the mercy of their employers.

If there was no coherent economic working class, how could a working 'class in action' reveal itself in June 1848 and March–May 1871? Its roots lay in social class, in the solidarity of workers based around their trade and their locality. The uniting factor was not manual work; it was the need to survive. Poverty was a permanent threat: one Parisian out of eleven and one Lillois out of six were reckoned to be destitute in 1830. Solidarity was built around family and kin, neighbourhood (*quartier*), fellow tradesmen, workplace and market square, cafés and bars (*cabarets*). Because guilds had been abolished by the French Revolution, artisans replaced them with friendly societies which provided mutual help, and by associations called *compagnonnages* which looked after their members as they moved round the country in a circuit called the *tour de France.* Although this system declined over the century, the need for solidarity grew among migrants to the cities. Seasonal migration peaked around the mid-century, when there were an estimated seasonal 880,000 migrants, after which migrations became permanent. To take one example, the Creuse regularly supplied major cities with stone-masons, of whom Martin Nadaud became the most famous. He made his first journey to Paris in 1830 to work for his uncle, then moved to the same lodgings used by his father in his youth, and shared a room with a dozen migrants from his native commune. In 1831 Nadaud broke both his arms when he fell from the third floor of a building, and he depended on the care of his landlady, father, and a cousin to survive. This fraternity could last to the graveside: in 1851, a journalist in Lille was surprised to see several workers (who were usually anticlerical) spontaneously form a funeral procession behind the coffin of an old man from the poorhouse because he had no other mourners.

It was this broader solidarity beyond the workplace which Alain Cottereau identified as the solution to a paradox in workers' protests: there was no shortage of political militancy, but even when trade unions were partially legalized in 1864 (and fully authorized in 1884), membership remained low. When there was a conflict in a firm, workers often simply left it. They could do this because of the short-age of skilled workers in the second half of the century, because they could practise another trade, and because they received support from their community. This community was keen to prevent employers breaking unwritten agreements about working conditions, and this collective defence succeeded in keeping mechanization at bay for longer than in Britain and Germany (hand-weaving collapsed in Britain in the 1830s, but it survived in France into the 1870s). This communal pressure acted on workers as well as employers. William Sewell found that workers' sons in Marseille were less likely to take non-manual work than the sons of migrant workers or even of migrant peasants, despite the lower literacy of peasants, because of the stronger community forces at work on natives of Marseille. The political militancy of French workers aimed to improve conditions for all, in contrast to the individualism of American workers and the trade union solidarity of Britain.[8]

In the countryside, community rested primarily on the family, especially in the regions of scattered settlement in the north, and of complex families in the west and south-west; in regions of concen-trated settlements such as the Mediterranean, village sociability played a greater role. In the evenings, families and neighbours met at a farmhouse, to share light and warmth, to work and tell stories; these rural gatherings, called *veillées*, had their village equivalent in *cham-brées*, meetings halfway between the *veillée* and an urban club. Over the century, the economic importance of communal activities grew less as rural wealth slowly rose and as common land was broken up. Annie Moulin has characterized the years from 1815 to 1870 as an evolution from 'poverty to mediocrity' in the French countryside. About twenty million people (55 per cent of the population) lived off agriculture in the mid-nineteenth century, peaking in the 1861 census. There were about fourteen million separate landholdings in France according to the 1865 tax rolls, making about 8.4 million landowners (some people owned more than one holding). Eighty-five per cent of holdings were smaller than ten hectares, the size needed for

---

[8] W. Sewell, 'Social Mobility in a Nineteenth-Century European City: Some Findings and Implications', *Journal of Interdisciplinary History*, 7 (1976), pp. 217–33.

self-sufficiency, so these owners rented extra land, worked as labourers on other farms, or worked in rural industry. There were also two million domestics, 900,000 day-labourers, 400,000 tenants, and 200,000 share-croppers employed in agriculture.[9] Under the Second Empire, standards of living improved visibly: cotton clothes became common, housing and diet improved. The culture of the peasant world became more varied with this extra wealth and as urban influences were adapted to local traditions. For example, festivals and dancing had relieved the routine of farm life for centuries. In the nineteenth century, traditional group figure-dances were rivalled by couples dancing waltzes or polkas together, variations which came to the countryside from the cities, and which worked best if dancers could afford leather boots instead of wooden clogs. Such intimacy scandalized priests, but added greatly to the joy of village youth.

Economic change and the invention of Camembert

The main economic stimulus to the countryside was the growth of a national market, at the centre of which lay the rapidly growing city of Paris, whose population reached one million in the middle of the nineteenth century. At the start of that century, French agriculture was both varied and monotonous. Variations came from the different conditions of land and climate: half of the land was under the plough, a sixth was woodland, another sixth marsh, heath, and moor, a tenth pasture, and a twentieth was covered by vines. Monotony came from the self-sufficiency of small farms; since bread was the staple food, most farms grew wheat, along with other cereals like rye, oat, buckwheat, maize and barley. Wine was the staple drink, so vines were grown in all departments save nine along the Channel coast and the mountainous Creuse. During the century, greater specialization for sale in the market made farm landscapes more varied across France, though more monotonous within regions.

Specialization for the market was a result of vastly improved communications. Rivers and canals were improved in the first half of the century, and Thiers's law of 1836 obliged communes to maintain their local roads properly. In the first half of the century, this produced a transport network which moved bulk goods more cheaply, such as

[9] A. Moulin, *Peasantry and Society in France since 1789* (Cambridge, 1991), pp. 48–89.

coal, grain, wood, and wine; in the second half, the speed of transport accelerated so that fruit, vegetables, meat, and dairy products could reach cities from the countryside. For several decades, agricultural output increased by bringing more land under the plough, increasing labour input, and by the shift from self-sufficiency to commercial specialization, not by improved techniques or higher yields. Specialization came first to the hinterland of cities, where market gardening was long established, and spread further afield after the mid-century: Normandy and the Massif Central raised livestock, Languedoc planted vines, the Côte d'Azur grew fruit, vegetables, and flowers.

The creation of a national, commercial market caused a profound change in French agricultural life. Zola caught this in his novel *The Belly of Paris*, when he described the varieties of cheese brought from across the country to the main Parisian market, Les Halles.

Three Bries, on round slabs, were as sad as extinct moons; two, very dry, were full; the third, in its second quarter, ran, emptying itself of a white cream, spreading into a lake, laying waste the thin boards which were vainly used to contain it. Port Saluts, like ancient coins, bore the printed name of their maker. A Romantour, clothed in its silver paper, resembled a bar of nougat, a sugared cheese lost amongst these pungent fermentations. Under a glass dome, the Roqueforts had a princely appearance, of fat, mottled faces, veined with blue and yellow as if attacked by some shameful disease of the rich, from eating too many truffles; meanwhile, in a plate to one side, goats' cheeses, the size of a child's fist, hard and greyish, recalled the pebbles which billy goats set tumbling at the bends of stony paths, when leading their flocks. Then began the stenches: the light yellow Mont d'Or, reeking sweetly; the thick Troyes, bruised, already on the edge of a stronger pungency, adding the fetidness of damp cellars; Camemberts, with the aroma of over-hung game; the Neuf-Chatels, the Limbourgs, the Marolles, the square Pont-l'Évêques, each added their distinctive, sharp note to a phrase so harsh that it was almost nauseous; the Livarots, stained red, as terrible to breathe as sulphur fumes; finally, above all the others, the Olivets, wrapped in walnut leaves, like carrion which peasants had covered with branches by the side of a field, steaming in the sun.[10]

This extract can be taken as an example of Zola's naturalist style: realism taken to the point of nausea. It can also be seen as a celebration of a rich tradition of gastronomy and regional specialities, with a political significance made famous by Charles de Gaulle's question,

[10] É. Zola, *Le Ventre de Paris* (1st edn. 1873) (pp. 478–80 in the 1969 Lettres modernes edn., Paris).

'How can you govern a country that has 246 varieties of cheese?'[11] This image of *terroir*, of ancient tradition and local speciality, remains powerful today, but it is illusory. Zola wrote this passage in 1872; ten years earlier, it would have been meant nothing to most of his readers; fifty years earlier, he could not have written it at all. At the start of the nineteenth century, soft cheeses were only sold locally, especially in the Paris basin and along the Rhône and Loire valleys. From the Pyrenees, Massif Central, and Jura mountains came blue, smoked, and hard cheeses that could survive long journeys. Roquefort and Brie were already famous, but the other cheeses Zola named—even Camembert—were unknown outside their home region. The development of a national market encouraged commercial brands, so that by the 1860s the name of each region signified a particular type of cheese. Camembert's fame was established, and soon it had to be defended from unscrupulous farmers who made Camembert-like cheese outside Normandy. Zola's cheese shop was aptly set in the new market halls, built in the 1850s, for it depicted modern commerce and not immemorial rural custom.

There has been much argument and little agreement about the performance of the French economy in the nineteenth century. The economy performed badly in terms of what could be called 'great power' economics, both in comparison with its major rivals and in the militarily important sectors of coal, iron and steel. Because the French economy was well advanced in 1800 and its population was one of the largest in Europe, its total output was then second only to Russia. By 1900 it had slipped to fourth place, overtaken by its imperial and European rivals, Britain and Germany. This lag was most marked in the classic sectors of heavy-duty industrialization, coal, iron and cotton (its railway network was competitive).

By other measures, the French economy's performance was more respectable. Although France's cotton industry could not match Britain's, its silk industry was the biggest and best in Europe. Iron and coal production lagged behind British and German levels to some extent because France simply had poorer reserves. Once again, slow population growth was important, for when the growth of output is

---

[11] R. Gildea, *France since 1945* (Oxford, 1996), p. 133, citing E. Mignon, *Les Mots du général* (Paris, 1962), p. 57.

Table 2.1 The industrialization of France and its peers.

		France	Germany	Italy	UK
Output of coal	1831	2	2	–	32
(million tonnes)	1870	13	26	0	115
	1871	13	38	0	121
	1911	40	235	1	276
Output of pig iron	1831	225	120	–	600
(000 tonnes)	1870	1,178	1,267	20	6,059
	1871	860	1,424	17	6,733
	1911	4,470	13,845	303	9,679
Raw cotton consumption	1831	28	–	–	119
(000 tonnes)	1870	59	81	15	489
	1871	99	112	27	547
	1911	252	437	190	858
Length of railway line	1831	31	–	–	225
open (km)	1870	16,465	18,876	6,429	n.a.
	1871	15,632	21,471	6,710	21,558
	1911	40,635	62,734	18,873	32,223

Source: B. R. Mitchell, *International Historical Statistics: Europe 1759–1993*, 4th edn. (London, 1998), tables D2, D8, D14, and F1. Coal output is for hard coal, brown coal, and lignite combined.

measured per head, the French economy came close to the European average and its agricultural sector out-performed it.

The French economy developed differently to Britain's because it had different resources, limitations, and preferences. Because energy was expensive in France (pithead prices of coal were 50 per cent higher than in Britain and 20 per cent higher than in Germany, and transport costs were higher too), French firms tended to concentrate on finishing products instead of heavy manufacturing, since this used less energy. It used more skilled labour (French workers were at least as productive as British ones), and though this meant that its products were more expensive, they were of a higher quality. The emblematic British industrial firm might be a Manchester cotton mill which employed hundreds of mostly unskilled workers to spin thread; its French counterpart would be the Lyon silk merchant who supplied raw materials and bought finished cloth from skilled weavers working in small workshops or at home, using the Jacquard loom to make intricately patterned silk textiles. Large cotton mills gained economies of scale, but small firms were better for silk-weaving

Table 2.2 The compound annual growth rates of the major European economies.

	Output (GDP at constant prices, %)		Output per capita (%)		Agricultural output (%)	
	1820–70	1870–1913	1820–70	1870–1913	1830–80	1880–1910
France	1.4	1.7	1.0	1.5	1.1	0.9
Germany	2.0	2.8	1.1	1.6	1.5	2.2
Italy	n.a.	1.5	n.a.	0.8	0.2	0.8
UK	2.4	1.9	1.5	1.0	0.7	0.8
Europe	2.1	2.3	1.2	1.4	0.6	0.8

Source: C. Heywood, *The Development of the French Economy, 1750–1914*, 2nd edn. (Cambridge, 1995), pp. 7, 21. Heywood's source for gross and per capita output is A. Maddison, *Phases of Capitalist Development* (Oxford, 1982), pp. 44–5 ('Europe' here is the arithmetical average of Austria, Belgium, Denmark, France, Germany, Netherlands, Norway, Sweden, Switzerland, and the UK). His source for agricultural production is P. Bairoch, 'Dix-huit décennies de développement agricole français dans une perspective internationale (1800–1980)', *Economie rurale*, 184 (1988), p. 21 (no definition of 'Europe' provided).

since they had to adjust swiftly to changes in fashion. However, the fastest-growing international markets were for cheap cotton, not silk, and mechanization elsewhere was pushing prices down. Not for the last time, foreign competition would eventually force change upon French industry.

Recent scholarship has tended to discount the idea of fundamental limitations on the French economy: capital, labour, and raw materials were all available, and where there were relative weaknesses, the French economy adapted to allow for them, by using skilled labour instead of energy, or by using female, child, and foreign workers when adult male labour became scarcer. Yet problems remain with this more optimistic view, in particular the slowdown in growth that occurred around 1870 and lasted for about twenty years when industrialization in other countries was literally steaming ahead. There was at least one crucial long-term weakness in the French economy: a low level of demand for manufactured goods. Demand was weak because so many people lived in near-self-sufficient peasant farms, and in rural and urban poverty. Although wages rose above prices for the poorest workers between 1850 and 1880, much of this extra income was spent on food. When a bad harvest pushed up food prices, this reduced demand for manufactured goods, which could quickly turn into an industrial crisis because the bad debts of every firm that went bankrupt dragged other firms down too. The link between bad harvests and industrial crises was finally broken after the 1857–9 slump, by a combination of foreign food imports and greater surplus wealth. The slow growth of the population put another brake on domestic demand compared to the rest of Europe and the USA. Exports might have made up for this, but French goods were more expensive than mass-produced British, German, and American goods. Instead, manufactured products made up a smaller portion of French exports as the century progressed.

Beyond this long-term weakness, there were more specific reasons for the slowdown around 1870. The Franco-Prussian war itself had a major impact. It killed about 200,000 people, a smallpox epidemic took away another 200,000, while civil war, dysentery, and measles added to the slaughter. The cost of the war included an indemnity of five billion francs and the loss of three departments in Alsace and Lorraine (Bas-Rhin, Haut-Rhin, and Moselle) to France's immediate rival, Germany. These lost departments more than cancelled out Napoleon III's gains of 1860, Alpes-Maritimes, Savoie and Haute-Savoie, for they contained important textile and engineering centres, and substantial mineral deposits; Table 1.1 above shows the impact of their loss on industrial output. A further explanation comes from Maurice Lévy-Leboyer and François Bourguignon, who concentrate on the integration of the French economy into international markets between 1860 and 1886 just as it lost competitiveness: too much capital was taken up by railway construction, Haussmann's housing boom, and foreign investments when other countries were investing in new technologies. Other factors include the 1861–4 cotton famine (caused by the American Civil War), the vine disease phylloxera that first appeared in 1863, and another disease, pebrine, that struck the silk industry in the later decades of the century. From 1871, farm prices began to fall in an agricultural 'Great Depression' that lasted until 1896. The crash of the Union Générale des Banques in 1882 ended the banking boom of the previous three decades.

There were three other notable features of the French economy. Perhaps the key oddity was multiple employment, which was the second main device by which workers and peasants survived, after community support. It was a form of insurance for workers against economic cycles and against a decline in any one industry, and it was no accident that Frédéric Le Play's studies of family budgets found that those in mixed employment had the best diets. Employers too favoured multiple employment because wages could be kept down when industrial work was only a supplement to farm income, and the *fabrique collective* enabled them to control their workforce without needing to impose factory discipline.

A second distinctive feature was the role of the state. The Bourbons were frankly hostile to economic change, Louis-Philippe was equivocal, and the Third Republic succumbed to the pressure of interest groups: only Napoleon III was fully committed to growth by a combination of liberalization and intervention. The 1842 law on railways, for example, served Paris better than industrial regions; the government hampered railway companies by treating them as profiteers, keeping their leases short and imposing taxes and strict regulations on them. The Second Empire encouraged more building in 1852 and guaranteed companies a return of 4 per cent after a crisis in 1857, with the result that while only one-tenth of internal trade went by railway in 1852, half of it did so by 1870. The Second Empire also furthered the work of the July Monarchy by a law of 1868 that enabled communes to borrow money in order to maintain local roads, and a banking boom began with the foundation of the Crédit Mobilier in 1852, followed by laws on banking in 1859 and 1864. State tutelage over the creation of limited liability joint-stock companies (*sociétés anonymes*) was gradually eased, until it was abolished in 1867. There were benefits for workers too. The *livret* was reformed in 1851 and 1854 so that employers could not control their workers by it. Louis-Philippe's ban on workers' associations (1834) was softened by the legalization of mutual aid societies in 1852, and by limited rights to form 'coalitions' and to strike in 1864, extended in 1868. A trade treaty signed with Britain in 1860 nearly doubled the value of imports and exports in a decade, and was followed by similar treaties with several other countries. Abroad, work began on the Suez canal in 1859, under the French engineer Ferdinand de Lesseps, and it was opened in 1869. Most famously, Napoleon III set Baron Haussmann (prefect of the Seine from 1853 to 1870) to work on redeveloping Paris, and Haussmann's works are today the most visible legacy of the Second Empire. They drove wide boulevards through mazy Parisian streets; erected new buildings, notably a flamboyant opera house; laid out parks; threw bridges across the Seine; dug a new water and sewage system. Department stores were founded to supply the increasingly elegant inhabitants of the city: Bon Marché in 1852, the Magasin du Louvre in 1855, Au Printemps in 1865, and Samaritaine in 1870. Haussmann also forced workers north and east when he demolished the narrow streets where they lived—and where barricades had been built in the 1830s and 1840s—but in so doing he created new workers' districts in Belleville and Montmartre, future strongholds of the Commune.

The final peculiarity of the French economy has its echoes today. Small firms making high-quality goods are still highly valued, if only in the French self-image; the industrial equivalent of *terroir* is artisanal production. Closely related to this is an emphasis on the quality of life. These ideas can be linked to another weakness in the French economy: the lack of desire to innovate. Because class was a question of lifestyle, not economics, it was more important to maintain that lifestyle than to achieve purely material gains. Though this did not apply to all, especially not to those who wanted to buy a more expensive lifestyle, its effect can be seen in all social strata. Peasant farmers were slow to introduce new methods which had negative side-effects: for example, reaping with a scythe was much faster than with a sickle, but it needed a strong man to wield it and left fewer gleanings for the village poor and no cover for treasured gamebirds. Workers rejected mechanization and social promotion in order to protect themselves, at the expense of the next generation. Members of the bourgeoisie turned their backs on industry to invest in land, government bonds, and the education of their sons for the civil service. Few nobles entered industry, unlike their eighteenth-century ancestors. Even businessmen were not all committed to increasing profit: while some were, others preferred to keep their firms as family enterprises. There was no shortage of scientific innovations, but these were not always applied, since scientists too aimed at cultivating the art of living instead of vulgar material success. What entrepreneurship was left was often smothered by the state, Napoleon III excepted. Yet Charles X and Louis-Philippe might argue that the end of all three of these reigns proved them right: economic and social change fed political instability. Within months of Napoleon III's fall, the boulevards of Haussmann's splendid new capital were red with fire and blood.

Revolutions, constitutions, and political life

The fall of Charles X

For all the fears of revolution and the regularity with which they came, the actual moment of catastrophe came as a surprise every time. Each regime was undone not because it was doomed to fail but by a combination of disputed political legitimacy and endemic political violence. Was the ultimate source of legitimacy divine providence or the nation? If it was the nation, did this mean that every (male) citizen should have a vote, or just its elite? What should be the balance of power between executive and legislature? Who had the final word when both president and parliament were elected? These theoretical questions only became critical when combined with extreme political polarization and popular unrest. Thus, while Louis XVIII and Charles X believed the king to be sovereign over the nation, this caused no practical problems as long as they observed the charter which they had granted to the nation. Since Louis was far more interested in his food than in the details of government, he made a good constitutional monarch even if he denied that he was one. Charles, on the other hand, intended to govern in person, which he believed to be his right and his duty. His coronation at Reims made this plain, to the offence of many—especially since the Catholic church had already staged a vast mission to Besançon and laws had been passed to compensate émigrés and punish sacrilege by the time of the coronation. Though these acts did not amount to very much (no one was ever punished by the law on sacrilege), they aroused the fears of all those who did not want a return to the old regime, which was the vast majority of the population. This was shown by demonstrations in Paris in 1826 and 1827, when further laws that appeared to threaten the Revolutionary legacy (by restoring primogeniture for the richest families and by censoring the press) were rejected by the Chamber of Peers. This prompted Villèle to dissolve the Parisian National Guard, the institutional form of the middle classes' civic pride and a crucial weapon against popular unrest. Villèle called elections to strengthen his position in November 1827, but they returned only about 180 government supporters, 70 ultras, and 180 liberal-moderate opponents. He resigned soon afterwards.

In his place, Charles X appointed a caretaker head of government, Martignac, who managed to steer his minority government along a cautious path for over a year. However, Charles X replaced him in 1829 with a new ministry containing some of the most unpopular royalists in France, led by the prince of Polignac. The president of the Chamber of Deputies, Royer-Collard, organized a vote of no confidence in March 1830; Charles stood by his ministers and dissolved the Chamber. An appeal to the electorate to arbitrate between the executive and legislature could have been a further development in a parliamentary system, but when the opposition won the elections Charles rejected this verdict and mounted a royal *coup d'état*. He issued ordinances on 25 July that re-established censorship of the press, dissolved the Chamber again, and changed the electorate to increase his chances of victory. Protests by journalists and typesetters (directly affected by censorship) on the 26th were followed by scattered demonstrations on the 27th, then by insurrections on the 28th and 29th in the popular quarters of eastern Paris. Over 500 Parisians, mostly artisans aged 25–35, and 150 soldiers were killed in fighting during these 'three glorious days'. By the 30th, opposition politicians and journalists had recovered leadership of the revolt and called for Charles to be replaced by Louis-Philippe d'Orléans, head of the second branch of the royal family. The republicans wanted General Lafayette (a hero of the French and American Revolutions) to become president, but he rejected the title and on 31 July embraced Louis-Philippe at the Hôtel de Ville (town hall) of Paris, swathed in a tricolour flag. Although Charles X had once said that 'there is no middle course between the throne and the scaffold', he abdicated on 2 August and fled to England, perhaps remembering the riposte attributed to Talleyrand, 'You are forgetting the post-chaise.' On 9 August, Louis-Philippe was enthroned as king of the French (not of France) in the Chamber of Deputies, dressed in his National Guard uniform.

Was the fall of Charles unavoidable? Had he accepted the verdict of the elections, as Louis XVIII might have done, he could have kept his crown at the price of admitting the sovereignty of the people. But since he refused to recognize this, it was always possible that there would be a revolution some time. Yet the liberal philosopher Royer-Collard was not a man to start a revolution, and Charles only fell when he lost control of the streets of Paris. From 1789 onwards, political violence menaced every regime down to and including the Fifth Republic. The most extreme form of this was civil war, as in the Vendée rising of 1793, the rising against Louis-Napoleon in December 1851, repression of the Commune in May 1871, and the conflicts of the Second World War. Fears of the great Revolution lay behind the ferocity with which popular protests were suppressed, and once in power, new regimes were just as keen as their predecessors to stamp out the revolutionary movements that had been their allies just months before. Assassination was a very different form of protest. Louis-Philippe and Louis-Napoleon both survived several attempts on their lives, the worst of which were by Joseph Fieschi in 1835 and by Felice Orsini in 1858. Such attacks were the acts either of individuals or of the revolutionary conspiracies that flourished throughout the century, beginning with the *Chevaliers de la foi* on the right and the *Charbonnerie* (inspired by the Italian *Carbonari*) on the left. The main causes of the uprisings were economic, though they generally had a political dimension too, for the artisans of major cities were steeped in republican and socialist ideas, enriched by memories and traditions from the 1790s. The revolution of July 1830 occurred when high political protest intersected chronologically and geographically with popular protest. The economy had been in trouble since 1826, beginning with a series of poor potato and grain harvests. In the Seine and Loire valleys, bands of beggars attacked food convoys and blackmailed farmers by arson; at the same time, half a dozen mountainous departments were troubled by the imposition of the Forest Code of 1827. One of the missing elements in the Napoleonic codes, this closed access to common woodlands, pro-voking a violent response from villagers. The worst disturbances, in the Ariège, were known as the *guerre des Demoiselles* because bands of twenty to thirty men disguised themselves as women before attacking forest guards and timber merchants. This 'war' was quelled by 1832, although incidents continued until 1872. The authorities could sur-vive disturbances like this until they troubled Paris at a politically sensitive moment.

Why was there so much political violence in France even after the introduction of universal suffrage, which Victor Hugo said 'abolished the right of insurrection'? The simplest answer is that there was noth-ing exceptional about French politics in this. France may have been a turbulent country compared to mainland Britain or Switzerland, but its revolutions after 1800 were tame compared to the Russian Revolution and Spanish Civil War. Many aspects of life were brutal, such as military conscription, the prison system, and even daily life, so why should political protest have been different? For artisans and peasants, there was no other way to make themselves heard even with the vote. Men took up arms without hesitation in order to defend their country or their honour, so why not their ideals or their livelihood? In Paris, building barricades had become part of popular culture rather than a once-in-a-lifetime act of defiance; according to Tocqueville, it was 'the street urchins of Paris who generally start rebellions, and they usually do so gaily, like schoolboys off for the holidays'.[12] The problem posed by political violence was not how it began but how to end it.

Louis-Philippe: a king for everyone?

Louis-Philippe was made king because he offered a regime which might solve this problem by including nearly everyone in it. The Orléans family were royal yet accepted the Revolution: in the early years of the Revolution Louis-Philippe had joined the National Guard and fought in the Revolutionary wars at the battles of Valmy and Jemappes. During the Terror he had fled abroad, but remained distant from the Bourbons in exile and during the Restoration. In 1830, his supporters included many influential figures: Lafayette, Talleyrand, the bankers Jacques Laffitte and Casimir Perier, and the historian and journalist Adolphe Thiers. Guided by Thiers, Louis-Philippe added the Napoleonic legacy to this mixture of royalism and revolution, by completing the Arc de Triomphe, arranging for the return of Napoleon's ashes for burial in the Invalides in 1840, and appointing imperial marshals (Soult and Mortier) to lead his government. Catholicism became the religion of 'the majority of Frenchmen' instead of the official religion of France, and the tricolour replaced the white flag of the Bourbons. Louis-Philippe began his rule from the centre too, between 'Movement' and 'Resistance', as the wings were then termed. Restoration officials were purged and replaced with Napoleonic officials and soldiers, or by new men like Odilon Barrot, a barrister from the Orléanist left. The premier,

[12] A. de Tocqueville, *Recollections*, trans. J. P. Mayer (London, 1970), p. 29.

Laffitte, prepared laws which doubled the electorate to 166,000 by lowering the age limit to 25 and the tax level to 200 francs; deputies had to be at least 30 and pay at least 500 francs' tax. Over a million men were given the right to vote for municipal councils, and National Guard officers were elected by their men.

The July Monarchy's attempt to find a 'middle way' came under immediate pressure. The continuing economic crisis led to strikes and demonstrations by workers and peasants demanding reform; riots broke out in September 1830, during the trial of Charles's ministers, and in February 1831, when the Legitimists (supporters of the Bourbon dynasty) held a memorial service for the duke of Berry. International events also excited the left, who wanted to help nationalist rebellions in Belgium, Poland, and Italy gain their freedom from the Netherlands, Russia, and Austria respectively. This agitation pushed Louis-Philippe towards 'Resistance'; he dismissed Laffitte and Barrot, and appointed Casimir Perier in March 1831, who crushed a rising by Lyon silk workers that November. Perier's foreign policy was pragmatic: he abandoned the Polish nationalists, protected Belgian independence against the Netherlands in August, and occupied the port of Ancona in Italy in January 1832 to counter Austrian influence. Just as Perier stabilized the July Monarchy, he died on 16 May 1832 in the first cholera epidemic to hit France, along with 100,000 others. That month, the widowed duchess of Berry landed in Provence to raise the Legitimists there and in the Vendée; though her supporters were easily defeated, she evaded capture until November . . . when she was found to be pregnant, much to the scandal of Catholic ultras. The left was still the greatest threat, with risings in Paris in June 1832, major strikes in 1833 and 1834, then more insurrections in Lyon and Paris in April 1834. In 1831, Lyonnais silk workers had fought for a new tariff for their cloth; in 1834, the cause was a new law on associations that menaced their mutual aid societies. Paris followed the lead of Lyon, coordinated by the secret 'Society of the Rights of Man'. After the defeat of both risings, elections in June went heavily against the republicans, and a series of repressive laws was passed in September 1835 after Fieschi's assassination attempt. The failure of an attempt by Louis-Napoleon Bonaparte to raise the Strasbourg garrison in 1836 concluded this troubled period.

Since revolutionaries, royalists, and now a Bonaparte had all attempted to overthrow it, the July Monarchy had clearly failed to be all-inclusive, and it had abandoned the middle way. What sort of regime was left? It was a constitutional monarchy, based on the Charter of 1814 with two significant changes: the preamble no longer said that the Charter was granted by the king to the people, and the emergency powers used by Charles X in 1830 had been struck out. The difference between the Restoration and July Monarchy was more political than constitutional. Contemporaries called the latter a 'bourgeois monarchy' and Louis-Philippe a 'citizen-king', in contrast to the aristocratic monarchy of the Restoration. Even though many bourgeois did not have a vote and there was no meaningful social or economic difference between noble and bourgeois, it merited this title because of the political differences between the Bourbon and Orléanist monarchies. In the words of Robert Tombs, the '1830 revolution was not the triumph of one socio-economic class over another, but of one socio-political faction over another, that of the majority of notables who had accepted and gained from the changes of 1789, over the ultraroyalist majority that had rejected them and lost'.[13] Louis-Philippe's public style confirmed this, preferring the château de Neuilly to Louis XIV's vast and formal palace at Versailles, which was converted into a museum dedicated 'to the glories of France'. It was also more parliamentary than the Restoration in practice, for governments fell from office when they lost their majority, and though Louis-Philippe was an active ruler, he could be eclipsed by talented men like Thiers and François Guizot. What did not develop was a party system that would allow alternation between left and right within the regime. As a historian of England, Guizot hoped that 1830 would be France's version of the Glorious Revolution of 1688, but he undermined himself by following the example of Robert Walpole instead, using placemen and corruption to control parliament (about half the July Monarchy's deputies were also civil servants, of whom three-quarters voted for the government). Parties might also have rooted the Chamber of Deputies in the country, to compensate for the second main weakness of the regime, its lack of legitimacy. Louis XVIII claimed the legitimacy of divine right and Napoleon III claimed that of popular election, but Louis-Philippe was caught midway between these positions, and Guizot kept him there by refusing to extend the franchise.

[13] R. Tombs, *France 1814–1914* (London, 1996), p. 358.

There was an alternative to Guizot's scorn for party and populism, embodied by Thiers. The 1830s were marked by ministerial instability, though the same pack (Soult, Thiers, Guizot, Molé, and Victor de Broglie) was usually reshuffled, a trick repeated by the Third and Fourth Republics. When the economic prosperity of the late 1830s ended in 1839, a new period of instability began with an insurrection by the conspiratorial left of Auguste Blanqui and Armand Barbès in Paris in May 1839, followed by another attempt at revolution by Louis-Napoleon Bonaparte, landing at Boulogne in August 1840. In March 1840 Louis-Philippe was obliged to make Thiers premier, who broke with precedent by chairing the council of ministers instead of the king. Unlike Guizot, Thiers embraced the populism of the Revolutionary and Napoleonic eras; his southern warmth contrasted with Guizot's Protestant austerity, and his speeches entranced the Chamber of Deputies where Guizot had lectured to it. Thiers attempted to regain popularity for the regime by drawing on the Napoleonic legacy instead of extending the franchise or making notable social reforms, only to find that international events made this nationalism a liability. In July 1840 French opinion was outraged by the Treaty of London, an agreement between Britain, Russia, Prussia, and Austria to protect the ailing Ottoman empire by demanding that Mohammed Ali, the pasha of Egypt, withdraw his forces from Syria. This was a national insult to France because the treaty had been concluded without it, and because France had claimed an interest in Egyptian affairs ever since Napoleon's expedition; just four years earlier, an obelisk from Egypt had been erected in the place de la Concorde in Paris with great ceremony. Louis-Philippe was no more militarist than he had been in 1830, and dismissed Thiers rather than fight a war for national honour. Soult replaced Thiers as premier in October 1840, with Guizot as minister of foreign affairs and as the government's real director, until he became premier in name as well in 1847.

This ministry remained in office until the end of the July Monarchy, convinced by the experiences of 1830 and 1840 that any reforms which increased the strength of populism would lead to disaster, though conflicts with the Catholic church over secondary education prevented it from forming an alliance of 'throne and altar' as Charles X had done. A remarkable Catholic renaissance began, opposed to the regime, led by such diverse figures as the liberal priest Félicité de Lamennais, the politician Charles de Montalembert, and Louis Veuillot of the polemical newspaper *L'Univers*. The appearance of cheaper newspapers, led by Émile de Girandin's *La Presse* in 1836, made them the focus of a political world far broader than the Chamber of Deputies: by 1848, there were ten times as many newspaper subscribers in Paris as there were voters. The Soult–Guizot ministry also oversaw a period of sharp economic growth, which finally yielded a clear parliamentary majority for Guizot in the elections of 1846, when supporters of the government won 291 seats out of 459; such a result convinced Guizot that reform was superfluous, and his opponents that it was essential. At this point, fate turned against the regime. A poor harvest in 1845 was followed by a disastrous one in 1846, exacerbated by a potato blight (the same blight that caused famine in Ireland). This worsened the industrial crisis that began when the railway boom turned into a bust in 1846–7. In March 1847, the Chamber again rejected demands for two essential reforms, banning civil servants from sitting as deputies and widening the electorate. From July, Barrot led a 'banquet campaign' for reform around the country, where large dinners were held to circumvent laws on public meetings, just when the government was sullied by a corruption scandal involving two ex-ministers, Jean-Baptiste Teste and General Cubières. The banquet campaign began to grow out of the control of Barrot and his allies, who had no wish to overthrow the regime nor any expectation of doing so. Because the king had criticized the campaign in December 1847, they felt obliged to hold one last banquet in Paris to avoid losing face, and the government banned it for the same reason. As in 1830, radicals and workers then took the initiative, and popular demonstrations began on 22 February 1848. This turned into revolt on the 23rd, when the National Guard sided with the crowds. Louis-Philippe havered between conciliation and force, dismissing Guizot while appointing the hated Marshal Bugeaud to command the army (Parisians held him responsible for a massacre in 1834, when troops had fired on unarmed civilians). The change of ministry had come too late: a crowd invaded the Chamber of Deputies then swept off to the Hôtel de Ville to declare the republic. In his seventies, Louis-Philippe had no stomach for a fight, nor was there a popular heir since the accidental death of his eldest son in 1842; he abdicated on the 24th and took flight for England once more.

The brief life of the Second Republic

On 25 February 1848, Tocqueville was struck by 'the uniquely and exclusively popular character of the recent revolution', and by 'how little hatred, or indeed any other acute feeling, was shown in this first moment of victory'.[14] Four months later, the popular revolution was defeated in savage street fighting. What went wrong? The victory of the republic was initially welcomed by the provinces, nobles, and even the church. The provisional government was led by Alphonse de Lamartine, a royalist turned republican, a diplomat, poet, and historian, with Alexandre Ledru-Rollin as minister of the interior. It rapidly declared universal male suffrage, the right to work and the right of association, abolished the death penalty for political offences, and limited the working day to ten hours in Paris and eleven in the provinces (this rose again to twelve in September 1848). The socialist Louis Blanc headed a commission to examine social reforms and the organization of work, while 'national workshops' were opened to occupy the unemployed (over half the workers of Paris). Inspired by Victor Schoelcher, slavery was finally abolished in the French empire. As revolutions spread across Europe, the provisional government faced demands to support national movements in Italy and Poland, and suddenly appreciated the virtue of Louis-Philippe's inaction. The government was undone by money instead of war. The economic situation worsened further because investors and businesses lacked confidence in the new regime; they certainly did not want to lend it money, and since widespread disorder meant that indirect taxes were not being collected, the government resorted to an extra 45 per cent levy on direct taxes. Though this was needed to keep the cities fed, it alienated the countryside; further demonstrations by Parisian radicals on 17 March and 16 April convinced the rest of France that the Parisian left was a serious menace.

As a result, the elections of 23 April produced a Constituent Assembly dominated by landowners and social conservatives. It was only a matter of time before conflict between this Assembly and Parisian radicals erupted. The radicals made the first move when Blanqui, Barbès, and François Raspail led an invasion of the Assembly on 15 May, demanding support for the Polish revolution. The

---

[14] Tocqueville, *Recollections*, p. 70.

Assembly counter-attacked on 21 June, when it announced the closure of the national workshops, which by then employed over 113,000 workers. On 23 June, workers took to the streets of eastern Paris in a social revolution. For them, the popular triumph of February 1848 had been stolen by the elites sitting in the Assembly, despite universal male suffrage, and they believed that the only solution was a revolution that would remake society as a whole, not just its political regime. This time the army, the National Guard from non-working class districts, and the new *Garde Mobile* (also recruited from the unemployed) held firm under the command of General Cavaignac, and crushed the rebels. Eight hundred troops and 1,500–3,000 rebels were killed, and another 4,500 were imprisoned or deported.

The Constituent Assembly decided that the executive should be headed by a president, who was to be directly elected by universal male suffrage to give him some authority independent of parliament. The danger that this gave one man too much power was countered by limiting him to one four-year term only. The deputies who voted for this weighed up the chances of republicans like Lamartine and Ledru-Rollin, or Cavaignac, head of the government since 28 June, or even of a royalist candidate; what they did not expect was the rise of Louis-Napoleon Bonaparte, first elected to the Assembly in June though he only took a seat after re-election on 17 September. The presidential elections of December 1848 gave victory to Louis-Napoleon by 5.5 million votes against 1.4 million for Cavaignac and a mere 370,000 for Ledru-Rollin. Raspail, Lamartine, and the conservative General Changarnier won just 60,000 votes between them. Bonaparte won through the rejection of Parisian radicalism and taxes by the provinces, Catholics, and the peasantry, and through the prestige of a name that united populism, order, and glory.

Like the July Monarchy, the Second Republic had the potential to be an inclusive regime, with a Bonaparte at the head of a republic, underpinned by a massive popular vote. However, the government followed right-wing, not centrist policies for the next three years. In the spring of 1849 French troops toppled the new Roman republic and restored the city to the pope, in order to block Austrian ambitions. An outraged left demonstrated in Paris on 13 June, only for the government to break the protest by declaring a state of siege. The government helped the Catholic church even more in 1850 by a law in January which authorized members of religious orders to teach in primary schools and by Falloux's law on higher education in March, which gave the church a greater say in the administration of the university and allowed it to open its own schools and colleges. Furthermore, because the left was increasingly successful in elections to the new Legislative Assembly in 1849 and 1850, the Assembly limited the vote to those who paid personal taxes, had no criminal record, and had been resident in one place for at least three years. This cut the electorate from 9.6 to 6.8 million, losing millions who were presumed to vote left because of their poverty, criminality, or vagrancy. These and similar measures stimulated the formation of a rural left, the democratic socialists. The main left-wing areas stretched from the centre of France south across the Massif Central to the Pyrenees, east to the Swiss border, and south from there to the Mediterranean. The strength of the left and extreme left in the countryside is an oddity of French electoral politics which first became visible in the Second Republic, though its origins lay deep in the politics of religion, forms of landownership, and family or communal solidarities.

Louis-Napoleon had not simply drifted to the right with the Assembly, for he also had been remaking the political formula of Bonapartism. His first ministry was a talented one in line with the Assembly's majority; led by Barrot, it included Tocqueville and Falloux too. In October 1849 they were replaced by a weaker ministry led by General Hautpoul, who was not given the customary title of President of the Council of Ministers, which was in turn followed by ministries entirely dependent on Louis-Napoleon. He needed to be re-elected as president both as a step towards restoring the empire and to avoid personal bankruptcy, and when the Assembly refused to change the constitution in July 1851 he turned to a *coup d'état*. Saint-Arnaud, a general from Algeria, was made premier in October and the prefect of police was replaced with a notorious anti-republican. Despite a growing expectation of a coup, it was executed so swiftly on 2–3 December 1851 that there was little resistance from the Assembly or from Paris. The Assembly was dissolved and 220 deputies were arrested, including Thiers, Tocqueville, Broglie, Barrot, Falloux, and the stonemason Martin Nadaud, elected as deputy for the Creuse in 1849. This time the main insurrection came not from Paris, where Saint-Arnaud quickly though bloodily demolished the barricades, but from the provinces, where the democratic socialists rallied some

70,000 men. This was the largest rural rising of the nineteenth century, though it involved remarkably little fighting. Entire villages rose in support of the rebels, only to submit when superior forces arrived from outside. It took until 10 December to defeat these scattered risings, with about 120 fatalities in total; they were punished by 27,000 arrests and nearly 10,000 deportations. Like his uncle, Louis-Napoleon followed his coup with a plebiscite, on 21–22 December; like his uncle, he won it handsomely, by 7,145,000 to 592,000. If the bloodshed of the 2 December coup was the original sin of the Second Empire, the French people gave it absolution remarkably quickly.

The Second Empire

On 2 December 1851 Louis-Napoleon succeeded where Charles X and MacMahon failed, when he overruled parliament in the name of executive authority. He succeeded partly by the use of force and partly because of the fear of continued social conflict; in Marx's formulation, the bourgeoisie preferred 'an end with terror than terror without end'. The Provisional Government (the only truly left-wing government of the nineteenth century) and the June days had rekindled fear of either extreme, which could only be overcome by a strong but non-partisan executive (the Bonapartist solution) or by a weak executive controlled by broad party alliances (the Third Republican solution). The Second Empire was a deliberate copy of the first, for, as Louis-Napoleon proclaimed, 'Since France has only kept going for the past fifty years thanks to the administrative, military, judicial, religious and financial organization of the Consulate and Empire, why should we not adopt the political institutions of that era too?' Power was held by the emperor, who presided over non-elected ministers who were answerable to him only and kept separate from the legislature. Deputies were elected to a 300-strong Legislative Body every six years, by universal male suffrage without the limits of 1850. The Legislative Body had no right to initiate laws, could not elect its own president, and its debates were not published. The appointed Senate was even less active, serving only as a guardian of the constitution. Prefects' powers were increased further, especially in the manipulation of elections on behalf of official candidates and in their control of state employment: 55 per cent of posts in the ministry of the interior, 98 per cent in public instruction, 70 per cent in finance, and 40 per cent in agriculture, commerce, and public works lay in their patronage. Although municipal councillors were elected, mayors were once again nominated by the government. As with the First Empire, the aim was to 'freeze' political life, to rule above parties by the strong, centralized state, and to reconcile civil conflicts. Unlike the First Empire, Louis-Napoleon took the development of France as his goal, not the invasion of Europe. The Second Empire was declared on 2 December 1852 and the 'Prince President' Louis-Napoleon became Napoleon III, pretending that the Bonaparte dynasty was unbroken in the same way that the Bourbons had skipped from Louis XVI to Louis XVIII. A plebiscite held in November 1852 approved this by 7,800,000 votes to 250,000. Sustained economic growth, police surveillance of any remaining opposition, and the promise of peace enabled the regime to take root in the 1850s.

Napoleon III gave the Second Empire a dynamism that the July Monarchy had lacked. Louis-Philippe was a skilful politician, but he was not an adventurer or a visionary. Napoleon III was both. His political career began with two failed attempts to raise an insurrection; he had numerous love affairs (he fathered two children even when imprisoned between 1840 and 1846); as a follower of the socialist Henri de Saint-Simon he was devoted to economic and social change; he took ever-greater gambles in foreign policy. His court was the most flamboyant of the century, adorned by men like Auguste de Morny, the emperor's illegitimate half-brother and president of the Legislative Body from 1854–65, notable for his financial speculations, his strings of racehorses and of mistresses (he was Cora Pearl's first high-society lover).

Political stability and the temptations of imperial glory persuaded Napoleon III to abandon the pacifism he had professed in 1852, and which all regimes had practised since 1815 from the fear that war led to revolution. The aims of his foreign policy were little different from those of previous regimes: to restore French prestige and authority in Europe, revise the borders of 1815, protect French interests, and win allies. Louis XVIII had regained France's freedom of action and had intervened in Spain; under Charles X, Villèle successfully supported the cause of Greek independence in 1827, which restored France's influence in the eastern Mediterranean and drew it closer to Russia. Charles had hoped to use this friendship and the weakness of the Ottoman empire to reshuffle Europe's borders, gaining Belgium and the left bank of the Rhine for France, until the tsar rejected this. Instead, Charles turned to Algeria, to bolster his prestige and to support French interests in northern Africa. A diplomatic row with the bey of Algiers had provided the opportunity for Charles to send a large force of 635 ships to Algiers in 1830, and the city fell on 5 July. By the time the news reached Paris on the 9th, it was too late to save him; a new empire was born as the old monarchy fell. Louis-Philippe resisted the temptation to regain Belgium in 1830 because of British threats of intervention, and found enough allies to form a Quadruple Alliance in 1834 with Britain, Spain, and Portugal. However, the storm that broke over Egypt in 1840 isolated France once more. Guizot worked hard to recover British sympathies, symbolized by visits between Victoria and Louis-Philippe in 1843 and 1844, though he swam against a tide of anglophobia and francophobia in the French and British press respectively, and against a tempest whipped up by Palmerston over the marriage of the queen of Spain in 1846. The conquest of Algeria was also completed under the July Monarchy. It was not until 1834 that the government decided to keep its conquered territories, then limited to the towns of Algiers, Bône, and Oran. Expansion out of these bases was resisted by highly mobile Arab forces commanded by Abd el-Khader. In the 1840s, Bugeaud slowly squeezed Abd el-Khader by making his forces as mobile as the Arabs, and by the brutal devastation of villages suspected of helping the enemy. By the time Abd el-Khader surrendered in 1847, about 109,000 Europeans had settled in Algeria, just under half of them French. France had acquired a major new colony—and a colonial army with different values and loyalties from the mainland army. The revolutions of 1848 returned attention to Europe, but once again governments refused to support revolutionaries abroad; the 1849 expedition to Rome was about the defence of order and French interests, not revolution.

Napoleon III abandoned this caution in 1854. Hostilities between Russia and the waning Ottoman empire made Britain and France fear that Constantinople might fall to Russia, and they declared war in March 1854. Allied troops landed in the Crimea and, after a shambolic campaign on all sides, gained satisfaction when the Black Sea was declared neutral at the Congress of Paris in 1856. Although Napoleon might not have entered the war had Britain not led the way, and although it nearly ended in disaster, it gave him a taste for martial glory. Italy presented an opportunity to satisfy this taste, repel Austria, create another satellite state (along with Belgium), regain land lost in 1815, and make himself the true heir of Napoleon I. The romanticism of the Italian nationalist cause also played a part, but Napoleon III did not follow the principle of nationalities systematically throughout his foreign policy. At a secret meeting held in July 1858, the emperor agreed with Cavour, the premier of Piedmont, that France would help Piedmont expel Austria in return for Savoy and Nice. Narrow victories at the battles of Magenta and Solferino in June 1859 persuaded Napoleon III to sign the armistice of Villafranca with Austria the next month; as a result, he had to wait until 1860 to receive Nice and Savoy, when Cavour gained control of central and northern Italy. France's standing in Europe had reached its highest level since Napoleon I, with the borders of 1815 partially redrawn, reputedly the best army in Europe, Austria and Russia defeated, Britain and Prussia neutral. Imperial expansion began to accelerate too, by trading arrangements in Morocco and Shanghai, by expansion in Senegal, Guinea, Côte d'Ivoire, and Gabon, the capture of Saigon in 1859, and the creation of a protectorate over Cambodia in 1883. Napoleon even sponsored an attempt to found a new Habsburg empire in Mexico.

If these overseas ventures failed, they cost Napoleon relatively little (less than they cost Archduke Maximilian, who faced a Mexican firing squad in 1867 after the French abandoned him). Matters became more serious when he gambled against Bismarck in Europe. Napoleon attempted to capitalize on the confrontation between a waxing Prussia and waning Austria by secretly promising neutrality to both, in the hope of gaining an advantage on the Rhine. But when the Prussian army routed the Austrians at Königgrätz (Sadowa) in 1866 and Bismarck formed the North German Confederation in 1867, it was clear that France's newly recovered superiority was already menaced. In 1870, Bismarck proposed that a member of the Hohenzollern-Sigmaringen family (related to the Prussian royal family) take the vacant Spanish throne. When news of this reached Paris on 2 July, it provoked a furious reaction. Though the candidacy was rapidly withdrawn, Napoleon III sent his ambassador to King William of Prussia, then staying at Ems, to insist that it would never be renewed. William telegrammed his account of this meeting to Bismarck, who took his chance to provoke war between the two states: his edited version of the 'Ems telegram' outraged both French and Prussian opinion, and the French army began mobilization the next day, 14 July. In one sense the Franco-Prussian war was a vast duel fought over a slight to national honour; in another, it was caused by the geopolitical conflict of France and Prussia—indeed, it was only the first of three rounds in this conflict. A third perspective might see the war as a self-made trap: Napoleon had stoked the nationalist fires so feared by Louis-Philippe and had alienated other bases of support; unity could no longer be achieved on any other issue, so he had to pursue war. How had the promising domestic position of 1860 turned so sour by 1870?

Between 1860 and 1870, the Second Empire turned towards a parliamentary system, making it a precursor to the Fifth Republic. The first steps towards what later became the 'liberal empire' were taken in 1860–1, when Napoleon III gave the Legislative Body greater control of the budget, allowed it to debate general government policy, and authorized the publication of its debates. The aim of this liberalization, according to Morny, was to reduce the personal importance of the emperor so that the empire might be able to outlive Napoleon III, sacrificing the Bonapartist system for the Bonaparte dynasty. It was also a concession to growing opposition, giving it the oxygen of greater parliamentary, press, and electoral freedom. This freedom was exploited by a new mass-circulation press led by the *Petit Journal*, the first one-sou (5-centime) newspaper, printed on new, faster presses. Opposition came from Catholics, offended by the Italian expeditions that stripped the pope of his possessions outside Rome, from liberal Orléanist notables like Victor de Broglie and Thiers, and from the republican left. During the 1860s, urban elections swung increasingly to the republicans, both bourgeois and working-class. Bourgeois republicans defended the political liberties of 1789 combined with the new doctrines of positivism; derived from the teachings of Auguste Comte, this combined a scientific view of society with an anticlerical view of politics, and spread through freemasonry and the universities. The radical left contained different strands, uneasily wound together in the International Working Men's Association of 1864. Most French socialists followed Pierre-Joseph Proudhon or Blanqui, while a few were more influenced by Marx. Proudhon took the view that political revolutions had achieved nothing so far, and looked for an anarchist solution to the reorganization of society, based on small working-class communities and cooperatives. Blanqui (arrested May 1848, amnestied 1859, re-arrested 1861, escaped 1864) continued to work for a revolutionary coup in the spirit of 1793.

The advance of the opposition was shown by an increased number of strikes in 1868–70, as the economy faltered, and by the elections of 1869, when it won 40 per cent of the vote. Napoleon III responded by liberalizing his regime still further: he dismissed the authoritarian Eugène Rouher as his leading minister, and replaced him with Emile Ollivier on 2 January 1870; Ollivier had been one of the first republicans elected to the Legislative Body back in 1857. The revised constitution made the Senate a proper upper chamber, gave parliament the power to initiate laws, and made ministers answerable to it. Napoleon III remained head of the government as well as of the state, and reserved a double-barrelled weapon in case of a dispute between executive and legislature: he could dissolve the Legislative Body and could appeal directly to the nation by a plebiscite. Ominously, the Parisian streets were in ferment again on 12 January 1870, for the funeral of Victor Noir, a republican journalist shot by Prince Pierre Bonaparte when Noir delivered to the prince a challenge to a duel on behalf of another journalist. However, a plebiscite held to confirm this constitution in May was won by 7,350,000 to 1,500,000 votes. While this may well have given the Second Empire a potentially durable constitution, it also made the day-to-day conduct of politics harder and made the government more dependent on popular support. When anti-Prussian tempers flared in July 1870, Napoleon had little choice but to follow this mood, and hope for victory on the battlefield.

Within six weeks, the Second Empire had been destroyed instead. In the previous decade, the Prussian army had rethought the principles of European warfare. It used railways to deploy massive armies of civilian reservists with great mobility, equipped with new rapid-firing artillery; these armies then encircled their opponents rather than fighting pitched battles. One French army, under Marshal Bazaine, was trapped at Metz; a second army, led by Marshal MacMahon and Napoleon III himself, tried to rescue it, only to be defeated at Sedan on 2 September. When this news reached Paris on the 4th, crowds invaded the Legislative Body and then marched off to the Hôtel de Ville in ritual manner to proclaim the Third Republic. Napoleon III had to wait until March 1871 before he could follow the paths of Charles X and Louis-Philippe, to exile in England. This war was important for the rest of the Continent too, for the German empire was proclaimed in the Hall of Mirrors at Versailles on 18 January 1871; in the words of one commentator, Europe had 'lost a mistress and gained a master'.

The Paris Commune and civil war

Napoleon III's war of honour and political advantage was over, but the war of geopolitics was not. Bismarck demanded the cession of Alsace and part of Lorraine to Germany, which the new government of National Defence rejected. The fiery republican leader Léon Gambetta raised new armies, which were defeated one by one; Paris was besieged from 19 September until it surrendered after a winter of starvation on 28 January, when an armistice was agreed. Fatefully, its spirit was not broken, shown by the funereal atmosphere in the city when German troops paraded through it on 1 March.

On 8 February, elections for a new National Assembly returned about 214 Orléanists, 186 Legitimists, and 150 republicans; the Bonapartists were wiped out, winning just fifteen seats. This royalist victory was partly because the Bonapartists and republicans were both discredited by fighting a losing war, and partly because many of the local notables who were elected were instinctively royalist. Thiers, who had long called for peace, was the undisputed victor of the campaign. He was made 'chief of the executive power of the French republic' on 17 February, and persuaded the Assembly to accept that Alsace (except Belfort) and part of Lorraine should be handed over to Prussia, along with an indemnity. But Paris did not accept these humiliating losses, nor the royalist Assembly, nor measures which denied Paris the right to elect its own municipal council, ended the moratorium on debts and rent, and abolished National Guardsmen's daily allowance of 1.5 francs. The dangers of a Parisian rebellion were greater than ever before because the city was filled with the rifles and artillery used in the siege. On 18 March, government troops bungled an attempt to remove cannon placed on the heights of Montmartre, which provoked the feared rebellion. Although this move has often been seen as a deliberate incitement by Thiers, it was probably a badly executed effort to disarm Paris before a conflict arose.

The Paris Commune was proclaimed on 28 March and was

crushed by regular army forces in fighting during the week of 21–28 May. Between 10,000 and 25,000 Parisians were killed in the fighting and in subsequent reprisals ordered by the army's commanders. Forty thousand more were arrested, 10,000 were convicted, and half of these were deported to New Caledonia. The old Hôtel de Ville and Tuileries palace were destroyed by fire, along with many other buildings. What had the Commune done to deserve this? Ironically, it is often accused of having done all too little. It did not confiscate private property, not even the gold reserves of the Banque de France; its social legislation did little more than ban night-work in bakeries and the deduction of fines from wages. For the National Assembly, and for future generations, it symbolized much more than this, for good or bad. The Commune's political side was led by Blanquists (Blanqui himself had already been arrested), who looked back to the Commune of 1792. They were fiercely anticlerical, and executed the archbishop of Paris, Monseigneur Darboy, along with twenty-three other hostages (this job was dangerous—a previous archbishop of Paris, Monseigneur Affre, had died on a barricade in 1848 when attempting to mediate). The social side was led by Proudhonists, who restored the moratorium on debts and rent, and planned to set up cooperatives in abandoned workshops. Separately, neither the political nor the social side came to very much, but they combined to produce a social revolution through the direct rule of the Parisian people. Elections to the Commune on 26 March returned a left-wing body: thirty-five of the eighty members were skilled workers and most of the others were recognized veterans of the left (just under half the electorate voted, as many wealthy or conservative residents had already fled). The most striking feature was that the Commune lacked individual leaders, and arose from the *quartier* solidarity of daily life as June 1848 had done. This social revolution was the control of Paris by its populace, a revolution of hierarchy not of confiscated property, and a revolution repeated by communes in Lyon, Marseille, Bordeaux, and Saint-Étienne. But the National Assembly was determined to break this popular rule over Paris, and break Paris's rule over France. By the end of May, it had succeeded.

The royalist republic

On 13 November 1872, Thiers announced to the royalist-dominated Assembly: 'The republic exists; it is the legal government of the country . . . The republic will be conservative or it will not exist.' The prospects for a Bourbon restoration had faded in 1871, when Henri, count of Chambord (the grandson of Charles X), refused to give up the white flag of the Bourbons for the tricolour, thereby rejecting the whole Revolutionary heritage. While the Orléanists waited for the childless Chambord to die and thereby make the more accommodating count of Paris (the grandson of Louis-Philippe) into the sole royalist claimant, the republic took root. Thiers realized that monarchists would accept a republic if they ran it, while republicans could never run a monarchy: a conservative republic was the only way to avoid further revolutions. Thiers was given the title of President of the Republic on 31 August 1871, and for nearly two years he dictated government policy, buoyed up by his electoral success the previous February (he was elected by a record twenty-six departments) and by Bismarck's insistence that he would only work with Thiers. However, Bismarck's opinion ceased to matter when Thiers concluded an agreement to evacuate the last German troops from France in March 1873, and he was duly ousted by the royalist majority on 24 May. Marshal MacMahon was elected president by the National Assembly, and chose Albert de Broglie, son of Victor, to lead the government for a year. In November, MacMahon's term was extended to seven years (the term of office remained thus for the Fourth and Fifth Republics up to 2002), to give the royalists a chance to find a convincing candidate. Broglie's Orléanists and the republicans together wrote a new constitution in 1875, which established that France would be a republic, with a directly elected Chamber of Deputies and an indirectly elected Senate based on universal male suffrage, and with a president indirectly elected by the two chambers. Without direct election and without the right to call a plebiscite, the president was stripped of Napoleon III's ability to command a popular mandate, though he did have considerable powers, including the right to dissolve the Chamber of Deputies. The catch lay in articles 3 and 6 of the Constitution: article 3 stated that all of the president's acts must be countersigned by a minister, while article 6 decreed that ministers were answerable to the Chamber. The Chamber could thus vote against a minister who signed an order of which it disapproved.

It was only a matter of time before the president and Chamber tried their strength. MacMahon oversaw the period known as 'Moral Order', an attempt to revitalize the country by Catholic and conservative policies whose physical symbol was the Sacré-Cœur basilica, built on top of rebellious, red Montmartre. Opposition to this order gathered under Gambetta, the scourge of clericalism and spokesman for what he called the *nouvelles couches sociales*, the 'new social strata' (this term deliberately avoided the word 'class'). The elections of February–March 1876 returned about 362 republicans and 155 conservatives (half royalists, half resurgent Bonapartists), forcing Mac-Mahon to appoint the moderates Armand Dufaure, then Jules Simon, as premier. By the following spring, even Simon was too much for MacMahon. On 16 May 1877 he dismissed Simon and reappointed Broglie, and dissolved the Chamber on 22 June. Seventy-seven prefects and 1,743 mayors were purged in order to win elections held in October, but this could not stop the advance of the republicans, who won about 325 seats. MacMahon yielded, and recalled Dufaure. No other president of the Third Republic ever dissolved the Chamber of Deputies, though the Constitution intended that he should do this if need be. Had MacMahon acted as an arbiter, dissolving a Chamber which could not form a stable majority, he would have set a beneficial precedent; instead, he broke the power of future presidents by re-enacting the defeat of Charles X. The Third Republic was thus set for the alternative to Bonapartism, namely a weak executive and parliamentary rule. The double challenge that it then faced was to secure the victory of parliament against royalism and Bonapartism, and to defend property against social revolution.

3

Republic, state, and nation confront the Father, Son, and Holy Ghost: 1877–1914

Of all the many images that France can project, from the Lascaux caves to the Stade de France, perhaps the richest collection comes from the decades before the Great War: the Eiffel Tower, the Tour de France, the art nouveau signs of the Paris Metro, the can-can at the Moulin Rouge, Impressionist and post-Impressionist art. Across the country, towns and villages were remodelled by a new civic architecture of schools, army barracks, post offices, railway stations, town halls, and grand boulevards. Beyond these visual images lie two political ones: France was one of the two great imperial powers, alongside the United Kingdom, and one of the two great republics, alongside the United States of America. A sense that French history had finally 'come right' was promoted during the Third Republic by scholars led by Ernest Lavisse. Lavisse argued that French history naturally culminated in the unity of state, nation, and republic achieved after 1871, and his interpretation was fed to schoolchildren in a textbook known as the *petit Lavisse* because it condensed his lengthy studies into one primer. Modern historians have pursued these themes too: as mentioned in Chapter 2, François Furet wrote that the French Revolution 'came into harbour' with the Third Republic, while Eugen Weber argued this was the time when local loyalties were translated into 'Frenchness'. Achievements in science, art, music, and literature also showed the vitality of France: it was the age of Louis Pasteur, Marie Curie, Henri Matisse, Paul Cézanne, Claude Debussy, and Marcel Proust, to name but a few. France was Europe's leading car maker and the world's leading movie maker by 1914. After a prolonged agricultural depression lifted in the 1890s, the worst of rural poverty was finally dispelled. In towns, running water, sewers, electricity, heating, and telephones arrived. Later generations, scarred by war, called this period a golden era, the *belle époque*.

Not everyone shared this rosy view at the time. The left argued that workers and peasants still did not receive a just share of the nation's wealth, nor their due respect and place in society; they suffered from what became known a century later as social exclusion. Women did not have the vote and remained legally subordinate to their husbands by the Civil Code. Despite the triumphs of French engineering and science, the country was overtaken economically and militarily by Germany, while the wealth of the French empire was no match for Britain's: Indochina was not India. Even if the Revolution had come into harbour, France had not: it was fraught with unresolved tensions from its past and new challenges set by the present. In particular, Catholics felt politically excluded, alienated by militant anticlericalism: Lavisse's trinity was rejected by Catholics in favour of the Holy Trinity of Father, Son, and Holy Ghost. The Great War would be the supreme test of its abilities to overcome these tensions.

The triumph of the republic, 1879–1885

In the first few years after the resignation of MacMahon, the triumphant republicans set out a new political settlement that survived until 1940, and encouraged a social and economic transformation which at last penetrated the depths of rural France. Behind this settlement, there were profound shifts in the source of political power.

The main ministries of these years were led by the moderate republicans Charles de Freycinet and Jules Ferry. The moderates were mockingly known as 'Opportunists', a term applied to Léon Gambetta in 1881 to contrast his fiery oratory in opposition with the caution he showed in power (reforms would be made when they were 'opportune'). The moderates began with a series of partly symbolic acts to demonstrate that the republic had at last triumphed: in 1880, the government decreed that parliament should return to Paris from Versailles, and granted amnesties to 3,500 Communard prisoners; 14 July was established as a national festival. A sweeping electoral victory in 1881 confirmed this success: 457 republicans were elected against ninety-five royalists and Bonapartists. Such victories meant that the moderates faced more opposition from within the republican parties themselves than from the right. Freycinet and Ferry were pitted against the populists Gambetta and Georges Clemenceau. Gambetta, the flamboyant defender of republicanism under Louis-Napoleon and defender of France in 1870–1, only formed one brief ministry because more staid republicans distrusted him as a demagogue. Clemenceau, the other great leader of popular republicanism, spent the 1880s harrying governments, toppling Ferry over failures in his colonial policy in south-east Asia in 1885. He did not hold ministerial office till 1906.

Reforms came in four overlapping areas: education, anticlericalism, political freedom, and the economy. The main education acts were masterminded by Ferry, beginning with bills on higher education and Camille Sée's law on the provision of public and secondary education for women (passed in 1880). Amongst other measures, this founded the École de Sèvres, a version of the École Normale Supérieure, to train women teachers. Further laws followed in 1881–2, to make state primary education free, to make it obligatory to send children to primary school (either public or private), and to make public education religiously neutral. As a result of these laws, the number of teachers doubled over the next few decades, reaching 125,000 by 1912–13. Primary schoolmasters and schoolmistresses, the *instituteurs* and *institutrices*, were liberated from the grip of the church, and in 1889 they became employees of the central state instead of the local council. These changes gave them better conditions and a higher status, and henceforth they rivalled the priest and mayor as leaders of village life.

These reforms had three aims: to educate; to liberate children from the Catholic church; to instil republican and patriotic beliefs. This involved teaching Lavisse's version of history, and teaching the French language to the millions of children whose first language was not French: at least half the population spoke either patois (dialect) or another language. This instruction did not eliminate these other tongues for many decades to come; instead it often produced bilingualism or compromises where children spoke in patois but counted in French, because they learnt to speak at home and to count at school. The republic's emphasis on girls' education was largely driven by political aims: it was important to educate girls in state schools because if they were taught by Catholic orders, they would undermine the work of republican boys' schools when they became mothers. In principle, mass education was also inherently democratic because it opened new social and career paths to every child. In practice, the opportunities created by primary education alone were limited, and secondary education remained the preserve of the elites: only 5 per cent of children progressed that far.

Anticlericalism overlapped with educational reform in order to break the hold of the religious teaching orders; other anticlerical laws abolished obligatory Sunday rest, made cemeteries non-denominational, and legalized divorce. Political liberty was secured by laws of 1881 which guaranteed a free press and abolished the requirement that public meetings receive prior approval from the authorities. It was also secured by purges of the administration and magistrature, replacing royalists or Bonapartists with republicans. In 1884 trade unions were at last recognized, in a law piloted through parliament by René Waldeck-Rousseau. A new law on municipal government meant that mayors were henceforth elected by town councillors, not appointed by the prefect (with the exception of Paris, which was not to be trusted with such independence after the Commune). The army was also reorganized and re-equipped, with the ultimate aim of recovering Alsace and Lorraine. More contentious was Thiers's law of 1872 which formed a small, professionalized army with five years' military service. The victorious republicans changed this in 1889 to military service for all young men. This aimed to foster the republican nation by bringing men from every social class and every region together under the flag; it would revive the 'nation in arms' of the Revolution in place of the long-service army which was both discredited by defeat in 1870 and suspected of disloyalty to the republic. This became a vital issue for the left, especially when nobles entered the officer corps in large numbers because they had few other possibilities for employment by the republican state. The left's attachment to conscription never waned, and it fell to the

Gaullist Jacques Chirac to abolish it after his election as President of the Republic in 1995. Though France was a civilian democracy, military life was pervasive: regiments were garrisoned across the country, and 150 new barracks were built to house them. Brightly coloured army uniforms stood out against the dull black and blue of civilian clothing, and all men were liable to conscription and reservists' duties. Civic events were enlivened by military parades and bands, while civil disorder was suppressed by troops acting in support of the gendarmerie, which was itself a branch of the armed forces.

The political liberalism of the moderates was matched by their economic liberalism, for the main purpose of their economic policy was to encourage trade. Foreign trade was promoted by reduced import tariffs in 1881 and by new trade treaties agreed in 1882. Domestic trade was helped by Freycinet's massive public works programmes of 1878 and 1882, which spent four billion francs on railways and canals that finally linked the whole of France into a single economy.

The republican triumph involved several shifts in political power, in social, religious, and geographical terms, in the relationship between centre and periphery, and in the relationship between government, parliament, and civil service.

The social shift was a transfer of power away from the old notables to a combination of the traditional petty bourgeoisie of tradesmen, craftsmen, and small landowners and the growing middle class of white-collar workers, intellectuals, employees, clerks, engineers, teachers, lawyers, doctors—Gambetta's new social strata. These new strata became leaders of the older petty bourgeoisie: this was an age when the spoken and written word reigned supreme, and so it was inevitable that lawyers, journalists, and teachers would be asked to lead brewers and locksmiths. The republic was built on the petty bourgeoisie and the middle classes. It gave them full political rights (if they were male), freed them from control by the state or church authorities, protected their interests, and offered them social promotion through education. Their leaders were a mixture of the self-employed, such as lawyers or doctors, and employees, such as teachers. They joined forces in local electoral committees, in the Radical party and in freemasonry. As professional men, they were themselves bourgeois, but many of them had risen from humbler families through the republic's schools and by their own merit; the republic had made their ascent possible, and it received their loyalty in return.

The religious shift was expressed by the absence of Catholics from ministerial office until the Great War, while Protestants, Jews, agnostics, and atheists took their place in government. Freemasonry played an important role in both this social shift and the religious shift. The number of masons rose steadily: in 1914 there were 33,000 members of the main order, the Grand Orient de France, with 8,000 in the rival order, the Grande Loge de France. These two orders were almost exclusively male: very few lodges accepted women. French freemasonry became increasingly left-wing over the decades. The Grand Orient became officially agnostic in 1877, and then moved towards atheism under leaders drawn from the new middle classes. By 1900 freemasonry was dominated by the Radical party, till further shifts in membership passed control to the socialists in 1911. Freemasonry served many purposes, and many lodges were formed simply for charitable or social reasons (travelling salesmen often joined to give them a 'club' to visit on their journeys). The two most important political functions of freemasonry were first to act as a backbone for the otherwise amorphous Radical party and to be a nursery for its politicians, and secondly to act as a way to influence the authorities. The new strata ousted the old elites largely because they gained access to the official world of prefecture, parliament, and ministries, and freemasonry was an important way to gain this access.

The third shift, of geography, saw the regions south of the Loire gain influence, partly because the electoral system favoured the countryside over more urban regions (especially for the Senate), and partly because this half of the country contained many strongholds of radicalism and anticlericalism. As a result, it gained a larger share of public investment than the more developed Paris basin and industrial north and north-east; economic policy tended to favour the family firms and farms that proliferated south of the Loire, and religious policy went against the more devoutly Catholic areas of Brittany, the north, and the north-east.

The last two shifts represented changes in the balance of power. From the first to the third Napoleon, officials of the central government, especially the prefect, had held authority over the periphery. This was tempered by the need to accommodate local elites and by the sheer logistical problems of ruling the countryside, without good roads and before the telegraph. Essentially, central governments demanded little more than order, taxes, and conscripts, while the periphery wanted to be left alone. The Third Republic made matters more complex: governments and deputies needed votes, which gave the periphery much more sway. But now the centre had more tools for coercion: the telegraph relayed orders instantly, while roads and rail carried men to enforce them. It also had more scope for bribery: it could endow favoured localities with post offices, transport links, army garrisons, and state monopolies such as tobacco factories. The changed relationship in the triangle of government, parliament, and administration flowed from the same process that gave the periphery more power, namely the greater power of parliament at the expense of ministers. But this process affected governments much more than the administration. The state bureaucracy grew in size as the state's spheres of action grew, and the more feeble ministers became, the more they depended on their civil servants.

The new democracy

On the face of it, the most glaring weakness of the Third Republic was the instability of its governments: 108 came and went in seventy years. This was compounded by the nature of these ministries. They were all coalitions, and nearly all were formed as a collection of politicians who could deliver enough votes to win a majority in the Chamber of Deputies. This instability thwarted controversial reforms, long-term planning, and consistency. The Council of Ministers did not equate to a cabinet in the British sense of a body drawn from one party or allied parties and bound by collective responsibility. Each minister ran his ministry as his domain, headed by a personal office of political allies, and in French the term *cabinet* refers to this office. The Senate made matters worse by checking several of the Chamber's reforms: it was dominated by conservative rural landowners by design. It toppled a third of the ministries under the Third Republic, usually by rejecting important legislation. However, the rapid turnover in governments was not as severe as it might appear. For one thing, this turnover is exaggerated because most of the changes were reshuffles, not ruptures: 43 per cent of ministers returned in the very next government, over the Third Republic as a whole. Ministers were drawn from a core of long-serving deputies: of the 561 men who served as minister between 1879 and 1900, 122 served in five or more governments. There were acknowledged experts who stayed at their post as the rest of the council danced around, such as Théophile Delcassé at foreign affairs (who served continuously from 1898 to 1905), or who returned to the same portfolio repeatedly, like Joseph Caillaux at finance, Jules Ferry at education, and Jules Méline at agriculture. The ministers for war and for the navy were often generals and admirals from outside parliament.

Instead, the fundamental problem lay in the power accorded to the Chamber of Deputies without sufficient discipline upon it. The President of the Republic was reduced to a figurehead whose duty was 'to wear evening dress in the daytime', and who lacked the legitimacy of a directly elected leader. After the failure of MacMahon, no president called an early election again during the Third Republic. This removed one essential discipline from the Chamber: it could vote down as many governments as it liked without facing the electorate before its four-year term was up. Party discipline was also missing. In the early Third Republic, candidates were selected by local committees aligned with the major political forces, who then joined the appropriate parliamentary group or groups when they met in Paris; it was not until 1910 that deputies were restricted to joining one group instead of two or three. Both membership of these groups and their support for a ministry were flexible, so no one could be sure whether the government had won or lost an election until it faced its first vote back in the Chamber.

Political parties were formalized for the first time between 1900 and 1905. Reading from left to right, the parties formed were the socialist party, the left of centre Radicals, the moderate republican Alliance Démocratique, the centre-right Fédération Républicaine led by Jules Méline, and Jacques Piou's Catholic centre-right Alliance Libérale Populaire. Yet these parties did not reform political life, for only the socialists were at all disciplined. Before 1914, faction remained the primary force in politics, not party. These factions were based on powerful forces, such as locality, ideology, and the defence of specific interests, but they did not gain a mass following; the result was what Duverger termed 'democracy without the people'. Its consequence was that governments lacked strong popular mandates, and switched between the centre-left and centre-right. Chapter 1 described how rule by a single man, following the example of Napoleon I, is one of the two ways that France has been ruled by the centre since the Revolution, in order to avoid the extremes of left or right; this oscillation between coalition governments was the second.

Without mass parties to unite voters and deputies, professional politicians grew into a 'club', whose internal loyalty led Robert de Jouvenel to call the Third Republic the 'republic of pals'. He commented that there 'are fewer differences between two deputies of whom one is a revolutionary (let us say socialist) and the other is not, than between two revolutionaries, of whom one is a deputy and the other is not'.[1] This similarity was sealed by deputies' custom of addressing one another by the intimate *tu*, instead of the more formal *vous*. One of the key features of this system was the *cumul des mandats*, the accumulation of elected positions: one-third of deputies were also mayors, and another third were local councillors. This was a major element in the primacy of local politics, weakening central party organizations.

The creation of this political club did not lead to apathy among voters. 'The people' may have been excluded from the heart of democracy, but they were fascinated by it nonetheless. Politics had long been a matter of passion and gossip: now it became an object of mass consumption as well, by giving the vote to all men over 21, and by the development of mass circulation newspapers. The decades before the First World War, before radio and television, were the heyday of the printed press. Technological innovations were vital to this: the telegraph relayed news to local press offices across the country, and high-speed rotary printers invented by Hippolyte Marinoni between 1866 and 1883 made print runs of millions possible. A provincial city could support four daily newspapers (of four broadsheet pages each), one for each local faction. These reported national news across their front pages, with local news and advertisements inside. The Parisian daily newspapers reached a combined circulation of about a million by 1870, rising to five million by 1910. The biggest sellers were the *Petit Parisien* and *Petit Journal*, which put less emphasis on politics and more on sensational journalism, illustrated by artists' impressions of

[1] R. de Jouvenel, *La République des camarades* (Paris, 1914). Cited by M. Agulhon, *The French Republic 1879–1922* (Oxford, 1993; 1st edn. Paris, 1990), p. 126.

train smashes and crimes of passion. Newspapers proliferated because censorship had been lifted and it was relatively cheap to found them, but it was harder to make them profitable. Income from sales and advertisements were spread too thinly, opening newspapers to bribery. Governments funded newspapers as a matter of course, usually for domestic political ends but also to support foreign policy: large sums were paid to encourage French investors to buy bonds issued by the Russian government after its alliance with France. At their worst, some small newspapers were little more than devices for blackmail, helped by the 1881 press laws that made libel cases almost impossible. Newspapers found it cheaper and better for their circulation to indulge in polemics rather than in detailed reporting, and this sensationalized politics still further.

'How beautiful the republic was under the empire'

The republicans' supremacy appeared to be confirmed in 1885. After Victor Hugo died on 22 May that year, vast crowds swept through Paris for days, to mourn a hero of the republican cause; the same spirit swept through the country's ballot boxes the following October, when the republican parties won by 370 seats to 200. Yet new challenges were rising, from the economic depression, from both the left and right wings, from corruption within the regime, and from the German empire.

The economy performed poorly in the 1880s, in the midst of what became known as the Great Depression until the slump of the 1930s took that title. This depression lasted from 1873 to 1896; it was marked by falling prices, especially in agriculture, rather than by a collapse in employment or production. The price of wheat—France's staple crop—fell by a third between the 1870s and 1890s, putting many farmers out of business. Peasants often held out better than richer farmers, because their only aim was subsistence. But growth was weak, and agricultural output fell 0.8 per cent a year from the late 1870s to the early 1890s. One result of this was that rural migration changed its nature in the 1880s, and seasonal movements to cities became permanent. The rural population had reached its peak, and the long process of depopulation began. By 1881 the slowdown in the economy had forced a number of companies into bankruptcy, prompting many banks to tighten their lending. This credit squeeze then broke the Union Générale des Banques, which had over-stretched itself with loans for railway construction in the Balkans. A crash on the stock market and in banking resulted, which in turn led to bankruptcies in industry over 1883–5. Up to the 1860s economic downturns had led to a subsistence crisis, where unemployed workers could not afford to eat; from the 1880s onwards they led to banking and stock market crashes instead.

There were ominous political repercussions to this episode, and the tide turned against moderate republicans and their free-trade policies. The backers of the Union Générale were Catholic conserva-tives, some of whom claimed that the bank had been broken by a conspiracy of Jewish bankers, led by the Rothschilds. Anti-Semitism crept towards centre stage. Economic pressures led to bitter strikes in industries such as mining, for by 1884 the price of coal had fallen by a third from its peak in 1873. This prompted the Compagnie d'Anzin, based in the coal belt of the Nord department, to provoke a strike intended to break the miners' union and enable it to cut costs. The company had the sympathy of the government while the workers lacked resources: after fifty-six days, they went back to work. This strike served as a model for Zola's novel *Germinal*, published in 1885, which in turn presaged a much longer and bloodier strike in 1886, at the mines of Decazeville, in the southern department of Aveyron. This time, the strikers won after 108 bitter days.

These remained isolated incidents, for socialist parties and trade unions only recovered slowly from the defeat of 1871. Although the amnesty for Communard exiles revived the socialist movement, it remained too splintered in the 1880s to have much impact. The past failure of political movements made trade unions suspicious of socialist parties. When the main trade union, the Confédération Générale du Travail (CGT), was formed in 1895, it declared that it was outside all political parties, unlike unions in Britain, Belgium, and Germany. The long experience of state repression also made unions deeply suspicious of state actions, including the 1884 law that legal-ized them. Unions were further weakened by their failure to develop as bodies that provided assistance for their members. This was the intended result of Louis-Napoleon's authorization of mutual aid societies, which successfully provided aid but were forbidden to make political or industrial claims. French trade unions developed in semi-isolation from the state, political parties, and mutual aid bodies. The number of trade unionists reached a million in 1911, but the number rose and fell rapidly with major industrial conflicts. The level of unionization was about one-third that in Britain and Germany. Unions had a 'culture of confrontation': to make demands, not to provide assistance; to stand apart from politics; to destroy the state and capitalist society, not to reform it.

In opposition to the Second Empire, the republic had been a lofty ideal; once it existed, it was rapidly tarnished by corruption. The first major scandal broke in October 1887, when it was revealed that a republican deputy and son-in-law of President Grévy, Daniel Wilson, had been selling decorations for the Légion d'Honneur from the presidential Élysée Palace. The scandal forced Grévy to resign in December 1887. This was the first of many scandals that dogged the Third Republic to its grave.

Why did political corruption flourish? In brief, because the state was the source of money and favour, and because a great many people wanted to feed from it. State employment itself was one way to draw sustenance. The old elites held on to their positions as senior officials (*hauts fonctionnaires*), while the rapidly expanding lower bureaucracy provided jobs in post offices, schools, and the tax and legal systems. These were desirable jobs for young men educated by the republic's schools, who wanted to escape from the land or from their father's trade into a stable and respected job. Ministers were besieged by petitioners seeking posts for themselves, their families and friends, as well as by deputies lobbying for their constituents and allies. Secondly, many deputies themselves were liable to corruption if they did not have an independent income, because they were poorly paid yet were expected to maintain a bourgeois lifestyle and to fund their election campaign themselves; this was relieved in 1906 when their salary was raised from the level set in 1848 to 15,000 francs, a comfortable but not high income by bourgeois standards. The third and most diverse form of corruption came from the favours that central and local governments could provide, whether as public funding, favourable legislation, tax concessions or tariffs, municipal licences, colonial concessions, public works contracts, or protection from prosecution.

In the 1880s, the threat from abroad was more psychological than real. The war of 1870–1 left France seeking the recovery of Alsace-Lorraine from Germany, yet with no allies to help accomplish this. Imperial expansion meant that France came into conflict with Britain and Italy in Africa, and the reciprocal distrust between republican France and autocratic Austria and Russia kept them apart. Alsace-Lorraine poisoned diplomatic relations between France and Germany permanently: no French government could declare that it had no intention of recovering the provinces, even though that became the policy in practice as the decades passed, and no government could ally with Germany. This latent hostility welled up from time to time, for example in April 1887, when a French police commissioner, Schnæbelé, was arrested in Germany as a spy. The minister of war, General Boulanger, made a bellicose and undiplomatic reply that horrified the rest of the government, and that made him a popular hero when Schnæbelé was released.

Economic depression, social unrest, and the Wilson and Schnæbelé affairs produced a smouldering discontent with the republic; Boulanger was the spark that ignited a fire. Georges Boulanger was a career soldier who had served in Italy, China, and the Franco-Prussian War, and who also had a reputation as a good republican. He was made minister of war in 1886 to fulfil the republicans' twin goals of making the army democratic and national, and of matching the German army. When Freycinet fell in May 1887, Boulanger was despatched to the provinces, to the outrage of the Parisian crowds. After the resignation of Grévy and his replacement by Sadi-Carnot, diverse malcontents sought to use Boulanger to challenge the current republican order and to demand a revision of the constitution. Left-wing radicals and former Communards backed Boulanger for his militant Jacobin spirit; the right-wing Ligue des Patriotes of the nationalist poet Paul Déroulède fought for him as a new Bonaparte; royalists such as the duchess of Uzès funded him to undermine the republic. Anti-Semitism was introduced as a device to glue left- and right-wing protesters together, and to unite all classes against a common enemy; Maurice Barrès, a young writer and Boulangist deputy from 1889 to 1893, promoted this idea as 'national socialism'. Throughout 1888, Boulanger stood in a series of by-elections, winning then resigning when another by-election took place to create a rolling electoral campaign. The Boulangist campaign peaked with a massive electoral victory in Paris on 27 January 1889, which his supporters subsequently viewed as the moment when Boulanger should have led a march on the Élysée Palace. Instead, the government fought back by changing the electoral system to single-member constituencies that increased the emphasis on local politics. The minister of the interior put pressure on Boulanger by prosecuting some of his allies and by spreading a rumour that Boulanger himself would be arrested next; Boulanger did not wait to verify this, and fled to Brussels on 1 April 1889. Without its focal point, the Boulangist movement rapidly splintered, leaving the general to compensate for his unheroic flight by romantically committing suicide on his mistress's tomb in Brussels in September 1891.

The Boulangist movement flared up then fizzled out for the same reason: it had disparate, conflicting supporters who were all trying to manipulate Boulanger for their own ends. But the legacy of the Boulanger affair lived longer. Though his backers had not fused together in 1889, the same ingredients of former Communards, Bonapartists, anti-Semites, and royalists did merge to form a new nationalism in the crucible of the Dreyfus Affair, ten years later. The Boulanger affair also created a new form of mass politics, using the mass press, national organization, and dramatic rallies to galvanize supporters in a way that the old committee-based methods never could.

The new empire

The new republic also founded a new empire in the 1880s, building on the existing colonies in Africa (Algeria and Senegal), America (French Guiana), Asia (Cochinchina), and the Pacific (Tahiti and New Caledonia). Initially, imperial conquests were not popular, or were seen as a distraction from *revanche*, the recovery of Alsace and Lorraine. However, the empire became a source of national pride when it related to rivalries with Britain in the 1890s and with Germany in the 1900s: the empire enabled France to recover its glory once again.

The government's prime motivation for the conquests begun in the 1880s was economic: to search for new markets for French goods.

Jules Ferry declared: 'European consumption is saturated; we must create new bodies of consumers in other parts of the world, or else modern society will go bankrupt.'[2] The importance of economic motives in empire-building has long been disputed by historians. Though many colonies were economically disappointing and European trade remained far more important, Jacques Marseille has shown that colonies did rapidly develop as outlets for French industry, as Ferry and Méline had hoped, and also as sources of raw materials. By 1913, colonies took 13 per cent of French exports and provided 9.4 per cent of its imports; nearly 10 per cent of investment went to the colonies, and the state spent 7 per cent of its total budget on them. Imperial trade was worth nearly as much as trade with Germany and more than trade with Belgium, and it was growing fast. The empire dominated trade in certain goods, providing 95 per cent of the rice and 90 per cent of the wine imported by France, and buying over half of its exports of cotton cloth. The empire provided a reliable market when bouts of protectionism meant other markets were sometimes abruptly closed, and most of these investments proved to be profitable. Colonial demand was especially important for what Marseille called the 'motor' industries of food and textiles. Indeed, after the 1930s the empire supported industries that could no longer compete in Europe, and by the 1950s, colonies bought over a third of French exports and took nearly all France's foreign investment.

French imperialism was encouraged by a few key individuals and groups in Paris, plus lobbies in the ports of Bordeaux and Marseille. The ministers responsible for the expansion begun in 1879–80 were Freycinet, who had ambitious rail-building plans for Africa as well as France, and Admiral Jauréguiberry, minister for the navy and colonies. Over a much longer period, Eugène Étienne, deputy for the Algerian constituency of Oran, had great influence as leader of the colonial lobby, a mixture of explorers, journalists, colonists, and businessmen. Africa was the most successful region for the lobby—Indochina marked the limits of expansion in the east, not the beginning of a new east Asian empire. The strength of the colonial lobby weakened in 1905 when it split between those who supported the

---

[2] J. Marseille, *Empire colonial et capitalisme français: histoire d'un divorce* (Paris, 1984), p. 368.

rights of indigenous populations and the Algerian deputies led by
Étienne, who promoted the interests of white settlers.

The actual process of expansion owed most to local circumstances.
Many colonies were formally acquired to protect economic interests
when local order buckled under the pressure of European activities.
In 1881, a protectorate was established over Tunisia when Ottoman
rule there crumbled, to prevent Britain or Italy from taking control;
Egypt was the next Ottoman territory to fall, but the Chamber
rejected Freycinet's request for troops to protect the Suez Canal, and
Britain took control instead. In 1885, China yielded Tonkin and
Annam to France as protectorates. France's Asian possessions were
consolidated as the Indochinese Union in 1887, including Cochinchina, Tonkin, Annam, and Cambodia. In 1890, Britain and France
awarded one another Madagascar and Zanzibar, though it took a
major military expedition to secure French rule in Madagascar. Other
conquests in Africa were driven on by legends about the riches to be
found inland and by European rivalries, especially with Britain. In
1879–80 the explorer de Brazza pushed up the Congo river while
Jauréguiberry ordered conquest up the Niger, with the dream of a
trans-Saharan railway passing through the fabled city of Timbuktu.

The unique feature of French imperialism, compared to other
European empires, was the role played by the Colonial Army and its
conflict with Islam in West Africa. The Colonial Army was a separate
formation from the mainland army, imbued with its own sense of
adventure and mission. This led it to seek conquest rather than
compromise, which it justified by fostering economic and social
development in new colonies. However, it met unexpected resistance
in Islamic West Africa from the empire of Samori Turé. While most
African rulers commanded limited resources and had to yield rapidly,
Turé held out against France from 1881 till his death in 1900 because
he commanded an empire united by the Islamic faith; this extensive
conflict, in space as well as time, led the Colonial Army to conquer
and hold large territories even when they no longer had any
economic potential.

Another distinctive feature of the new empire is that most of it was
not for settlement. In 1911, just 850,000 settlers from mainland France
lived in the French colonies, compared to another 610,000 living in
other countries. Because of the low birth rate, emigration was low,
and France provided just 1 per cent of total European emigration in

the nineteenth century. The exception was Algeria, where the number of settlers rose from 119,000 in 1871 to 200,000 by 1900 (even here, many of these settlers were Spanish or Maltese). By the end of the century, the settlers had gained control over Algeria, ahead of the Colonial Army, the civilian administration, and Paris, as well as the local Algerian peoples. Jules Cambon made some reforms as governor from 1891 to 1897, until Étienne secured his transfer. The land granted to new settlers eroded Muslim land holdings and society until it fell apart. The old aristocratic families disappeared, artisanal industries collapsed, and constant land seizures wore away the peasantry. Muslim justice was replaced by the *Code de l'Indigénat* of 1881, and the Muslim clergy became state employees (the separation of church and state in 1905 did not affect them), which discredited them in Muslim eyes. After 1900 a small, secularized Arab elite began to reappear, demanding equality (as well as being subject to a separate legal code, Algerians paid extra taxes and had no vote) and more education. It took decades more for this elite to develop into a nationalist leadership, when the settlers would finally reap as they had sown.

Protectionism and the *Ralliement*, 1890–1898

As the turmoil of Boulangism faded, the republicans reasserted themselves. The centenary of the Revolution was marked by an international exhibition, the construction of the Eiffel Tower, and a grand banquet to celebrate the unity of the nation. Every mayor in France was invited to attend this event, and 11,000 of them dined together in Paris, toasting France and the republic. Political and economic stability was built on three pillars: protectionism, the *Ralliement*, and an alliance with Russia. Together, these outweighed the scandal of the Panama Canal affair, violence at the new May Day parades of the left (begun in 1890), and a series of anarchist outrages.

The first pillar was the *Ralliement* ('rallying'). This major shift in Catholic attitudes towards the republic meant that Catholics would accept the existence of the republic, and work within it rather than against it. This change was initiated largely by Pope Leo XIII's encyclical of 1892, *Au milieu des sollicitudes*, which declared that the republic was as legitimate as any other constitution, and that change could only come by constitutional means. It was fostered in France by Albert de Mun and Jacques Piou, who built a Catholic political movement that was conservative but not reactionary. In return, some moderate republicans rejected the anticlericalism of the 1880s, notably Jules Méline, premier from 1896 to 1898. The *Ralliement* was part of a wider change in Catholic attitudes to social and economic developments: the church realized that it was too rooted in rural society to be able to speak to the millions living in cities, and that it had to respond to the conflict between capital and labour. Leo XIII's encyclical of 1891, *Rerum novarum*, encouraged Catholics to reach out to urban, industrial workers and argued for an alternative philosophy to both capitalism and socialism, one that was not based on material-ism and conflict. It accepted that the state had a role to play, and broke with the view that poverty was intended by divine providence and could not therefore be eradicated. Despite innumerable initia-tives, this new approach generally failed. Christian democratic parties and Catholic trade unions did not succeed in France, in contrast to Germany, Italy, and Belgium. Men like de Mun persisted with charities and clubs for working men despite repeated failure, partly because such failure is to be expected in missionary work, and partly because working with industrial labourers fostered a masculine, 'hairy-chested' Catholicism to put against the feminized, emotional Catholicism that flourished in the late nineteenth century.

The second pillar was a new tariff law that Méline guided through parliament in 1892, when he was president of the Chamber of Deputies. This tariff abandoned existing trade treaties in order to protect French industries and farming from the depression. It created two tariff rates, a minimum one for countries that gave France 'most favoured nation' trading status, and a maximum for others. Over time, reciprocal agreements were signed with most trade partners, though only after tariff wars had been fought with Italy and Switzerland. Tariffs on imported raw materials, including coal and steel, stayed low to help French industries, but they were raised on agricultural imports and manufactured goods.

As with protectionism generally, short-term benefits were bought at the expense of long-term development. Imports of foodstuffs fell, from 35 per cent of all imports in the 1870s to 25 per cent by the 1890s, and the decline in France's own agricultural output was probably halted. Socialist and workers' movements objected that tariffs raised the cost of food for the urban population and for rural labourers, which cut the amount they could spend on other goods. In compensation, workers received greater social protection: the workers' *livret*, the identity card introduced by Napoleon, was abolished in 1890, a law on arbitration was passed in 1892 that helped to settle many labour disputes without strikes, and free medical aid for the sick and destitute was established in 1893. French industry also benefited from protection, with the consequence that it did not need to adopt new techniques so quickly. Though many industries did expand and modernize well after 1900, France lost the technological edge to Germany and the USA between 1885 and 1900. Protectionism could only be a palliative for both agriculture and industry, and it was the end of the depression in 1896 that led to a definitive improvement in rural living standards. Protectionism was part of a tendency to shield vested interests, caused by a desire to preserve social stability and by the vulnerability of the Third Republic to lobbying. A typical example was the support granted in 1881 for shipbuilders; most of these made sailing ships, not steamers, and this support was used to prop up their traditional output, not to develop their technologies. As a result, the French merchant fleet fell badly behind rival, steam-powered fleets in a couple of decades.

The third pillar of stability was an alliance with Russia that ended France's diplomatic isolation. Divided by ideology, France and Russia were united by a mutual fear of Germany in Europe, and by a mutual rivalry with Britain outside it (Britain clashed with France in Africa and with Russia on the north-west Indian border). The alliance soon developed its own emotional power and vested interests. It was initiated in 1891 and sealed by Tsar Nicholas II's state visit in 1896—a political triumph for Méline. Financial interests were created by French investment in Russia, which was encouraged by Delcassé, and which reached a staggering twelve billion francs by 1914, or 26 per cent of all French investment abroad.

The regime's integrity was then challenged by the biggest scandal of all, the Panama affair. Construction of the Panama Canal was begun by two of France's leading engineers, Ferdinand de Lesseps of the Suez Canal and Gustave Eiffel of the Tower. However, their plans were over-ambitious (to dig straight across from the Atlantic to the Pacific ocean with no locks) and under-capitalized (they began with

600 million francs, where other experts recommended twice that amount). Progress was slow, hampered by weather and disease: sixty out of every thousand workers died, mostly from malaria and yellow fever. By 1888, de Lesseps sought to raise another 720 million francs by issuing bonds that paid interest and through an extra payment awarded by an annual lottery. This, because it contravened existing laws, needed parliamentary approval which was obtained by massive bribery of newspapers and politicians. The issue failed to raise the necessary funds and the Panama company went bankrupt in January 1889. In September 1892, Édouard Drumont's anti-Semitic newspaper *La Libre Parole* began an exposure of the corruption, because several of the leading bribers were Jewish, notably Cornelius Herz and Jacques de Reinach. This campaign exploded in November with the suicide of de Reinach and the flight of Herz abroad. The ensuing inquiry revealed that 104 deputies had received payments one way or another, but the 'republic of pals' closed ranks and only one parliamentarian was among those eventually convicted of corruption. The accusations made by Boulangists against the republic appeared to be justified in the eyes of the public; anti-parliamentarianism and anti-Semitism leached into mainstream opinion. Stability was further shaken by a series of anarchist bombings between 1892 and 1894, including an explosion in the Chamber of Deputies in 1893 and the assassination of the President of the Republic, Sadi Carnot, in 1894. Repressive laws and police infiltration ended the bombings, at the cost of left-wing opposition to these measures.

The Dreyfus Affair: citizenship and nationality

By the end of the 1890s, the republican regime had successfully weathered several storms, only to face its most serious challenge yet when the Dreyfus Affair broke. This case, of an army officer accused of spying, racked France for years because it posed a much deeper question than Boulangism had done. The Boulanger Affair had questioned the nature of the regime: the Dreyfus Affair questioned the meaning of the nation.

In a famous lecture of 1882, the scholar Ernest Renan asked, 'What is a nation?'[3] He concluded that it was not based on race, language, religion, common interest or geography. The French were not a single race either ethnically or anthropologically. The country did not speak with a common tongue: there were fourteen major dialects of *langue d'oïl*, the dominant language of northern France, and eight of *langue d'oc*, the language of the south. Moving clockwise round France, other regional tongues included Flemish, Alsatian, Franco-Provençal, Corsican, Catalan, Basque, Gascon, and Breton. These languages were further divided into village patois (without counting Parisian argot, street slang). Religion most certainly did not unite the country; common material interests were lacking until a single market formed late in the nineteenth century, and even this could pit north against south, town against country, employer against worker; the geographical territory of France was not a single whole but had been composed piecemeal over several centuries.

Instead, Renan argued that a nation was founded on 'a soul, a spiritual principle', which consisted of two things. 'One is the common possession of a rich inheritance of memories, the other a continuing consent, the desire to live together.' Did France possess these two vital ingredients? Here lay the fault-line between right and left, for the right emphasized inheritance and the left emphasized consent. The right's view of the nation excluded those who did not share this inheritance, such as Jews, who were rooted neither in French soil nor in its religious tradition. The left excluded those who did not consent to their trinity of republic–nation–state, such as the militant Catholic right. The Dreyfus Affair split the country because it activated this fault-line: for the right, Dreyfus could not be truly French because he was Jewish; for the left, he could not be more French because he had chosen to live and serve under the French flag.

In the 1890s about 80,000 Jews lived in France, with another 45,000 in Algeria. French Jews belonged to several disparate communities, from the old-established, assimilated Sephardic Jews of the south-east and south-west to the poor, Yiddish-speaking Ashkenazi refugees from eastern Europe, who arrived in France in the 1880s and 1890s, driven by the pressures of their own increasing population and by persecution. This population had never been more diverse, stretching

---

[3] Ernest Renan, 'Qu'est-ce qu'une nation?', *Œuvres complètes*, i (Paris, 1947).

from the ennobled and fabulously wealthy Rothschilds to penniless immigrants. Dreyfus belonged to a third group of about 12,000 Ashkenazi Jews from Alsace who had moved to France after it was annexed by Germany. Jews such as Dreyfus were ultra-loyal to the combination of republic, nation, and state. They had been emancipated by the French Revolution, chose France over Germany in 1871, and repaid their debt by choosing a military career in the service of France. They had changed their ancient attitude of being a people in exile to being citizens with a homeland.

Republicans accepted Jewish membership of the national community because they understood Frenchness to be a question of citizenship and rights, as established by the French Revolution. It could be acquired by anyone who gained the legal status of a citizen—and in 1889, the basis of nationality was changed from nationality by parentage to nationality by residence. This was the attitude of the USA, where every naturalized immigrant became an American, but the reverse of Germany, where nationality depended (and still depends) on ancestry. The German interpretation was shared by writers such as Maurice Barrès, who believed that Frenchness lay in 'the land of our dead', the soil where one's ancestors had been born, lived, and died for hundreds or thousands of years. For Barrès, Jews did not have this ancestry, and so could never be French. The success of many Jews under the Third Republic and their loyalty to that regime meant that anti-Semitism was a way to attack the republic. As Pierre Birnbaum has argued, this was the distinguishing feature of modern French anti-Semitism: it was primarily political, rather than religious, economic, social, or racial, though elements of these four other types were also present.[4]

The Dreyfus Affair itself concerned the innocence or guilt of Captain Alfred Dreyfus, arrested on 15 October 1894 for passing secrets to the German military attaché in Paris, Colonel von Schwartzkoppen. The evidence against Dreyfus was weak, but the minister of war, General Mercier, pressed ahead with the case after *La Libre Parole* publicized it out of its own anti-Semitism. From this decision onwards, senior army officers committed a series of irregular and illegal acts rather than admit Dreyfus's innocence and Mercier's original sin. Dreyfus was found guilty at a court martial in December

---

[4] P. Birnbaum, *Antisemitism in France* (Oxford, 1992).

1894, despite two irregularities. First, Commandant Henry of the counter-espionage service declared in court that he knew Dreyfus was guilty but that he could not reveal his proof, which made this hearsay evidence without value. Secondly, a secret dossier of circumstantial evidence was presented to the judges without the knowledge of Dreyfus or his lawyers. A discreet campaign led by the Dreyfus family prompted Henry to forge evidence against him, knowing how weak the case against Dreyfus was. The *dreyfusard* campaign broke into the open in November 1897, when the identity of the real culprit, Commandant Walsin-Esterhazy, was revealed by Dreyfus's brother, Mathieu—more than a year after another officer in the counter-espionage service, Colonel Georges Picquart, had identified Esterhazy as the spy. Picquart's superiors had rewarded him for this awkward discovery first by despatching him to the Tunisian deserts, then by arresting him and dismissing him from the army. Esterhazy was acquitted of spying by a court martial on 11 January 1898, defeating the *dreyfusards*' tactics.

At this moment one can say that the Dreyfus case, a miscarriage of justice, became the Dreyfus Affair, a battle for the soul of the nation. Émile Zola replied to Esterhazy's acquittal with one of the most famous newspaper articles ever published, 'J'accuse', printed by Clemenceau in the newspaper *L'Aurore* on 13 January 1898. It inflamed public opinion with its vehement denunciation of the army officers involved and of clerical influences behind them—there were sixty-six riots across France in the next few weeks. Tens of thousands of newspaper articles, speeches, meetings, and rallies ensued as 'the Affair' was debated in public and in private, splitting social circles and families. The dividing line ran through parties, classes, faiths, and families as well as between them, defeating simple attempts at explaining why one person chose one side rather than the other. One commentator, Julien Benda, believed that this choice was a matter of temperament, a preference for authority or anarchy. Those whose nature preferred authority sided with the army commanders, while those who preferred anarchy were *dreyfusards* because they wished to make their own minds up by arguing over the evidence. Most press, parliamentary, and public opinion remained hostile to the *dreyfusards*, and though the elections of 1898 were generally favourable to the left, leading *dreyfusards* such as the moderate republican Joseph Reinach and the socialist leader Jean Jaurès were defeated, and several nationalist and anti-Semitic *antidreyfusards* won (Drumont was elected as a deputy for Algiers, Déroulède won in the Bonapartist south-west). The tide turned suddenly at the end of August, when Henry's forgery was exposed, and he committed suicide on the night of his arrest. It took another year to complete the legal procedures needed for a retrial, which took place in Rennes in August 1899. The complexities of the case on one hand and Mercier's continued insistence on Dreyfus's guilt on the other produced the curious verdict of 'guilty with extenuating circumstances' by five votes to two; a presidential pardon freed Dreyfus in September. In 1906 a full inquiry was established under pressure from Jaurès, which definitively established the innocence of Dreyfus; he and Picquart were readmitted to the army.

The significance of the Dreyfus Affair has been much debated. Throughout, the 'silent majority' of French citizens were little concerned by the Affair, though virtually every politically aware person had an opinion about it. It had little effect on the 1898 elections, and though some ministers fell over the Affair, that was no great matter in the Third Republic. Nevertheless, it had two profound effects, in the separation of church and state (the end of the Napoleonic Concordat) and the creation of a new nationalism. Like nationalism in Italy and Germany, French nationalism as a political force was born on the left, because it made the people sovereign at the expense of monarchs. For the historian Zeev Sternhell, defeat in 1870–1 was crucial because it turned French nationalism inwards, becoming tribal and exclusive now that it could no longer export universal ideas as the Jacobins of the French Revolution and Napoleon had done. The new nationalism of the Dreyfus Affair differed from the royalist right because it acknowledged popular sovereignty, and from the traditional nationalist left because it was authoritarian; the two fused in the Bonapartist solution of rule by a single man elected by the people. Never organized into a party, its leading figures were Déroulède, Barrès, and Charles Maurras, with the new royalist newspaper and organization Action Française. Simultaneously, the far left broke from the nationalism of the Jacobins by advocating internationalism and antimilitarism, and shed its own anti-Semitism.

Today, the *dreyfusards* are victorious, and the centenary of 'J'accuse' was marked with great ceremony, joining the Declaration of the Rights of Man and de Gaulle's Appeal of 18 June 1940 in the canon of historic texts. But the Affair should not be seen in simplistic terms of '*dreyfusards* good, *antidreyfusards* bad'. While the 1906 inquiry proved the absolute innocence of Dreyfus, few people outside his family had reason to doubt the court's verdict in 1894, and the truth was then obscured by so many lies and forgeries that it was quite possible to believe in his guilt in good faith. Some *dreyfusards* exploited the Affair to promote anticlericalism, which drove moderates such as Méline to the right. Henry himself may initially have acted in what he thought was the best interest of the army, only to find himself trapped by his own deceit. Only a few writers (notably Jaurès) kept to the facts of the case, while many others (including Zola) launched into conspiracy theories that forced people to take sides according to their political loyalties rather than their reason. The polemics of both sides fed off each other to become ever more poisonous. The use of conspiracy theories has been a staple of French political language for centuries. During the Dreyfus Affair, they went beyond an explanation of the case according to the actions of a few plotters to fantasies about global conspiracies run by freemasons, Jews, or Jesuits. These served to demonize opponents, their interests, and their vision of French identity, whilst simultaneously inflating the claims of one particular faction to represent the true interests and identity of the nation—for each side believed that the very identity of France was at stake. Which identity would prevail? The country born of revolution, based on republic, state, and nation, or traditional, Catholic France loyal to Father, Son, and Holy Ghost?

Nor were the *dreyfusards* as generous as they might have been. The imprisonment of Dreyfus on Devil's Island was seen to be horrible because he was innocent, but the idea of transportation was not itself criticized. The penal colonies, called *bagnes*, were a distinctive feature of French criminal punishment. Louis-Napoleon ended the naval *bagnes*, forced-labour camps at navy bases, and created colonial ones instead. These failed on almost every measure: they did not reform, they did not colonize, they had high death rates, and they even had high escape rates; they simply punished in the crudest ways. The *bagnes* were nothing like the ideals of a prison that observed its inmates while dispensing exact doses of discipline and punishment developed earlier in the nineteenth century. They were the polar opposite of this, subjecting prisoners to the random punishments of climate, disease, and brutality. Eighteen thousand men and women were deported to French Guiana between 1852 and 1866, and nearly half died there. In the 1880s, public anxiety about crime concentrated on habitual criminals (those who had collected seven jail terms in ten years), who were deported to Guiana by a law passed in 1885; advocates of this law included the future *dreyfusards* Reinach and Waldeck-Rousseau, in the belief that it would offer the chance for moral rehabilitation. Fifteen thousand criminals were sent to Guiana under this law, and 10,000 to New Caledonia in the Pacific. Reform only came after the journalist Albert Londres exposed their dreadful conditions in 1923; the last convoy sailed for Guiana in 1938, although the *bagnes* were not finally closed until 1953. There was a racial aspect to this as well: over a third of the deportees from mainland France and its colonies were non-white: between 1886 and 1938, 63 per cent of deportees were of French or other European origin, 25 per cent were Arab, 7 per cent black, and 5 per cent Asian. The French prison system generally was harsh, and unsuitable converted buildings were often used as prisons. (This included Mont-Saint-Michel off the coast of Brittany, used as a prison from 1792 until the Second Empire, when the jail was closed to protect the historic buildings, not the inmates.) A major source of abuse was the system that contracted prison labour to private entrepreneurs, against which Martin Nadaud campaigned when he was a deputy. Reinach, Waldeck-Rousseau, and their fellow reformers created a tolerant penal regime outside the jail walls, through suspended sentences, parole, and better reform institutions for children, but once inmates were out of sight, whether in France or Guiana, they rapidly slipped out of mind.

The political outcome of the Dreyfus Affair was a revival of republican solidarity in the shape of a ministry led by the highly respected senator and barrister René Waldeck-Rousseau, formed to settle the Dreyfus Affair and restore order. An austere, taciturn man (Barrès likened him to 'a turbot in aspic'), Waldeck-Rousseau took two crucial ministries himself, the interior and public worship, and made three other notable appointments: a young Joseph Caillaux as minister of finance, the veteran general marquis of Galliffet as minister of war, and the socialist Alexandre Millerand as minister for trade and industry. The government barely survived its first day in the Chamber in June 1899, where the left was outraged by Millerand's participation in a non-socialist government and by the presence of Galliffet, who had helped to liquidate the Commune. A personal friend of Waldeck-Rousseau, Galliffet commanded the loyalty of the army; he also had an aristocrat's disdain for upstart troublemakers and contempt for those who had dishonoured the army by their lies. After this difficult start, this cabinet went on to be the longest-lived of the whole Third Republic. Nationalist rioting was cut short by the arrest of thirty-six leading troublemakers, including Déroulède, and the anti-Semite Jules Guérin, after a siege of Guérin's party headquarters that lasted nearly six weeks. They were charged with conspiracy against state security, although Waldeck-Rousseau privately admitted that this plot was 'moral' rather than 'material', and that their chances of success were minimal. Waldeck-Rousseau restored order but not did not make much more progress: despite Caillaux's support, income tax did not advance, though a progressive tax on inheritance did pass the Senate in February 1901. The main legislation was on the religious question, in the form of a law of 1901 that required all religious orders to be approved by parliament. Waldeck-Rousseau intended to apply this law selectively through his control over the Chamber, but his plan backfired after the elections of 1902 produced a much more left-wing Chamber, and when he had to stand down through ill health. His magisterial cabinet was replaced by a far more militant one led by Émile Combes, a former country doctor, a radical and freemason who had trained for the priesthood in his youth. Combes's government was left-wing but not socialist, and it followed the anticlerical policies of the 1880s rather than social reform. He used the legislation to ban all congregations that came before the Chamber. Two hundred thousand members of 3,216 orders were banned, including the main teaching order in boys' schools (the *Frères des Écoles chrétiennes*), and innumerable female orders that provided most of the country's child care, female education, medical care, and welfare. A third of Catholic schools were shut. It was an act of social vandalism committed by men who did not have to bear the consequences.

Combes's attack on the Catholic church provoked resistance from Rome, where Leo XIII had been succeeded by Pius X in 1903. Diplomatic relations broke off in 1904, and Combes swiftly ended the Napoleonic Concordat. On 9 December 1905 the Catholic, Protestant, and Jewish churches were legally separated from the state. Opposition focused on the expulsion of the religious orders (parish clergy remained) and by the 'Inventories', when officials documented what

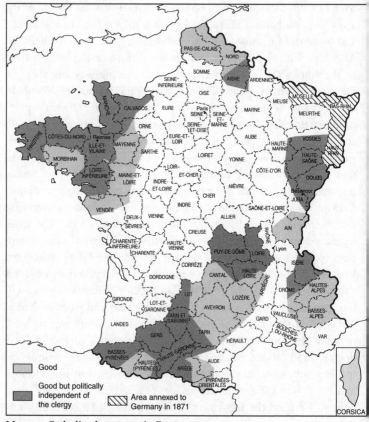

Map 3.1 Catholic observance in France, 1877.

Source: Jacques Gadille, *La Pensée et l'action politiques des évêques français au début de la Troisième République* (Paris, 1967), vol. I, following p. 152.

was Church property and what belonged to the state. There were thousands of local dramas across the country as groups of nuns and monks departed, schools were closed, and churches were entered, sometimes by force, in front of protesting crowds. This turned the Catholic community against the republic much more than the legislation of the 1880s had done because it created an immediate physical impact and loss across the country. From the election of 1906 onwards the maps of church attendance and of right-wing voting matched one another. Map 3.1 shows the areas of good Catholic practice as recorded by bishops and prefects at the start of the Third

Republic; they also marked where Catholics did not follow the clergy politically. With the expulsions and the inventories, prayers and votes went together once again. Another consequence of this was the continued exclusion of women from the vote: the left opposed female suffrage because they believed that women would vote for Catholic parties since they attended church more than men. Many women were politicized by the Republic's anticlerical policies, both ideologically, if they were practising Catholics, and practically, for example if their children were at schools run by religious orders. (Tactlessly, the new girls' state lycée in Orléans was installed in buildings confiscated from the church.) Hundreds of thousands of women supported local protests against anticlerical policies, which were soon organized into national movements.

The impact on the church was profound. Financially, it lost 35 million francs in salaries, and 411 million in assets. Even this massive figure disappointed anticlericals because the church's total assets were worth over a billion francs; half was transferred to other owners before it could be seized, while disorganization and fraud meant that only 205 million francs had actually reached the government by 1912. The law on separation established 'religious associations' as the legal basis to retain property and rebuild parish activities, but Pius X forbade Catholics to form such associations because the French government had sought to impose them instead of negotiating about them. In the long run, separation was arguably positive because the church was freed from state control and created its own lay organizations. These grew after the First World War (Pius X's ban was lifted in 1924) and flourished after the Second World War.

The limits of republican solidarity, 1905–1914

Moderate republicans, radicals, socialists, and anarchists had rallied in defence of Dreyfus and against the Catholic church, bound by the shared values of the Revolution. With the traditional right soundly defeated by 1905 and centre-left republicans in power until the First World War, divisions inside the left surfaced. These centred on four major issues: the state's traditional concerns of tax and conscription, plus social conflicts around welfare reforms and strikes.

Rupture came with the fall of Combes in January 1905 in a scandal known as the *affaire des fiches*, or the 'case of the card index'. The Dreyfus Affair had exposed widespread anti-republican sentiments in the army officer corps. In order to promote good republicans and to block reactionaries, the minister of war, General André, had used masonic lodges to gather information about officers in their local garrisons. When this was exposed, socialist deputies did not support Combes because they believed that he had not made enough social reforms, and he was forced to resign. The major governments that followed were led by the veteran republican Clemenceau (1906–9) and the former independent socialist Aristide Briand (1909–11). Clemenceau formed his first ministry at the age of 65, boasting a batch of talented Radicals and independent socialists including Caillaux, Briand, and Viviani, with the rehabilitated Georges Picquart as minister of war.

A number of major social reforms were made in these years, but they were granted by bourgeois republicans at their own pace and discretion. Workers' and socialist movements wanted more and faster reform, and they wanted it in the name of justice, not by the grace of the bourgeoisie. In 1905, aid was granted for the old or incurable poor, and for the unemployed. Military service was cut from three years to two. A compulsory weekly day of rest (not necessarily Sunday) was restored in 1906; both trade unions and the church had long campaigned for this, but mutual loathing had stopped them from joining forces. The working day was limited to ten hours. Aid for large families and for maternity was approved in 1913, to stimulate the birth rate. The most important reform came in 1910, when pensions were created for workers and peasants. However, these were opposed by trade unions because they were created by the state (i.e. the enemy), because workers would have to contribute as well, and because they would be 'pensions for the dead': they would only be paid from the age of 65, which was above workers' and peasants' life expectancy.

A crucial question raised by even these limited reforms was how they should be funded. An income tax was proposed by socialists and Radicals, led by the patrician Caillaux, as the fairest system of taxation; it was opposed by the right and much of the republican centre as an invasion of privacy and a confiscation of wealth to be squandered on the poor. In order to prepare for an income tax, a first survey into income was conducted in 1894–5, which revealed how unequal earnings were: 9.5 million households earned under 2,500 francs per year; half a million earned over 5,000 francs (the minimum level needed to live a bourgeois lifestyle) and 3,000 earned more than 100,000 francs. Up to the late nineteenth century, the bulk of state expenditure went on services that applied to everyone, such as defence, justice, or public transport, and that in practice benefited the rich most. Central government spending had risen from about 10 per cent of gross national product in 1800 to 15 per cent by 1900, and now governments were proposing to spend even more money on services to help the poor only, at the expense of the rich. In fact, direct taxes cost the urban bourgeoisie very little, taking about 2 per cent of their total expenditure; the rural bourgeoisie was hit much harder by land taxes, which could take as much as 20 per cent of their income when the harvest was poor. Time and again an income tax was approved by the Chamber of Deputies to be blocked by the Senate, though it is likely that many more deputies would have voted against it if they had not had the Senate to stop it for them.

Conflict also arose over conscription. The socialist and anarchist left had become increasingly anti-military, breaking with the old Jacobin, Revolutionary tradition of 'the nation in arms' in preference for international working-class solidarity. They opposed conscription as a cruel burden on working-class and peasant families. Far from uniting the classes, they saw military service as class war by other means: workers and peasants served in the ranks under harsh conditions, commanded by an officer corps drawn from their class enemies, the bourgeoisie and nobility. Protest against abuse was almost impossible, since conscripts were regulated by military justice. Worse still, soldiers were used to break strikes: workers and peasants were set to fight one another in the clothes of striker and soldier. But in 1913 the government sought to extend the term of service back to three years. This was needed to keep the French army at the same size as the German army: faster population growth in Germany meant that it could call many more men to arms each year, forcing Frenchmen to serve longer in compensation. Socialists, who were more internationally minded than the Radicals through their contacts with socialist parties in Germany and elsewhere, believed that the three-years law increased the danger of war by feeding an arms race between France and Germany. The left finally gave its support for the three-years law in return for progress on income tax: if workers and peasants gave France their blood, the rich could give it their francs.

The most brutal expressions of the rift within the republican camp came in a series of strikes from 1906 onwards. Clemenceau tried negotiation with a miners' strike in 1906, but when this failed he turned to force. Briand, previously an advocate of the general strike, broke a train workers' strike in 1910 by mobilizing the railway workers: anyone who then struck could be arrested as a mutineer and tried by a military court. Those who did strike were subsequently sacked. Major strikes were concentrated in the years 1906–11, while 1910–14 was the peak when measured by the number of strikers: about 5 per cent of the workforce struck each year in this period. These smaller-scale strikes usually ended in victory for the strikers or a compromise, in large part because the economy was growing and companies were eager to get their output going again. Big-city workers struck more than those in small towns and the countryside, with mining the most militant industry. Women were notably absent: though 30 per cent of all workers were female, fewer than 4 per cent of strikers were women.

Strikes changed with the nature of work. As mechanization spread, skilled artisans were replaced by semi-skilled workers; as workers settled permanently in the cities, multiple employment ended. Postal workers and railwaymen had no other potential employers. These factors meant that workers were increasingly dependent on their employer and could not walk out to earn a living elsewhere as easily as in the nineteenth century. More and more disputes were about control of the workplace rather than wages: rejecting paternalism, protesting against foremen, or resisting the introduction of new machinery. Protests involved new methods, such as massed strikers brought together by railways, coordinated action instead of locally based protests; state employees unionized and struck more readily than private-sector ones because they shared a single employer and working conditions, unlike private-sector employees scattered in small companies.

The end of multiple employment in industry had its equivalent in farming, which led to the Languedoc wine-growers' protests of 1906–7. This was essentially a strike of self-employed farmers who had shifted from peasant-style farming of several crops for self-sufficiency to commercial farming of a single crop for sale. They had replanted their land with vines after the phylloxera disaster, until a glut of cheap wine flooded the market, and they could no longer sell their only product. This protest also drew on provincial opposition to Paris and the central state, rural and urban tensions (growers blamed dealers who adulterated the wine, watering it down and adding extra sugar to eke it out), and north/south conflicts (northern farmers grew the sugar beet that ended up in cheap wine). The campaign peaked in May–June 1907, with a rally of 70,000 people in Montpellier, and when the prefecture in Perpignan and the sub-prefecture in Béziers were sacked. A regiment in Béziers sent to quell protesters mutinied when it thought that it would be used against its own home town. However, the movement's success outran its leaders' ability and experience, and Clemenceau was able to defuse it adroitly. The wine-growers were satisfied by a law to combat fraud in the wine industry: unlike the Catholic protesters of 1906, they remained loyal to the Republic and wanted it to help them, not to leave them alone.

The socialist and workers' movements in France enjoyed a rare advantage, namely widespread support from rural voters, including small farmers and peasants. However, they failed to exploit this before 1914, weighed down by their history of bloody defeat. When the various fragments of the socialist left united in 1905, as the Parti Socialiste, Section Française de l'Internationale Ouvrière (SFIO), its dominant figure was Jaurès, a powerful speaker and an eloquent writer. One of the reasons for his success was that he was a socialist for reasons of humanity, not ideology, which allowed him to be more flexible than his more rigid Marxist rival, Jules Guesde. Jaurès was able to appeal to France's millions of independent peasants, men who abhorred any suggestion that the land they held so dear might become common property. Jaurès wooed small farmers by advocating cooperatives: each farmer still held his own land but he shared equipment, bought fertilizers, and sold produce jointly. This was preaching to the converted, since the 1884 law on associations had been used to form agricultural cooperatives much more than to form urban trade unions. The success enjoyed by socialists in the French countryside was most unusual in Europe. Hervé Le Bras and Emmanuel Todd explain this in anthropological terms: socialists did well in non-Catholic regions that had strong communal traditions, such as the Limousin, an area of share-cropping and complex

families, and the Mediterranean coast, a region of nucleated settlement traditionally opposed to whatever happened in Paris. These
regions voted for parties that emphasized community, unlike the
more individualist north, and frequently combined this with protest
votes. Since they were also anticlerical, they could not vote for the
extreme right, which was dominated by Catholics. This led them to
vote for the most extreme left-wing candidate standing.

Support from rural as well as industrial areas gave the SFIO
tremendous electoral gains: its representation in the Chamber of
Deputies rose from thirty-six in 1905 to fifty-one at the elections the
next year and 102 in 1914. However, the long shadow of defeat in 1848
and 1871 led it to reject participation in 'bourgeois' governments: its
policy was to overthrow the existing order, not to tinker with reforms.
Though Millerand had broken this code sensationally in 1899, the
partisans of non-participation had regained the upper hand by the
time the SFIO was formed. It wasted its electoral success by abstaining from government, with the perverse but inevitable effect that the
Radicals had to turn to their right to win a majority in parliament.
Republican solidarity had reached its limits.

Women and feminism

The later nineteenth century saw the revival of feminism in France,
after a brief efflorescence in the Second Republic, and a number of
reforms were made to improve the condition of women. Arguably the
caution of the feminist movement itself and the slow pace of reform
were more notable than the actual achievements. In addition to the
dominant strand of middle-class, cautious reformers there were more
militant feminists, often left-wing and/or working-class, and conservative Catholic women's groups. Both the reformers and Catholic
groups concentrated on moral reforms and welfare projects that were
far closer to charity than to the turbulence of the British suffragettes.
The hesitancy shown by French feminism had two primary sources.
The first was a question of belief: most feminists shared the overall
conservatism of the Third Republic with regard to social change, and
distanced themselves from extremists in the same way that the bulk
of republicans distanced themselves from the Commune. Secondly,

women's interests were divided by social class. Even if they shared the same disadvantages in terms of civil and political rights, the comfort of wealthy women came at the expense of their dressmakers, house-maids, and cooks just as the fortunes of their husbands came mostly from male labour. This was vividly depicted in the memoirs of Jeanne Bouvier, who worked both as a housemaid and as a dressmaker. This sketch of her fellow workers, the *midinettes*, described how the only things they shared with the ladies who bought their dresses were fashion and TB.

They imposed strict diets upon themselves so that they could afford to make themselves look beautiful. This love of finery owes itself to the fact that they only made luxury goods. Most of them entered the trade between the ages of 12 and 15. They grew up in this speciality of the clothing industry, which is one of the glories of French business. How could they not love the finery, the beautiful dresses and hats and everything that made up the toilette of a lady, when these children grown into young women spent all their days making dresses that adorned other women! If the *midinettes* had been better paid, they could have dressed well without skimping on their meals. Their strict diets weakened them, and they developed tuberculosis. This was the cause of many deaths in the trade. Its consequences were not only to be feared by the workers—they could afflict their customers as well.[5]

Demand for reform can be grouped into three areas: political, economic, and sexual rights. The chief political grievance was that women had no vote, either in local or national elections. This was demanded as a right in itself and as a means to other ends; for example, the state paid female schoolteachers less than male ones, essentially because men were represented in parliament and women were not. Unfortunately for suffragette leaders such as Hubertine Auclert and Madeleine Pelletier, left-wing politicians did not support them because they feared that women would vote for Catholic parties, and right-wing politicians were not prepared to sacrifice their male chauvinism for electoral gains. Madeleine Pelletier herself adopted all the values of the Third Republic: she qualified as a doctor and fought for the equality of rights, thus embodying the republic's belief in science and the legacy of the Revolution. Yet she achieved

[5] J. Bouvier, *Mes mémoires* (Paris, 1983 edn.; 1st edn. 1936), p. 97. Born in 1865, Bouvier worked on her parents' farm, as a factory worker at the age of 11, as a housemaid, then as a dressmaker for the rest of her working career. She was also a trade union activist from the 1900s to 1930s, a writer, and an archivist.

this despite the republicans, not because of them. Women's education was not designed to liberate them or to educate them as equals, so that one day they could win the vote; it was designed to break the hold the Catholic church had over them so that they would not lead their sons astray or conflict with their husbands. The meagre funding provided for girls' schools revealed how cheaply the republic valued them.

Economic issues were a second area of concern, with reformers aiming to improve working conditions and pay (a woman working at home in textiles earned in one day what a male Renault mechanic earned in an hour). State employees were best able to organize themselves, whether they were manual or white-collar workers, as was the case for the schoolteachers' union organized by Marie Guillot. Female unions received some support from socialist and syndicalist leaders, but the rank and file were much more hostile to them, as they were to immigrant labour, because women and migrants undercut men's pay. They made little headway in the two main sectors of women's employment, domestic service and textiles. Only 3 per cent of textile workers were unionized by 1911, partly because many worked at home. There were about a million domestic servants in 1900, of whom 80 per cent were female and half were under 30; they usually quit service at marriage. Most were 'maids-of-all-work', the only servant in a household. These factors of gender, age, lifecycle, and dispersal made it almost impossible to unionize them, while those who stayed with one family through their lives were typically fiercely loyal to their employers. The most important changes to women's working conditions came neither from governments nor union pressure, and instead emerged from the labour required by the new economy. A multitude of white-collar jobs was created, as shop assistants, schoolteachers, clerical staff, and in the post office. While these jobs were still badly paid compared to men's wages, conditions were often poor, and few led to a career, they were still an improvement on factories, farms, and domestic service. One long-standing economic injustice at least was corrected in 1907, when married women were finally given control over their own earnings.

The third area where reforms were demanded was birth control and sexual rights. The demographic history of France showed that birth control was widely practised, but when it failed for single women or servant girls, they turned to illegal abortions. This was

dramatically illustrated in 1893 when fifty-three women were prosecuted in the case of a woman from the disreputable Clichy district of
Paris, who was alleged to have carried out over 10,000 abortions over
several years. In contrast, men were sheltered by law as well as nature:
until 1912 it was illegal to pursue the father of a child. Similarly,
prostitutes were regulated, checked for venereal diseases, and forcibly
treated for them, not their male clients. There was little equality
within marriage either: men had rights while women had duties;
husbands' affairs were indulged while wives' affairs were punished.
The main reform was the divorce law of 1884, which permitted
divorce when one partner was at fault (divorce by mutual consent was
made legal in 1975). This did bring relief to some women, for eight
out of ten cases were initiated by women. Divorces were concentrated
among middle-class and bourgeois women living in the towns of
northern France. Within this population divorce was not uncommon
by the time of the Great War: there were 7,300 divorces in 1900, rising
to 15,000 in 1913. In other communities and social groups, it remained
a rarity and a scandal.

Republicans were right to fear that many women opposed them,
for they gave them little reason to do otherwise. Their lukewarm
efforts to improve the position of women were undercut by their
failure to do more and by their attacks on the Catholic church. French
Catholicism became increasingly feminized over the nineteenth
century. The number of female clergy overtook male clergy in 1880,
thanks to the rise of female orders; women's lay organizations also
outstripped men's. The cults of the Virgin Mary, Bernadette of
Lourdes, and Teresa of Lisieux both feminized and sentimentalized
worship, to such a point that some priests delivered separate sermons
for all-male congregations. The Dreyfus Affair and the separation of
church and state mobilized Catholic women, many of whom joined
two national organizations, the Ligue des Femmes Françaises and its
larger offshoot, the Ligue Patriotique des Dames Françaises, which
claimed 200,000 and 545,000 members respectively by 1914, making
them larger than most trade unions or political parties, and far larger
than the liberal feminist Conseil National des Femmes Françaises,
which had 100,000 members by the outbreak of war. Hundreds of
thousands of Catholic women made pilgrimages to Lourdes, which
stood for everything that the republic rejected: it represented
Catholicism, locality, femininity, and faith against the republic's

secular, centralized, male, and positivist values. One and a half million pilgrims, mostly female, went to Lourdes for the fiftieth anniversary of the visions there, in 1908. For them, Lavisse's trinity was no match for the Holy Trinity.

The bicycle and the cobbler

The slow emergence of new opportunities for women and demands for their rights typified how the social and economic characteristics of the twentieth century were emerging. Two emblems of these changes were the rise of the bicycle, and the rise and fall of the village cobbler.

The modern bicycle was a result of new engineering techniques and factory-based mass production. It increased people's mobility substantially at a time when cars were still luxury goods, and carried with it economic and social gains. It also played an important role in the growth of organized sports, notably with the introduction of the Tour de France in 1903; this was special because it toured the frontiers of France to emphasize both the unity of the nation and the lost regions of Alsace and Lorraine. Sports, including football, running, and boxing as well as cycling, emerged as part of a distinctive youth culture different from the old patterns of apprentices' leisure. Cycling helped to change women's lives too because they were also permitted to ride bicycles, giving them more personal freedom. Another staple of modern leisure appeared in this period, when the Lumière brothers showed the first film in 1895; by 1914, there were 260 cinemas in Paris.

The bicycle was just one element in a second industrial revolution that took place in Europe and the USA around 1900, though its full impact was not felt across the world until after the Second World War. It was based on four new technologies: electricity, the internal combustion engine, chemicals, and radio. From the 1890s, and certainly from 1906, the French economy took part fully in this new revolution. The annual growth rate in non-agricultural activity was 2.5 per cent over 1906–13, the best rate since 1875–82. Trade too rose after stagnating between 1871 and 1900, to double its level by 1913. Growth was built on greater investment and mechanization, raising labour productivity to compensate for the shortage of workers. Car production boomed in the 1890s, beginning with the Peugeot brothers, Panhard, and Levassor, followed soon after by Renault. In 1898 1,500 cars were built, rising to 45,000 by 1913, employing 60–70,000 workers; this made it the biggest single metal-working industry. France was Europe's leading car maker and exporter, well ahead of Britain and Germany (making 34,000 and 23,000 cars in 1913 respectively); the USA, however, produced 485,000 cars a year. The humble sewing machine transformed clothes-making, which shifted out of central Paris for provinces such as the Loire valley because wages were lower there. In contrast, Paris became a centre for car manufacture, chemicals, and electricals, forming a belt of factory districts and workers' housing around the central twenty arrondissements, which were still dominated by craft industries, commerce, public administration, and residential districts. Gérard Noiriel has called the result the 'modern worker', whose life was built around 'factory, suburb and housing estate'. In the north and east of France, the heavy industries of coal and steel used unskilled workers, often immigrants, to supply raw materials to the skilled mechanics and engineers of Paris. War in 1914 accelerated the growth of heavy industry for arms production. Factories became mechanized, organized around rational assembly lines on the principles of the American engineer Frederick Taylor, the pioneer of time and motion study and scientific management.

And yet France was slipping internationally. Its share of world trade fell from 12.7 per cent to 7.6 per cent between 1871 and 1914, and it slipped from being the world's second largest exporter in 1875 (behind the UK) to number four, behind the USA and Germany. Although industrial production had overtaken agricultural output, this had come from increased productivity, for the shift of workers from agriculture to industry was slow: workers leaving the land often went into service industries instead. This international decline and slow internal change at the end of the nineteenth century reinforced the view that French industry was fundamentally weak. However, productivity per worker was above the European average: slow population growth remained the problem. By 1914, the birth rate had fallen so much that any growth came from increased life expectancy and immigration. As described in Chapter 2, this squeezed the supply of labour and domestic demand over the whole of the nineteenth century. The labour shortfall was filled by the more efficient use of workers, high levels of skill, immigrants, and women. By 1911 there were about 1,160,000 immigrants in France, and a further 250,000 had been given French citizenship. About 40 per cent of French women worked, against just 10 per cent in Britain and Germany. The restriction on domestic demand explains the interest in colonial markets as additional outlets for French production. Domestic demand could only increase if wages rose, which cut into companies' profits and slowed further investment. Wages doubled over the second half of the nineteenth century, well ahead of price rises, but French workers still spent about 60 per cent of their income on food, against 40 per cent in Britain and Germany, leaving less to spend on industrial goods and services.

The rise and fall of the village cobbler stands for another transformation under way. With the end of the depression in 1896, the countryside entered a period of prosperity, and in many ways rural life reached its apogee. Roger Thabault's classic study of the development of his native village encapsulated this in the example of the village cobbler: as mentioned in the previous chapter, during the Second Empire peasants began to wear leather boots and shoes instead of carved wooden clogs (*sabots*).[6] Greater prosperity increased this demand, and the number of village cobblers rose to a peak around 1900. It then fell back as cheaper mass-produced goods reached the countryside, and cobblers went out of business, giving way to shoe shops and shoe-menders. From the late 1890s on, the new economy definitively reached the countryside. Peasants became farmers, producing crops for sale, working larger farms, and substituting machinery for labour.

The penetration of the urban economy was matched by urban lifestyles. In a highly influential book, the historian Eugen Weber argued that the transformation of 'peasants into Frenchmen' finally took place in the half-century around 1870–1920: before then, the rural depths of France were not primarily French but local or regional in their sentiments, their daily life, politics, and language. Moreover, he argued that the 'end of the century saw the wholesale destruction of traditional ways', such as festivals and dialects, replaced by imports from Paris or drilled out by authority. Villagers

[6] R. Thabault, *Mon village: ascension d'un peuple* (Paris, 1982 edn.; 1st edn. 1943), p. 163.

were at last integrated into the national community by roads and railways, by schools and military conscription, by the new mass press and democratic politics, by markets and the church. Most of these forces were familiar features of Napoleon's new regime, which had integrated towns into the nation decades before, but they only reached the countryside under the Third Republic. Other historians have rejected Weber's assumption that 'modernity' flowed from town to countryside. Xavier de Planhol argued instead that, far from being ravaged, rural France reached its apogee before the First World War. Urban habits did indeed reach the countryside, where they were adapted to fit local traditions to create even greater variety. Until the late nineteenth century, sheer poverty had enforced a degree of uniformity on peasants: now they could afford to be different. For example, the lace headdresses that are part of the 'traditional' costume of Breton women were themselves inventions of the nineteenth century: Breton peasants could not afford lace in 1800. After the First World War and especially after the Second, such rural diversity was worn away.[7] In many ways, Weber's argument has received a new twist today, with globalization cast in the role played by the national market a hundred years earlier, crushing small farmers and the values of their locality in favour of uniformity.

The outbreak of the Great War

By 1914, many of the trends that characterized France in the twentieth century were clearly visible. Some, like the structure of the state, the parliamentary republic, and the religious settlement, have endured . . . with interruptions and deviations. Other developments, such as the emancipation of women, the new empire, the second industrial revolution, and contemporary leisure, did not have their full impact until the 1950s and beyond. The main reason for this delay is to be found in another vital theme: relations between France and the rest of Europe. In 1914, France was one of Europe's leading powers but not the predominant force that it had been in Napoleon's day.

[7] X. de Planhol and P. Claval, *An Historical Geography of France* (Cambridge, 1994; 1st edn. Paris, 1988); E. Weber, *Peasants into Frenchmen* (London, 1979).

Its army had been humiliated by Prussia in 1870, its economy and population outstripped by Britain and Germany, and cultural leadership had passed from Paris to Vienna. Politically, republicanism and anticlericalism kept the liberating mission of the Revolution alive, though this appealed more to rebels than to foreign governments. Worst of all, the rise of nationalism across Europe meant that international affairs were dominated by antagonism instead of co-operation. From 1914 to 1945, France's relations with Europe revolved around war with Germany and its consequences. War from 1914 to 1918 bled the country white, leaving it too weak (psychologically as much as materially) to withstand Germany in 1940. France—and Europe—could only build for the future once this calamitous duel was over.

The outbreak of the Great War was both long expected and a dreadful surprise in France. French fears of Germany had revived in the 1900s as Kaiser Wilhelm II took an increasingly aggressive approach towards international affairs. In particular, Germany attempted to force Britain and France to improve relations with it, by building a larger fleet to challenge the Royal Navy and by threatening French control over Morocco in 1905 and again in 1911. This strategy backfired, and instead encouraged Britain and France to settle old colonial disputes through the *Entente cordiale*, from 1904 onwards. The increase in military service to three years in 1913 showed how seriously the threat was taken.

On the other hand, the actual outbreak of war was unexpected. The roots of the conflict lay in the conflicting nationalisms of south-east Europe. The retreat of the Ottoman empire from the Balkans created new and ethnically diverse states such as Serbia and Montenegro that sought to embrace their cousins inside the now tottering Austro-Hungarian empire, notably in the province of Bosnia-Hercegovina. When the Habsburg Archduke Franz Ferdinand was assassinated by Serbs in Sarajevo on 28 June 1914, the Austrians took the opportunity to threaten Serbia with invasion, to stave off the collapse of their empire. However, Tsar Nicholas II of Russia was also under pressure from Slav nationalists, who demanded that their fellow Slavs in Serbia be defended. German leaders, especially the army command, believed that they had to back Austria-Hungary, their only reliable ally, against Russia. They then escalated the conflict into an all-out European war, gambling that they could defeat France quickly in order to launch their offensive against Russia.

In France, little attention was paid to these developments. Elections in May 1914 produced a left-wing majority for the Radicals and social-ists under leaders who supported peace and accommodation with Germany, Caillaux and Jaurès. Viviani became premier and foreign minister rather than Caillaux, because the latter's wife was on trial for the murder of the editor of *Le Figaro*: she had shot him because he was running a scandal-mongering campaign against the couple. This sensation gripped popular attention far more than Balkan affairs. The President of the Republic, Poincaré, sailed to Russia with Viviani in late July, but this made matters worse because Austria waited till they had left St Petersburg on their return journey before delivering its ultimatum to Serbia: at the vital moment of the crisis, French foreign policy was, literally, all at sea. By the time they returned on 29 July, the day that Henriette Caillaux was acquitted, the eastern powers had begun to mobilize their armies in a race against each other. On 3 August, Germany declared war on France.

4

The stranglehold of the Great Patriotic War: 1914–1926

The American diplomat and historian George Kennan described the Great War as the seminal catastrophe of the twentieth century. It destroyed the Austro-Hungarian, German, Ottoman, and Russian empires, out of whose ruins came the unstable nation-states of eastern Europe and the Middle East, the Bolshevik revolution, Fascism, and Nazism, which in turn led to the Second World War, the Cold War, and Middle East conflicts. Though western Europe fared better than the east, the burden of the Great War still lay heavy, and it dominated life well beyond the armistice of 1918. The war held France in a political and financial stranglehold until 1926, while its psychological and demographic grip on the country lasted much longer, until it was overtaken by the disaster of 1940.

The *Union sacrée*

In 1914, France was a dynamic country with a political regime that had been established at the cost of bitter internal divisions. War reversed this position: it united the country, bringing republicans and Catholics together in a 'sacred union' or *Union sacrée*, while at the same time bleeding it of its vitality.

There were good reasons to doubt that the republic could unite the country for war. It had systematically alienated its Catholic citizens;

socialists and unionists preached international solidarity and pacifism; despite tensions with Germany, forty-four years of peace had rendered abstract the inescapable calls for *revanche*. Moreover, the keenest supporters of *revanche* were mostly the republic's nationalist enemies. Instead, the French people rallied together in August 1914, vindicating the republic. Jean-Jacques Becker has shown how surprised France was to find itself at war, overturning the view held for many decades that the country was eager for battle.[1] A major factor in this surprise and this solidarity was the trial of Mme Caillaux, which captivated public opinion; paradoxically, this surprise helped the country to rally to arms because the workers' movement was caught off guard. Socialists and unionists hastily organized meetings in defence of peace and pressed the Socialist International to do the same across Europe, but when German socialists supported the hard line taken by their government, in order to defend German workers against tsarist oppression, Jaurès announced that French socialists would rally to the cause of national defence. This was not enough to stop a nationalist from assassinating him on 31 July. The CGT was even more extreme in its opposition to mobilization, but it adopted Jaurès's position nonetheless, and its leader, Léon Jouhaux, defended this policy dramatically at Jaurès's funeral. Since the socialists had not succeeded in maintaining peace, they had to accept a defensive war.

Becker showed how rapidly one attitude followed another: astonishment at the outbreak of war was followed by unenthusiastic resignation, which was in turn followed by a sincerely patriotic determination when the time came for troops to depart. National reconciliation took place on a grand scale, in the certainties that France was rightfully defending itself and that the conflict would be brief. Achieving this reconciliation was essential for a regime that had divided opinion for nearly half a century. Poincaré, who could justly flatter himself as one of the creators of this state of opinion by the resolutely patriotic policy he had adopted since 1912, swiftly invented the political form to be taken by this national reconciliation. In his solemn message read to the Chamber of Deputies on 4 August, he affirmed that 'nothing will break the sacred union formed in face of the enemy'. Though the *Union sacrée* began as a brief political truce,

---

[1] J.-J. Becker, *1914: comment les Français sont entrés dans la guerre* (Paris, 1977).

the length of the war turned it into an ideology that celebrated a rediscovered national unity in which political factions had melted away, and it went on to become a vital formula in French politics throughout the twentieth century. The brotherly union of conscripts demanded a corresponding 'truce between the parties'. The government aided it by suspending a plan to arrest over 2,000 pacifist militants recorded in a list known as the *Carnet B* (the 'B-list'), by participating at Jaurès's funeral, and by widening its coalition on 26 August. Its expansion to the right (giving the ministry of war to Millerand, who had by now moved to the right, returning Delcassé to foreign affairs, and bringing the Catholic Denys Cochin into government in October 1915) was less spectacular than the entry of two socialists into the government, Marcel Sembat and the veteran Guesde. The CGT and Action Française sat together on the Comité de Secours National. Unity was sealed by the military reverses of the opening weeks of the war, when offensives against the German borders failed and the French army was forced back to the Marne in the first weeks of September, just thirty miles from Paris: France was in peril. The occupation of the north-eastern departments of France throughout the war also helped to prolong this consensus.

The energies of the first six governments of the war, until Clemenceau took power in November 1917, were absorbed by management of the *Union sacrée* and their relationship with the army command. For there was another *Union sacrée* at work: of the political and military worlds. Parliament resolved that it would remain in session until the end of the war, though 220 deputies were mobilized, and that it would impose parliamentary control over the army—which the latter rejected. At the start of the conflict the army had complete authority, but, since it could not promise victory in a single campaign, the terms of the constitution meant that civilian politicians would recover their powers. The politicians' return to authority was gradual, beginning with temporary missions to the front, then by surrounding Millerand (who was accused of protecting the army command) with junior ministers, and finally by dismissing him. Briand succeeded Viviani in an even more 'sacred' government because he had no fewer than five ministers of state (senior figures appointed to lend their political authority to the government) including three former presidents of the Council of Ministers. However, he found that he was constantly harassed by the Senate's army commission, chaired by Georges Clemenceau. Briand had to accept joint meetings of the Chamber and the Senate in secret committees that debated diplomatic and military questions at length. In this way parliament and the government recovered their prerogatives during the war, though in a clearly different system.

Political parties, which were weak enough at the best of times, had been stripped of all substance by mobilization, first because at the start of the war the Chamber postponed any elections till it ended, and secondly because public debate ceased: the *Union sacrée* spelt an end to political factions. Furthermore, parties that depended on militants withered when their leaders and members were sent to the front. Only Action Française repositioned itself by concentrating on its newspaper (also named *Action Française*); its speciality was the denunciation of real and imaginary traitors, which swelled its readership well beyond its core royalist audience. Other parties, especially on the left, were menaced by the bellicose ideology of the *Union sacrée*, but now realized that they could not quit the union without appearing to abandon ship. This was made even worse by press censorship, which had been entrusted to the military authorities when France was declared to be in a state of siege, from 2 August 1914 onwards. Censorship grew ever more frequent, extensive, and absurd, and this provoked one of the major political debates of the war. In October 1914, Clemenceau changed the name of his newspaper *L'Homme libre* to *L'Homme enchaîné*, in protest. Censorship helped to support morale by tranquillizing public opinion, by insisting that it was impossible to stop fighting, and by constantly stressing Germany's responsibility for the war. But censorship was not complete: for one thing, the mass-circulation dailies serialized novels which realistically evoked the horrors of the war, such as Henri Barbusse's *Le Feu*; for a second, *Le Canard enchaîné* was published for the first time on 5 July 1916.[2] Along with the decline of political parties and press censorship, the state of siege transferred the powers of mayors and prefects to military authorities, and from civilian courts to summary justice. The eclipse of liberal democracy was the price paid by the republic for mobilizing the nation.

---

[2] *Le Canard enchaîné* is still one of France's leading satirical and investigative publications.

Clemenceau reinvents the *Union sacrée*

In November 1917 the *Union sacrée* changed profoundly, with the appointment of Clemenceau as President of the Council of Ministers. By then, the political direction of the war had run into the mud almost as much as the war at the front. The failure of the campaigns on the Western Front led some politicians to think (but not speak publicly) about negotiation with Germany. However, the attempts to negotiate made by politicians such as Caillaux, Painlevé, and Briand were doomed because the German commanders themselves never for an instant considered restoring Alsace and Lorraine, which was the minimum war aim of France. By the spring of 1917 the strains of an unsuccessful war had fostered a wave of pacifist sentiment, and this was blamed on Louis Malvy, minister of the interior since 1914. Malvy's soft approach to the left (it was his decision not to apply the *Carnet B* in 1914) was undermined by the exposure as a spy of an anti-militarist with whom both he and Joseph Caillaux had links. The atmosphere became increasingly fevered as more and more spies were denounced (rightly or wrongly), most famously Mata Hari. *Action Française* gleefully mixed negotiation, defeatism, and treachery together, and its leading polemicist, Léon Daudet, inflamed his readers' indignation with the poisonous result.

The campaigns of Daudet, and others such as Maurice Barrès and Clemenceau himself, finally took effect in 1917 as ministry after ministry became entangled in scandals about espionage and treason, for scandal had replaced conventional politics under the *Union sacrée*. It became impossible to rule against the wish of Clemenceau, who doubled his campaigns in the Senate's army commission with his editorials in *L'Homme enchaîné*. By November 1917, the failure of centrist governments left Poincaré with the clear alternative of Caillaux, an advocate of a negotiated peace who was tarnished by his dubious acquaintances, or Clemenceau, an unbending believer in war to the end. This was no choice at all for the patriotic Poincaré, who appointed Clemenceau. Clemenceau's government transformed the *Union sacrée* so much that it has provoked an important historiographical debate: was it simply a wartime dictatorship, or France's first modern government? From the perspective of today's Fifth Republic, 'modern' implies a system that was both authoritarian and efficient, in contrast to the Third and Fourth Republics, which depended on compromise. Clemenceau used a huge majority (418 deputies against 65, 64 of whom were socialists) to form a Radical government without a single leading deputy in it; the *Canard enchaîné* made sport of this by depicting Clemenceau holding every ministry. He ruled with the aid of a small group of collaborators, consulted his ministers individually, and rarely met them all together. He kept Poincaré away from discussions and embodied an absolute, all-encompassing *Union sacrée* with even more confidence than Poincaré, its inventor, had ever done. The 'modernity' of this ministry largely lies in the way that this revitalized authority was balanced by accountability to the Chamber and Senate, especially sitting in their commissions, which were given patient explanations on the government's overall policy, but not on matters of daily detail. Censorship was reformed, to repress both pacifists and defeatists for military reasons, but to restore freedoms otherwise. Clemenceau's accountability to parliament was a substantial change in the link between the legislature and the executive, and it gave the latter significantly more independence; however, the circumstances of war limited the scope of this renewal. No one could challenge the patriotism of 'the Tiger', as Clemenceau was known, nor dare to expose themselves to his merciless condemnation. Like it or not, every deputy had to vote for him. Moreover, it was hardly 'modern' for Clemenceau, the defender of Dreyfus, to arrest Caillaux and send Malvy for trial, nor for this ancient figure, risen from the 1870–1 war, to have such a personal, menacing grip over a paralysed Chamber.

Society adjusts to the war: the wartime economy and morale

From 1914 onwards the government found itself confronted by new and varied problems, all of which stemmed from the nature of the war and from its length—or rather, from its indefinite continuation. Plans for human, economic, and financial mobilization existed, but they only covered a matter of weeks because the high command had never imagined that the war could last for longer than a single campaign. The solutions to these problems were always improvisations, either modified depending on their effectiveness or left as they were because other problems became more urgent.

After the shock caused by the outbreak of war and the dramatic rescue of Paris at the battle of the Marne in the summer of 1914, public opinion rapidly accustomed itself to war. In the countryside, this was aided by the generous allowances made to needy families, which also reassured soldiers about the families they had left behind; the rise in food prices helped the agricultural sector further. In cities, an economic recovery stimulated by the gigantic industrial programme begun in September 1914 had the same effect. Both military and civil authorities moved quickly to control opinion through the press. Newspapers' internal censorship and government instructions soothed the population, and soldiers wrote home about their imminent return from the front. But reports of new offensives created worries at the front and inside France. Very soon, the endless lists of the dead disappeared from newspapers, and death became either a private, family matter or an abstract concern when seen in total. People coped with the war by treating it as a series of short-term difficulties to be overcome. For example, they gave generously to special collections with an immediate focus (the 'day for Belgium', the 'day for the 75 mm cannon' . . .). Inquiries into civilian morale carried out by prefects revealed that the main worries in towns from the second year of the war onwards were the immediate problems of the price of food and short supplies. One short term succeeded another, and thus the war grew long.

The case of state finance illustrated the way that policy developed through series of short-term measures. The law on mobilization allowed the Banque de France to make advances to the treasury at the outbreak of hostilities, but the budget for 1913 had only amounted to five billion francs, whereas the average annual budget for the five years of war was thirty-eight billion francs. The Banque de France's advances were spent in a matter of days, so they had to be renewed and increased; they amounted to forty-six billion francs by the end of the war. Gold reserves remained stable, so payments for imports were met by voluntary gifts from French citizens (Mme Poincaré set an example by donating her wedding ring). The proportion of the currency covered by gold reserves had been set at 71 per cent in case of war: it fell to 21 per cent by its end. Short-term loans met most of the costs: fifty-one billion francs were raised by defence bonds, paying interest at 5 per cent, supplemented by twenty-four billion francs' worth of national defence loans, which were perpetual loans issued annually and promoted by patriotic advertising posters. In total, domestic loans raised seventy-five billion francs, compared to a miserly one billion from the income tax that had been approved in 1914 but was only levied from 1917. The net external debt that financed imports rose to forty billion francs, of which fifteen billion were owed to Britain and twenty-five billion to the USA. With this debt, financial questions became of fundamental importance in ordinary politics, and a potent historical actor reappeared on stage for the first time since the 1880s: the holder of government bonds. Bond-holders, French and foreign, became central characters in the 1920s. This debt was also one of the major causes of inflation, which had been germinating during the *belle époque* and which burst forth during the war with grave effects.

As with finance, the transition to a war economy began as a series of piecemeal measures designed to meet specific problems; because it was generally believed that any war would be short, policy-makers had no plans for the development of a war economy in 1914. These measures had a profound impact on some sectors which modernized their production methods to meet the war's limitless demand for arms and munitions. Some ministers hoped that this could lead to a more fundamental shift in the nature of the French economy by developing industry through state organization (the policy of Saint-Simon in the previous century), and by integrating workers and their unions within society. However, this shift did not long outlive the war, and industrial sectors that did not aid the war effort decayed.

There were two specific obstacles to the development of a war economy. First, the north-east, which produced nearly three-quarters of the coal, iron, and steel that were the staples of modern warfare, was occupied for four years. Secondly, mobilization affected a higher proportion of the workforce in France than in any other country. These two difficulties were met, like others, by a rapid expansion of the state. Though the reduced number of ministers changed little, Viviani's five under-secretaries of state became fourteen under Clemenceau, and each individual problem spawned a new administrative body: there were at least 281 governmental bodies by the spring of 1918. The state lost its traditional reticence in economic matters in two ways: it provided finance and it organized distribution. But actual production remained entirely in private hands. This collaboration between the public and private sectors was invented by a pairing that would have been highly unlikely before the war. It stemmed from a joint initiative between Albert Thomas (a socialist, historian, and under-secretary of state first for artillery and then for armaments) and Robert Pinot (secretary-general of the Comité des Forges, the iron and steel makers' association, who was often known as the secret minister for industry). Begun in November 1915, this initiative gathered war industries together into consortia, one for each sector. Their aims were agreed in common and the factors of production, such as raw materials and basic products, were distributed amongst them, or imported if need be. After the disorganization of the first few weeks, a shortage of labour became a permanent problem in industry as in agriculture. Half a million soldiers were specially assigned to war production, and women replaced men in the fields—they did so much less often in factory workshops, which preferred to employ workers from the empire, foreigners, youths, and wounded men returning from the front.

For industry, success depended on greater productivity, and companies sought to achieve this through the rapid adoption of Taylorist methods. Circumstances favoured development: government orders were as large as possible, prices were high and guaranteed, investment was supported, and profits were considerable. French industry equipped and armed Russian, Serbian, Romanian, Italian, and American soldiers as well as Frenchmen. This magnificent opportunity was eagerly seized by modernizing employers. Its political creators shared the same productivist vision, but had different ideas about the way to realize it. For Thomas, this was the long-dreamed-of chance to marry the scientific organization of labour with social democracy. He wanted to accelerate the institutionalization of trade unionism and thus integrate the working classes within the nation. The CGT leader Léon Jouhaux accepted the vague title of 'delegate to the nation', and in September 1914 the CGT founded an 'action committee' that worked with the public authorities to regulate problems created by mobilization and the war. Its use of arbitration committees to resolve disputes prevailed against the strikes of 1917, overturning the principles of class war set down in the CGT's Charter of Amiens in 1906.

The organized economy was thus part of the socialist project. It was also supported by Étienne Clémentel, minister of commerce from 1915 to 1919, who supported the formation of consortia as a way to organize French capitalism under the tutelage of a strong state. But after Thomas regretfully resigned (over Clemenceau's rupture of the

Union sacrée), Louis Loucheur took over his position; an industrialist and graduate of the École Polytechnique, he embodied a liberal 'anti-state' tradition that was keen to dismantle this mixed economy rapidly at the end of the war.

The economic outcome itself was mixed. Modern economic activity took a new surge forward, visible in military success itself, in the fortunes of the textile-maker Boussac and the engineers Citroën and Renault, in the development of the regions around Paris and Lyon, and in the incredible growth of isolated centres of war industries such as Toulouse or Bourges (which expanded from 46,000 to 110,000 citizens). But this must not be allowed to hide the serious difficulties of sectors and companies that did not benefit from the war's demand. Agriculture was weakened by a shortage of men and of horses, its productive area was cut by a quarter and its productivity by at least as much, and its reduced output was then drained by the enormous rations needed to feed the troops. Prices rose fast from the spring of 1916 despite massive imports; partial rationing was introduced, followed by food coupons in June 1918. The modernization of some sectors of the economy was thus accompanied by an overall reduction in production, by ageing capital equipment, by the destruction of workshops and factories, and by the massacre of men.

Mutineers and strikers

Civilian and military morale held out against the rising toll of war dead, shortages, and inflation till the spring of 1917. After nearly three years of stalemate in the trenches, it became clear that victory on the Western Front was impossible, and that all the French and British offensives had come to nothing. One voice alone must speak here for the experiences of millions of soldiers on all sides throughout these terrible years.

Sunday 14 February 1915

Dear friend,

When we came by here in November, this plain was still magnificent with its fields stretching as far as the eye could see, full of beet, strewn with rich farms and lined with ricks. Now it is the land of the dead, all its fields are torn up, mangled, the farms have been burnt or are in ruins and a new crop has been born: little mounds topped with a cross or simply a bottle turned upside-down in which the papers of the man who rests there have been placed. How often has death brushed me with his wing when I raced along the ditches or sunken roads to avoid their shrapnel or the rat-a-tat of their machine guns. For a long time I slept in a newly dug tomb, until we moved camp and I am now in a hole that I dug in an embankment. I carry my blanket attached to my saddle, my mess kit on the other side, and off we go. The other day I was in the trenches called Les Joyeux. I have never seen anything so horrible. They had shored up their trenches with dead bodies covered with earth, but in the rain the soil slipped down and you could see a hand or a foot emerge, black and swollen. There were even two large boots coming out of the trench, toes in the air, at head-height, like a coat-rack. And the 'Joyeux' hung their haversacks from them, and laughed at using the corpse of a *boche* as a coat-rack. I'm only telling you things I've seen, otherwise I wouldn't believe them myself.

Taupiac
Brigadier, 58th Regiment, 48th Battery, 68th Sector[3]

France's greatest victory had been the costly defence of Verdun, the fortress that anchored the north-eastern corner of the French lines. It was attacked by the German army between February and December 1916, its leaders correctly guessing that the French would defend it to the last and bleed themselves white in the process. Over the course of the battle, three-quarters of the French army fought at Verdun under the command of General Philippe Pétain, sustaining 377,000 dead and wounded. From June to November 1916 the British army mounted its greatest attack of the war on the Somme, sustaining 420,000 casualties—alongside another 195,000 French losses. Other fronts provided little hope: there was no progress on the Italian and Balkan fronts; unrestricted submarine warfare was begun by Germany in February 1917; and in Russia the tsarist regime was overthrown the following month. Now the short term stretched out to infinity. A series of mutinies affected more than half the French army, born out of the disillusionment which followed the collapse of hopes placed on General Nivelle's offensive on the Chemin des Dames area of the Aisne and Champagne regions in April 1917. The mutinies began behind the lines, in transit stations and convoys between Soissons and Reims; they revealed a general exhaustion, but were limited in their scope and duration. Essentially, the mutineers refused to attack, or to advance to the front lines: Guy Pedroncini described it as

[3] Letter of Brigadier Michel Taupiac in J. P. Guéno and Y. Laplume (eds.), *Paroles de Polius: lettres et carnets du Front* (Paris, 1998), p. 90.

a 'general strike' against the way that the war was being fought.[4] Some mutineers marched behind a red flag, to the cry of 'Long live peace!', and a solitary division wanted to march on Paris. But they never refused to defend their lines, nor did they abandon their posts: the Germans opposite never knew of the disorder. Military commanders blamed the mutinies on the bad influence of the home front, on the weakness of civil authorities personified by Malvy, and on the pacifist activities of the socialists. Even if Pétain, who replaced Nivelle as the head of the French armies, paid some attention to these superficial explanations, he also saw the mistakes made by the army command. This twofold explanation produced a repression which was both firm and relatively humane (3,427 soldiers were found guilty, 544 were condemned to death, but only 49 were executed), combined with an end to the recent offensives, reforms to soldiers' conditions (clearer terms for leave, better troop convoys and supplies), and a substantial propaganda drive inside the army. The military tactics of Pétain and Foch also preserved their troops' lives better, and the arrival of American troops in 1917 slowly swung the balance against Germany.

In the cities, social unrest occurred in two phases in 1917, followed by another phase in 1918, as escalating prices finally led to demands for higher pay. The first wave of strikes began in January 1917 among the seamstresses of Paris's *haute couture* companies (still active in the depths of the war), then spread to munitions factories in the region. Albert Thomas intervened rapidly by creating a minimum salary for the Seine region and an obligatory arbitration procedure, which was soon extended across France. This challenged the right to strike, and had to be imposed on a hostile CGT. Following the Chemin des Dames offensive, when price rises began to accelerate, the unions' May Day celebrations were a great success for the first time since 1914. The startling cry of 'Long live Germany!' was even heard at a meeting of the Comité de Défense Syndicaliste, a minority faction within the CGT. The strike movement swelled during May, and again largely involved women, spreading from fashion houses to services and thence into the arms industries, where seventy-one factories were briefly affected. The strikes became more political, with pacifist, even revolutionary or defeatist demands added to complaints about pay in some cases. This unrest was part of a much wider crisis of morale that

---

[4] Guy Pedroncini, *Les Mutineries de 1917* (Paris, 1967).

covered the whole urban world, workers and middle classes alike. Everyone knew what was at stake in the war, but increasingly people wanted peace even more than they wanted victory.

In the spring of 1918, strikes broke out in metal-working factories with more political demands than those of 1917. The watchwords were now revolutionary and pacifist: rule by workers' soviets, strikes until peace was signed. These protests split the labour movement. Alphonse Merrheim, leader of the socialist-revolutionary minority, moved closer to the CGT leadership because he feared that the supporters of these strikes were too inexperienced and he mistrusted the effect of these slogans. He was worried that their action compromised the patriotic line and threatened France's chance of victory. When confronted by the last German offensives of 1918, patriotism won the day and the strikers rallied to the national cause. Clemenceau let the movement blow itself out, believing that it was not a serious threat. The CGT emerged from the war incontestably stronger. It had finally become a mass organization, it had succeeded as a partner of the government, and it had changed its own direction, adopting a reformist strategy of negotiation that had yielded considerable benefits. Thus the war made a resolution of the social question possible, as Albert Thomas had intended. It was now possible that the working classes would be integrated into the republic through the national solidarity of wartime.

From the *Union sacrée* to the *Union nationale*

Clemenceau maintained that victory would come to the side that could hold out fifteen minutes longer. The appalling strain of war first broke Russia in 1917, then Austria-Hungary, Germany, and the Ottoman empire in 1918. France, Italy, and Britain emerged victorious, thanks to American intervention. When the armistice came on 11 November 1918, the republic had survived the ordeal of war and emerged with honour. The parliamentary regime had been able to mobilize its citizens for a fight to the death and to organize the country for victory; it had borne the heaviest of burdens and had triumphed. Clemenceau's methods of government had changed the institutional balance considerably, giving the regime a flexibility that left the essentials of the political system intact whilst pursuing victory. But in the words of Nicolas Rousselier, 'the moment of truth was ... less the period of war than the moment when peace returned'. Most French citizens dreamt of a return to life before the war—only factory workers and socialists had gains from the war that they wished to defend and extend. Instead, they found that the legacy of the war dominated their lives, and it took many years to pass away. It took a severe financial and political crisis to end the illusion that the *belle époque* could be restored, and to force the French to confront the realities of the postwar world.

The first challenge was to agree a peace treaty. Clemenceau intended to win the peace as he had won the war, and continued to limit the powers of parliament. Elections were postponed until November 1919, censorship was extended until October 1919, and the Chamber gave him full authority to negotiate the peace treaty. But his position in the negotiations was weakened by the way that the armistice had emerged from an exchange of notes between the Americans and Germans, and by President Woodrow Wilson's programme for 'peace without victory', which was popular with the socialists. The goals of the French negotiators, in addition to the return of Alsace-Lorraine, were security (which was to be achieved by control of the left bank of the Rhine) and massive reparations (to pay for the costs of the war and for reconstruction). Clemenceau only managed to win a military occupation of the left bank of the Rhine for fifteen years and the demilitarization of the right bank to a depth of fifty kilometres, supported by a military guarantee from the Allies. On the matter of reparations, André Tardieu clashed violently with John Maynard Keynes: Tardieu demanded compensation for the damage done to France, while Keynes wanted to take into account the ability (or rather inability) of Germany and Austria to pay. After a hundred meetings, the French position—which was both absurd and inescapable—eventually won. While the treaty was harsh enough to embitter Germany, it did not satisfy France either, and public opinion soon turned sour when Britain and the USA appeared to favour Germany.

The second challenge was to elect a new Chamber of Deputies. The election campaign began after the Treaty of Versailles was signed on 28 June 1919, and at first it seemed that the *Union sacrée* might live on in peacetime. The Alliance Démocratique proposed a broad coalition, a 'National bloc', running from the Catholics to the Radicals, with the Alliance as its pivot. This coalition could benefit from the new electoral system, which was proportional representation by department (previously used by the Third Republic in 1871 and 1885), by forming lists of candidates drawn from several parties. This eclecticism meant that the coalition had little coherence and the election was based on personalities not principles; the republic remained a parliamentary system without real parties. Criticisms of Clemenceau's 'dictatorship' grew louder as the war faded, and while Millerand wanted to exploit Clemenceau's name to underpin a very broad union, Édouard Herriot rejected this wide coalition because he was painfully rebuilding the Radicals' left-wing identity. The Radical party wanted to reduce the National bloc to the limited formula of 'republican concentration' used by Waldeck-Rousseau and Combes, to produce a loose alliance of parties that would restore republican values.

The only real novelty was the presence of a socialist list in 93 out of 100 departments, which pushed the Radicals into an alliance with the moderates to their right in areas where the socialists were strong. However, internal divisions meant that this strength was dissipated. When the socialist party met in an extraordinary congress in Paris in April 1919, it was split between revolutionaries inspired by the Russian Revolution and reformists encouraged by progress made during the war. To avoid a complete divide, the congress agreed to a revolutionary programme and rejected all electoral agreements with what they termed 'bourgeois parties', including the Radicals. Thus the socialists entered the election in isolation, having voted in favour of an electoral system that was weighted against isolated lists because they thought it would be more representative and more just! There was a direct confrontation between the National bloc and the socialists in only eighteen constituencies: elsewhere, differences between Radicals and moderates created a three-way contest. Ernest Billiet's business lobby, the Union des Intérêts Économiques, ran a campaign against communism using melodramatic posters depicting a Bolshevik with a dagger between his teeth; however, anti-Bolshevism was much less important to electors than recriminations about war pensions, the cost of living, and postwar reconstruction. In these circumstances, the question of relations with Germany, which kept the national union alive, was more important than the right's attempt to exploit fears about social agitation.

The Chamber of Deputies produced by the elections of November 1919 was nicknamed *bleu horizon* because it was crammed with war veterans wearing their sky-blue infantry uniforms. Its make-up was, however, very cloudy indeed. The right won by 4.3 million votes to 3.5 million, which translated into a much bigger victory in terms of seats won because of the electoral system in use. This system and its electoral pacts produced perhaps the most tangled parliamentary groupings of the whole Third Republic, along with two distinct ways to form a majority. The first was based on the wartime coalition, the National bloc proper. This ran from Léon Daudet on the royalist right to the moderate republican Louis Barthou, and centred on the large Entente Républicaine group; this majority was internally divided on social and religious questions because it contained staunch republicans and Catholic *ralliés*. An alternative majority was based on the traditional republican coalition, and ran from the centrist Alliance démocratique to the Radicals and independent socialists. Victory for the right in the Chamber was then tempered by other elections held in the autumn of 1919 on five Sundays out of six to renew every assembly from village councils to the Senate, and finally to replace Poincaré as President of the Republic. A wave of support for the Radicals swept through local communities and, exceptionally, placed the Senate to the left of the Chamber. In this sense, France returned all too easily to the prewar habits of weak parties and shifting coalitions. The last chance for a revitalized executive lay in the election of a strong leader as president either of the republic or of the Council of Ministers.

The election of Poincaré's successor as President of the Republic created an opportunity for this, because it was widely expected that Clemenceau, 'the father of victory', would win. However, he was too anticlerical for the conservatives of the Entente Républicaine; for the Radicals he was the persecutor of Caillaux and Malvy; for the socialists he was a nationalist dictator. For everyone, he embodied a system of extra-parliamentary government that could only be permitted in wartime. When the Chamber of Deputies and Senate met for the election, Clemenceau's young supporters began by demanding changes to the assembly's rules to speed up procedures and debates. This rapidly turned into an argument about personal power, substituting Clemenceau for Boulanger. The preliminary votes of the republicans favoured Paul Deschanel over Clemenceau—Deschanel was the President of the Chamber of Deputies and so represented the precedence of parliament. Clemenceau retired from the contest.

This was a major step towards the restoration of the parliamentary system, and put the burden of leadership on the president of the Council of Ministers. Alexandre Millerand took up the challenge by forming a National bloc government whose cabinet went beyond his natural right-wing majority by opening up to the centre-left. He thus avoided control by the numerous and disciplined group of the Entente Républicaine (which was given a single ministry) at the risk of creating a conflict between the right-wing majority in the Chamber and the broader base of his government. He took this risk in order to re-establish what he saw as the contract negotiated between the president of the Council of Ministers and the French people through their elected representatives. This was the opposite of a party system because the president of the Council built his own parliamentary majority through this contract instead of acting as the leader of his party. Such a move was necessary because the 1919 election had shown that effective parties did not exist outside the SFIO. Millerand defined the nature of his majority during a long initial debate, which hinged on a hard-line policy towards Germany and thus anchored it in the *Union sacrée*. He took part in numerous debates, and the Chamber was thus brought back into the government's deliberations. In turn it showed its capacity to govern: Millerand kept his majority despite an increase of 71 per cent in the tax burden and the first revisions of the Treaty of Versailles, made by conferences on reparations in 1920. The parliamentary system appeared to be working well under his direction, so why change it?

The rule of the National bloc and the primacy of foreign policy

The main aim of the National bloc was to perpetuate the *Union sacrée*. Everything was seen through the perspective of foreign policy: revolutionaries were defeatists; the bitter question of reparations pitted France against its allies as much as against Germany; the battle for the franc succeeded the battle for the peace. The war was not over yet. Millerand defended the increased powers of the executive in order to fight these new battles, and he refused to be a prisoner of the parliamentary majority by appointing Radicals to his government. When

Deschanel was forced to retire through ill health, Millerand stood for election as an active president, in the manner of Poincaré or MacMahon instead of Deschanel or Grévy. Millerand was elected President of the Republic on 23 September 1920 by a large majority— a majority which therefore acknowledged the merit of such leadership. He duly appointed his protégé Georges Leygues as the head of government, and later forced Briand to resign as his second premier. Finally he summoned Poincaré to be President of the Council of Ministers, the first time that a former President of the Republic took this office. Though Poincaré had a great deal of support, this derived from his past record, not from the parliamentary majority of the National bloc. Millerand was therefore able to remain at the head of this majority for the electoral campaign of 1924, when he proposed constitutional reforms that would increase the authority of the executive.

By the principle of national reconciliation, Millerand damped the fires of anticlericalism and re-established diplomatic links with the Vatican, despite some obstruction from the Senate. The wartime *Union sacrée* had had a religious dimension because it united Catholics, Protestants, Jews, and anticlericals across party divides, and because the clergy had rejoined the national community by their role in the war (45,000 priests had been mobilized and 5,000 killed). After the war, the clerical question, which had dominated politics right to the end of the 1900s as almost the only force capable of uniting the left, was eclipsed by international and financial questions. This religious peace aided the unity of the National bloc and allowed Catholics to enter it; it also explained why Clemenceau disappeared from public life, since he remained opposed to *rapprochement* with the Vatican. This reconciliation did not extend to Caillaux, who in 1920 was condemned by the Senate, sitting as the High Court, for his wartime connections with traitors. The strikers of 1920 (discussed below) were also severely punished by the same logic: the anxious nationalism of the *Union sacrée* saw their protests as mutiny.

Internal pressures were compounded by difficulties in foreign policy and monetary policy, which were inseparable. The monetary front opened in spring 1919, when first the British then the Americans ended their wartime solidarity of stable currency exchange rates. The first crisis of the franc was logical enough: it had to be devalued in order to balance the rapid growth of francs in circulation, reduced purchasing power, the scarcity of goods, and the swollen national debt (which had been incurred both to meet the costs of war and to fund reconstruction). The war distorted policy-making because governments wanted to restore the franc to its prewar level through foreign policy, not monetary policy, and because the fate of the franc was seen in nationalist not economic terms. Since 1918, finance ministers had drawn up an ordinary budget, which was balanced, and an extraordinary budget . . . which would be balanced by German reparations. In 1920, Germany did not pay these reparations, and Britain and America did not support French demands for them. Abandoned by its allies, France fell back on a rigid interpretation of the Treaty of Versailles. Clemenceau had never believed that reparations would work, and had emphasized security above all, especially the occupation of the Rhineland. Millerand was forced to reverse these priorities by the crisis in the franc's strength: occupation of the Rhineland became a device to make the policy of reparations work. When Germany rejected the amount of reparations due in 1921, Briand (then premier) ordered the occupation of three Ruhr towns and threatened to occupy the whole of this key industrial region. Without support from Britain, Germany accepted the sum owed but proposed to pay it in kind rather than in cash. Briand entered into negotiations at the Cannes conference in 1922, though this ran counter to his parliamentary majority, which opposed any concessions. Attacked by Poincaré and maligned by Millerand, Briand resigned. Poincaré was appointed in his stead, solely on the basis of his foreign policy: the payment of reparations was his absolute priority. The Treaty of Rapallo, signed between Germany and Soviet Russia, and the manoeuvres of the German government—first refusing to pay, then asking for a moratorium—pushed the French and Belgians into invading the Ruhr in January 1923. This occupation was solely designed to secure reparations by holding the Ruhr hostage, for France had no consistent policy regarding the Rhineland, such as separating it from Germany. Although Poincaré was able to overcome the passive resistance ordered by the German government, he could not settle the question of reparations, he faced financial difficulties at home, and feared isolation abroad. In order to resolve this position, he had to accept British and American mediation through the Dawes Commission: France could not execute its policies alone.

This lesson was not immediately accepted because the great

international deflation of 1921 levelled France's trade balance by substantially lowering the price of raw materials, weakening sterling and the dollar: the franc regained its strength, and prices fell inside France in 1922 and 1923. The franc seemed to have returned to its true value, as public opinion had always believed that it would. However, a second crisis of the franc began when the occupation of the Ruhr ended and the Dawes Commission met, at which point speculators attacked the overvalued franc. When Poincaré united the ordinary and extraordinary budgets in the name of financial rigour, he revealed the scale of the deficit and thereby redoubled speculative attacks. Supported by a bellicose press and opinion, which invoked the battle of the Marne and denounced foreigners, Poincaré balanced the budget brutally by numerous cuts in state spending and by an increase in taxation of 20 per cent just a few weeks before the elections of 1924. He secured a loan on the condition imposed by the Morgan Bank: France must accept in advance the conclusion of the Dawes plan to reduce reparations. The success of his rescue plan transformed the crisis into victory, making it a 'financial Verdun'. This warlike image revived Poincaré's status as a leader and enhanced his reputation as a statesman because he had carried through necessary reforms at the risk of electoral defeat. But it was also a financial Verdun because the battle exhausted the victor. The war was never-ending.

The return of the left: the *Cartel des gauches*

While the right wished to return to the way of the world before 1914, the left had been transformed by the war and by the Bolshevik revolution in Russia. Almost inevitably, this transformation also involved new schisms between those who valued the gains made by wartime participation and those who wanted revolution. When the SFIO met for its annual congress in February 1920, it was split three ways: one minority was loyal to the old socialist (Second) International, one wanted to join the communist (Third) International, and a majority wanted to unite them both. A merger was of no interest to the Bolshevik leadership in Moscow, and the twenty-one conditions that Lenin posed for membership of the Third International scandalized traditional French socialists. Nevertheless a massive majority voted for the Leninist model at the Congress of Tours on 20 December 1920, even though this belittled the trade union movement, purged reformists, and opposed the empire and the republic (many delegates voted this way because they were wrongly convinced that Lenin's conditions were purely formal). The majority faction became the Section Française de l'Internationale Communiste, soon renamed the Parti Communiste (PC). The minority group, whose case had been brilliantly argued by Léon Blum, kept the old SFIO party machinery and most of the parliamentary deputies, but not most of the militants. While this split followed the division within French socialism since the Bolshevik revolution of 1917, it also followed much older fractures which pre-dated the unification of 1905.

Its political consequences were profound and immediate. Although the Parti Communiste had most of the members, it lacked leaders, was deeply divided internally, and was subordinate to the orders of Moscow; it rapidly shrank until it existed only as a bogeyman for the National bloc. It rejected the Revolution of 1789 and its liberal, democratic gains, and it mobilized against both the army and the nation when it opposed the occupation of the Ruhr and the use of troops in Morocco to maintain French rule there. It was therefore outlawed from the nation. It also gave the reconstructed SFIO a neurosis about being outflanked on the left that lasted for the next sixty years. Gradually, the PC became mired in its own Marxist vocabulary and in tortuous discussions on the old question of participation in government. The SFIO preferred to leave this problem unsettled rather than rupture the party; and in order to avoid a repetition of its electoral suicide of 1919 it adopted the formula of a 'one-minute cartel' with the Radicals in 1924: it allied with the Radicals for the one minute it took to vote, then lapsed back into opposition.

These divisions of the socialist left meant that the Radical party was the sole alternative party of government to the National bloc . . . even though it belonged to the bloc! The *Union sacrée* had severely weakened the Radical party, leading its new president, Édouard Herriot, the mayor of Lyon, to rebuild it on its left. Herriot had reconstructed the party from the bottom up, from its local committees and regional federations, in preparation for a revival of the old formula of republican concentration. However, he managed the remarkable feat of continuing to govern within National bloc ministries at the same time: the Radicals were both a pillar of the government's majority and active members of the parliamentary opposition. This again illustrates how often the logic of parties did not operate under the Third Republic. A few months before the elections in June 1924, Herriot broke with the government and proposed an electoral alliance to the socialists, which became known as the *Cartel des gauches*. The left (without the communists) presented lists for this cartel in three-quarters of all constituencies, united by opposition to the National bloc. Newspapers and local activists took up the battle more willingly than the party machines did, in a contest against a right that was divided between a Millerand 'constellation' and a Poincaré 'constellation'. The right won in votes but lost in seats, by the logic of the electoral system. Once victory was secured, the Radical press vigorously attacked Millerand because he had broken with the doctrine of presidential impartiality. It forced the Chamber into a contest with Millerand, which the Chamber won. Millerand had fought the same battle as MacMahon almost fifty years before, and fared no better. This success for the left was dampened by the election of the Senate's moderate candidate, Gaston Doumergue, as President of the Republic, instead of the Chamber's candidate, the Radical-socialist Paul Painlevé. In contrast to the period of the National bloc, the Senate was henceforth to the right of the Chamber.

Herriot could not secure the participation of the socialists in his new ministry, and had great difficulty in guaranteeing their support for his cabinet of Radicals and Republican-Socialists. He inherited the Dawes plan and the failure of the Ruhr occupation, and wished to improve relations with France's wartime allies in order to make Germany pay. Over the summer of 1924, he negotiated the French withdrawal from the Ruhr and the resumption of German payments, which earned him enormous success in public opinion . . . and the most severe criticisms of contemporary historians. The charge laid against this 'amateur' diplomat was that he did not try to link cuts in reparations with cuts in France's war debts to its allies—but why should a link which had been refused to Clemenceau, Millerand, Briand, and Poincaré have been granted to Herriot after the failure of the policy of enforcement, namely the occupation of the Ruhr? Herriot's aim was to place France within a vast international guarantee of security sealed by the League of Nations; this became French foreign policy for both left and right until 1934. This policy was made possible by Poincaré when he accepted Anglo-American mediation, was realized by Herriot, and was then put into practice by Briand over seven years, earning the name of 'Briandism'. Although the Geneva Protocol, a system of obligatory arbitration supported by sanctions, was stillborn because Britain withdrew its support after the electoral victory of the Conservatives, rapprochement with Germany was an undeniable success. The Treaty of Locarno in 1926 guaranteed the borders of Germany's western neighbours; it simultaneously reinforced France's alliances in the east and enabled Germany to enter the League of Nations, sponsored by France. Finally, the diplomatic recognition of Soviet Russia during the more moderate period of the New Economic Policy also helped to foster international détente. As far as diplomacy was concerned, the cartel ended the war, and gave real substance to the peace.

The cartel also sought to throw off the war's stranglehold on domestic politics, by sweeping away the nationalist excesses of the bloc. Herriot passed an amnesty for victims of the policy of national exclusion: Malvy and Caillaux, condemned by the High Court; deserters; and railwaymen dismissed for striking during and after the war. He also ordered that the remains of Jean Jaurès be placed in the Panthéon. For the opposition, and for the veterans' leagues allied to it, these acts trampled underfoot the sacrifices of the men who fought in the trenches. Herriot also began a policy of renewed laicization, which anchored the cartel in the traditions of the prewar left. The Concordat was abolished in Alsace-Lorraine (it had survived separation in 1905 because it was then part of Germany), the French embassy in the Vatican was closed, and unauthorized religious congregations, which had been discreetly tolerated, were dissolved. However, this policy foundered when confronted by a formidable Catholic opposition, rebuilt around the Fédération Nationale Catholique of General de Castelnau. But times had changed for secularists too: Catholics had rallied to the nation during the war and the church no longer appeared to be a major threat. Secularism was no longer enough to unite the left, which was deeply divided on economic and financial questions. The war had left its mark here too.

As far as state finances were concerned, Poincaré's 'financial Verdun' obviously could not make the enormous debt disappear, nor remove the menace it posed to the franc as a currency. A third crisis of the franc was always possible, and it was sparked in April 1925 by the Banque de France itself (still a privately owned institution). The

Banque was alarmed by the fiscal programme of the *Cartel des gauches*, which included a tax on capital (a policy that united the Radicals and socialists). It retaliated by revealing that it had advanced more francs to the ministry of finance than the law allowed—even though these illegal advances had begun well before Herriot took office. The Senate immediately overturned the government, while holders of francs protected themselves by placing their funds in foreign currencies and investors sold government bonds. The cartel then began a long drift towards the centre. Cabinets led by Poincaré and Briand which dared not risk the opposition of business leaders were condemned by Herriot instead. This instability, especially severe at the ministry of finance, where six ministers followed each other in as many months, was additional evidence of governmental hesitation or powerlessness, which fed the crisis of confidence even further. The franc lost two-thirds of its value once again. The experts convened by the minister of finance, Raoul Peret, gave their very orthodox verdict to his successor, Caillaux (restored to political life after Herriot's amnesty), whose request for full financial powers was rejected by the Chamber. On the very day that Herriot formed a second cartel government (21 July 1926), he had to ask the Banque de France to increase its advances to the government at the same time that he proposed the tax on capital demanded by his socialist allies. The opposition of the Banque de France, leading newspapers, and Catholic associations incited a mob of investors, who besieged the Chamber of Deputies. Sterling leapt from 200 francs to the pound to 235 francs. The 'bond-holders' plebiscite' overthrew the government more surely than the deputies who rejected it by a vote of no confidence. Herriot was forced to leave the Chamber by a back door under cover of night. The cartel had run its course.

The episode of the cartel transformed political life. On the left, anticlericalism was no longer the unifying force it had been, while social and monetary questions divided it more than before the war. Pressure groups multiplied and intervened forcefully in public debate, notably war veterans, Catholics, taxpayers, and bond-holders. These groups generally stood on the political right, and on 21 July 1926 they ousted a government that had been produced by democratic election but had proved incapable of governing.

For the franc, this was no longer Verdun: it was Waterloo. The fall of the franc had a profound psychological impact: it signified that a return to the power and stability of France before the war was impossible. And it said this to a public anxious for a return to a prewar idyll in order to give meaning to the sacrifice of the dead.

Mourning

The shadow cast by the war was at its darkest and longest for the veterans of the trenches, the disabled, the bereaved, and the displaced. The losses of the war were massive: 1.4 million men died. These deaths were concentrated on soldiers on active service more than for any other war in modern French history. Epidemics and the destruction of the communes had killed civilians too in 1871, as did the bombings and deportations of the Second World War. So while the dead amounted to 3.5 per cent of the total population, they made up 10.5 per cent of the working male population and 16.5 per cent of mobilized troops—one soldier out of every six. Two social groups were hit hardest: peasant-infantrymen (41 per cent of casualties from 30 per cent of the army) and the middle classes (teachers, clerks, and foremen) who supplied the field officers. Geographically, the death rate was highest in the rural south-west, and lowest around the big cities, where many men worked in industries essential to the war effort. In addition, a little over three million men were wounded, of whom a million were disabled and 415,000 were pensioned off as invalids. This terrible toll was completed by 680,000 women who were widowed, 360,000 of whom never remarried, and 762,000 children who lost their fathers.

The faces of the 1.4 million dead haunted the nation. Before the war, the republic had failed to establish true republican ceremonies, despite 14 July: now it found the object for its cult. Antoine Prost has expertly explored this cult: born spontaneously, it was ritualized by the great ceremony of the *Union sacrée* held on 11 November 1920. This also commemorated the fiftieth anniversary of the Republic and ended the war between republicans and Catholics that had raged before 1914. On a single day, Léon Gambetta's heart was transported to the Panthéon and the body of an unknown soldier, brought from Verdun, was buried at the foot of the Arc de Triomphe, in front of a 'family' which stood as a metaphor for all French families: parents who had lost their son, a widow, an orphan. In every village, monuments to the dead were swiftly erected, a lead that was followed by towns with more ambitious plans. The initiative came from the public rather than from the authorities: the veterans called for, subscribed to, and raised these memorials. Monuments to the fallen took several forms, among which Prost has distinguished four main types: civic (honouring the republic), patriotic (honouring France), commemorative (remembering the dead), and, most rarely, pacifist. They became the altars of a civil liturgy and of the remembrance ceremony of 11 November, which borrowed heavily from Christian funeral rites. The names of those who died for France were read out in alphabetical order, to underline the equality of citizens, in front of flags flying at half-mast. This celebration of citizenship united the republic and the nation, because here the nation honoured the citizen, who was the most important character in the republic. The surviving citizens paid homage to those amongst them who had died. Naturally war veterans occupied the first rank at these ceremonies, and their sheer number ensured that they became a new, potent social force.

The demography of France was profoundly affected by the war for the rest of the twentieth century. The slow population growth that marked France in the nineteenth century was weakened still further, which in turn weakened the French economy and army relative to Britain and Germany. Replacing lost Frenchmen by immigrants reinforced an anxiety that France was in decline. Shortages of food and fuel during the war increased the civilian mortality rate too, culminating in the epidemic of Spanish 'flu during the winter of 1918–19, which killed 130,000 people from a weakened population. The number of births fell from April 1915 onwards (from 700,000 in 1914 to 360,000 in 1916), accompanied by an even sharper fall in the number of marriages (from 306,000 in 1913 to just 75,000 in 1915). The war thus cut two deep notches into the age pyramid: into the male generations born between 1870 and 1900 who were lost in battle, and in the 'hollow years' of low births of 1915–19, unbalancing the structure of the French population for a lifetime. Peace stimulated a considerable increase in the marriage rate (660,000 marriages in 1920 and another 455,000 in 1921), but there was no postwar baby boom. The rise in the birth rate was neither large nor sustained, and by 1924 the number of births and marriages had returned to the low levels seen before 1914. The male:female ratio was profoundly uneven, especially amongst the young, consigning hundreds of thousands of young women to an enforced spinsterhood. Over the decade, the excess of births over deaths was not even half the number of births lost to the war. An extremely severe law passed in July 1920 suppressed both abortion and propaganda advocating birth control, but evidently little could be changed by legislation. Already, the centre-west of France recorded a natural deficit in its population between 1920 and 1924. The war reduced the population in 90 per cent of communes, especially small rural communes, where depopulation continued after the peace. The Île de France was the only region in the whole country that was more populous in 1921 than in 1911.

The occupation of several departments in the north-east led to a lasting exodus of more than two million refugees. The shortage of labour provoked the organized immigration of more than 100,000 Europeans plus 220,000 colonials (mostly Algerians, Indochinese, and Madagascans) and Chinese, who worked under highly militarized conditions. These labourers returned home quite quickly, and the war changed neither the size nor the composition of the foreign population resident inside France. However, it did begin a period of active, authorized immigration (by a law of June 1919), organized through bilateral agreements with Poland, Italy, and Czechoslovakia: there were 1.5 million immigrants in France in 1921, compared with 1.1 million in 1911, and 200,000 new immigrants arrived every year up to 1930. By 1931, France had a higher proportion of foreigners in its population than any other country in Europe, or even the USA, at 6.7 per cent.

The war veterans

The hardship and trauma of the trenches could have created a new and unbridgeable division in French society, between those who had served in them and those who had not. Certainly, letters written by men in the trenches sometimes expressed a fear that their tragic fate was not understood, or a bitter riposte to the carefree attitude of the interior. They showed above all a concern to put the battlefield into writing, to express their ordeal by fire and to share this hardship, as shown by the letter cited earlier. But in fact the nation cohered as a single body because the interior shared the same anxieties, the same patriotic sentiments, the same belief that France was defending civilization. Republican loyalty was joined to another sentiment that was both general and above all personal: the fulfilment of a duty. Faced by an excess of suffering and of death, this loyalty united the faith of the soldier with the faith of the interior. Conversely, the strikers of 1918 were drawn from the workers who remained the least integrated part of this body, yet even they suspended their protests as soon as the German offensive of that year became threatening. There were 6.5 million surviving veterans in 1920, more than three million of whom quickly formed large associations. The divides between them reflected the wider political tendencies of the country rather than party loyalties, and their wartime solidarity meant that they were more united than these divides might suggest. The Union Nationale des Combattants tended to the right, the Union Fédérale to the centre-left, and the Association Républicaine des Anciens Combattants (ARAC) was close to the communist party. These bodies grouped together innumerable specialized associations (for men who had been blinded, lost a limb, suffered head injuries . . .), and all united in 1927 in the Confédération de la France Meurtrie.

They had an impact on the politics and society of France in two main ways. The first was a visceral rejection of any new war. The Great War had been 'the war to end war',[5] and hence they opposed further conflicts. This explained their bitterness towards the peace treaties because they seemed unlikely to guarantee peace, for reasons which differed according to the left and the right, but which were blamed on France's Anglo-American allies in either case. Some on the left became absolute pacifists, such as the young pupils of the École Normale Supérieure who fell under the influence of Alain, and rejected all war.[6] Inside the ARAC, the communists tried to maintain the pacifism of revolutionaries, to whom all generals were murderers; this met with mixed success because it implied that the sacrifices made during the war were meaningless. Veterans introduced their

---

[5] The 'last of the last', or *dernière des dernières*, known in short as the *Der des Der*.

[6] Alain (Émile Chartier) was Radicalism's leading thinker and professor of philosophy at the prestigious *Khâgne* (the class preparing for entrance to the École Normale Supérieure) of the Lycée Henri IV in Paris.

pacifism to the rest of society, which had a profound effect on France's response to Hitler in the 1930s. The second impact was a new hostility to politicians. Historians are divided on the importance of this attitude: was it latent hostility to the parliamentary system or just the surliness of the infantryman? Whatever the case, veterans criticized political parties for dividing a society which had been united during the war; they contrasted their silence to the gossip of elected politicians, their virtue to the latter's corruption, their ability to win the war to politicians' inability to win the peace. They showed a bitterness of principle that made them a natural seed-bed of anti-parliamentarianism; this was soon exploited by certain leaders of associations drawn from the conservative right, using veterans' sentiments against the republic as a whole.

Economic progress and social anxiety

In the early 1920s, strong economic growth brought substantial material benefits to the country, especially the middle classes and peasantry. Key sectors of industry continued the modernization fostered by the war economy and greatly improved their productivity. Yet the breakthrough achieved by modern industrial sectors should not foster any illusions: the transformation of social structures was limited, and the war had accelerated movement across social boundaries rather than erasing the boundaries themselves. The war had shaken the foundations of the old social order without creating a new one in its place, disappointing both those who wished for a return to the prewar world and those who wanted a new world to reward their wartime sacrifices.

The French economy of the 1920s

Economic growth in the early 1920s was erratic. It began with a marked crisis in 1920 and 1921, followed by rapid, irregular growth which levelled out twice, during the second crisis of the franc in the spring of 1925 and then again during Poincaré's stabilization at the end of 1926. GNP grew in real terms by 7 per cent a year from 1921 to 1925, and then by 3 per cent a year during the rest of the decade. Such high growth rates were not seen again before the 1950s. Historical disputes on the causes of this growth focus on the role of inflation. On one side, monetarists and liberal economists deny that inflation had any positive effect on growth. Other historians have argued that recovery was rapid because of a loose monetary policy and generous indemnities for war damages, while depreciation of the franc aided industries that produced for export. Inflation reduced the debts of all borrowers, including the state, companies, and farmers, at the cost of creditors, savers, and banks. But this old debate (did growth occur because or in spite of inflation?) hides the essential point. Monetary policy was not tight, despite the indebtedness of France, because the problems of debt and the strength of the franc were bound up with reparations, national prestige, and foreign policy. This lack of restraint produced rising prices and a falling franc, which favoured recovery. From 1922, the middle classes gained access to the new consumer goods of motor cars and electrical equipment, which were the foundations of a real industrial renewal.

The contribution made by industry to growth was especially strong, even though the size of the industrial workforce expanded little: rapid growth in productivity was the most important factor. Modernization, which was only effective in certain sectors during the war, became the watchword of industry, powered by increased investment. Mechanization became a general phenomenon, accompanied by American working practices. Its heroes were a cohort of big business leaders who were fascinated by the USA, and who married the traditions of Saint-Simon with the innovations of Henry Ford. In 1919, Clémentel supported the creation of a vast employers' union, the Confédération Générale de la Production Française, to promote these modernizing ideas. Few companies had been large enough to undertake such programmes until industrial concentration began at the start of the century and then accelerated during the war; it was further encouraged by the law of 1925 on limited companies, *sociétés anonymes*. The automobile sector shrank from 150 companies in 1924 to 98 in 1929, with two-thirds of production coming from the three leaders, Citroën, Renault, and Peugeot. Péchiney consolidated the aluminium producers in 1921, and the chemicals firm Rhône-Poulenc was born in 1928. Integration advanced in the metallurgical industries too. Even retail traders, the economic emblem of the Third Republic, met competition from the expanding Monoprix and Uniprix chains.

Three industries besides car making seemed to meet the criteria for modernization. Iron and steel making, which had been a dynamic sector since the beginning of the century, was swelled by modern German factories in the recovered territories of Lorraine. France held third place in the great international steel cartel formed in 1926. Chemistry also profited from the Treaty of Versailles, which restored the potash deposits of Alsace and which distributed patents seized from Germany. Chemists then developed new products for mass consumption, such as photography, pharmacy, and the first synthetic textiles. Electricity rapidly became essential in an economy built upon small firms that had always been short of coal. Electricity production went from two billion kilowatt hours in 1913 to fifteen billion in 1930, half of which came from the great hydroelectric dams built in the 1920s across the main rivers of the Massif Central. Electrification of the countryside developed spectacularly: over 80 per cent of all communes were connected by 1930. The automobile and electric sectors stimulated many other branches of industry, and in this way acted as true dynamos of development. These modern sectors sought to conquer foreign markets too, aided by French diplomacy, particularly in eastern Europe. The government wished to find allies on Germany's eastern border and to take over German investments which had been confiscated at the end of the war: this policy was most successful in Czechoslovakia, where the iron magnate Schneider won the lion's share of business.

Ambition and anxiety

Below these determinedly modern sectors, France still had a traditional economy of small and medium-sized companies in a structure that had survived since the 1830s. Fourteen million peasants, fourfifths of whom owned land, and seven million independent workers in the trade and service sector were the legacy of the venerable republican social project. The cult of the 'little man', independent and therefore free, and the myth of a democracy of citizen-owners triumphed as much as ever, in the face of opposing forces at work in postwar France. The 'French-style' company, the exact opposite of the big American trust, was praised more than ever by the Radicals as the economic foundation for the ideal citizen. Craftsmen survived and small retail shops proliferated, often serving as a refuge for war veterans who were supported by preferential loans. This model brought together town and country because small craftsmen and traders were often close to agricultural production, and because both were protected by the political world through customs tariffs and tax advantages. The over-crowded world of agriculture was rescued by the bloodshed of the war and the rise in food prices; this helped small family farms and produced a brief but real prosperity, as shown by a greater diversity in food consumption, the wearing of city clothes, and the advance of electrification. Country people aspired to the urban way of life, but aspirations outstripped monetary incomes, which were still tight and were primarily reserved for investment in land. Thus considerable frustration built up, and peasant discontent was harnessed by the major agrarian organizations, always ready to demand increased protection.

Rural desires for a bourgeois lifestyle were also shared by the worlds of employees and factory workers. There was a move towards social homogenization inseparable from the general urbanization of society, which had accelerated since the 1880s and speeded up again during the war. Education remained the fundamental method of social promotion and reproduction. But there was a complete separation between the public and private systems of schooling; a decree of 1923 even reinforced the study of Greek and Latin in secondary education, which successfully closed it off to the children coming out of state primary schools. However, the republic's creed of opportunity open to all through education was given new impetus by the experience of the trenches, where men had lived, fought, and died side by side, regardless of their qualifications. Among the 180,000 lycée pupils of 1925, enough were on scholarships (13 per cent) for this ideal to survive.

Education was only one aspect of social promotion. It was coupled with an apprenticeship in the rules of bourgeois life, of genteel conversation, and of the well-set dinner table, and with the imitation of new forms of consumption. Such behaviour was endemic to the social mobility of the Third Republic; the inflation and flux of the 1920s made it worse because insecurities about social position led people to adopt or cling on to markers of speech, dress, or possessions that were steeped in snobbery. Writing decades later, Simone de Beauvoir recalled how her father reacted to his lost social status by rejecting the conventional markers.

The war had passed and had ruined him, sweeping away his dreams, his myths, his justifications, his hopes. I was wrong when I thought that he was resigned to this; he never stopped protesting against his new condition. He valued a good education and fine manners above everything; yet, when I was with him in a restaurant, the metro, or a train, I was put out by his exclamations and his gesticulations, by his brutal indifference to the opinion of his neighbours. This aggressive exhibitionism was his way of showing that he did not belong to their type. When he had travelled first class, he had indicated that he was well-born by his refined politeness; in third class, he showed it by denying the basic rules of civility. Almost everywhere he put on a bearing that was both astonished and provocative, to signify that his true place was not there. In the trenches he had naturally spoken the same language as his comrades; he recounted with pleasure that one of them had declared: 'When Beauvoir says *merde*, it becomes a distinguished word.' To prove his distinction, he said *merde* more and more often.[7]

Changes in women's dress, inspired by a new generation of designers such as Coco Chanel and Elsa Schiaparelli, encouraged women everywhere to adopt bourgeois dress codes, spread by the women's magazines which were by then in full spate. New leisure activities held a distinct social significance: it was fashionable to drive to the seaside, where young people played tennis. But divisions within the school system, the development of a cult of material objects, and the desire for leisure generated considerable frustration when wishes could not be satisfied.

Moreover, the imagination of millions of self-employed people and the mass of salaried employees was haunted by more than their social position. They were stalked by two menacing figures born out of the war. On one side was the *nouveau pauvre*, whose life savings had been held in bonds made worthless by the war and by inflation—which led them to call for protection. On the other side lay the *nouveau riche*, scandalously enriched by the war—which led them to call for justice. In fact, the remaking of the bourgeoisie was much more limited than the remaking of bourgeois values. Industrialists such as Citroën and Boussac made fortunes in a matter of months, which contradicted the nineteenth-century values of patience, wisdom, security, and inheritance. Their boldness and their opportunism were matched by their cynical exploitation of hundreds of thousands of deaths. They

---

[7] S. de Beauvoir, *Mémoires d'une jeune fille rangée* (Paris, 1958; reissued 1990), pp. 244–5.

had, literally, profited from the war. The depreciation of the franc, the slump in the value of government bonds, and the cancellation of debts owed by the Russian and Ottoman governments overturned bourgeois morality as much as they overturned a way of life.

The defeat of the factory hand

The gains made by factory workers and the CGT during the war were rapidly undone by the peace. The reformist approach of Thomas and Jouhaux had never been accepted by all, as the strikes of 1917 had shown. During the war, the left-wing minority had evolved into an anti-war tendency that accused the CGT leadership of 'social patriotism' (i.e. fighting for their country, not their class) and of collaborating with their mortal enemy, the state. This tendency was especially strong in metal-working industries and was reinforced by an influx of young militants who joined the CGT as a result of the strikes of 1917 and 1918. The majority group drew up a compromise policy that combined both the revolutionary demands of the Russian Bolsheviks and the war aims of Woodrow Wilson. Inevitably this compromise could only hold during the war, and social agitation recommenced in the transport sector at the start of 1919 as prices rose and as patriotic solidarity weakened. Clemenceau no longer had the same scruples that had restrained him in 1918. On the eve of 1 May 1919, he rapidly pushed through a law on collective bargaining and established the eight-hour day, which was the traditional demand of the Second International. But at the same time he denounced the hand of Moscow in revolutionary social agitation, and he banned the May Day demonstration. Despite this, the demonstration was a success, until it degenerated into violent clashes that in turn produced a long series of protest strikes. The eight-hour day was not enough for the CGT's new members, for whom the Russian revolution held out the grand promise of eternal peace. Simultaneously the French navy blockaded Odessa as part of a *cordon sanitaire* thrown around Russia. The whole population feared a new war, but an engineer, André Marty, led a mutiny in the fleet and the expeditionary force was called home. This success encouraged the radicalism of the revolutionaries, whose claims henceforth knew no bounds.

At the Congress of Lyon in September 1919, the two tendencies confronted each other. The CGT leadership produced a reformist programme that called for collective bargaining, a national labour council, nationalizations, and social insurance. The revolutionaries responded in the spring of 1920 with more strikes. Young militants launched a strike first on the PLM (Paris–Lyon–Mediterranean) railway network, which was forcefully repressed by the company and by Millerand's government (300 workers were sacked); they then called a general strike for 1 May 1920. The CGT leadership hesitated, then rallied itself to the policy of a general strike in order to avoid being overtaken by a movement that it fundamentally opposed. Employers and the government prepared themselves for the struggle; Millerand was backed by the mass-circulation press, which was very hostile to the strike movement. He requisitioned the railways, arrested militants, and manned the trains with engineers and students from the *grandes écoles*. Faced with a disorderly return to work as the strike crumbled, the CGT called an end to the conflict on 22 May. Eighteen thousand railwaymen were dismissed and the Council of Ministers prosecuted the CGT, which was heavily punished. The majority condemned the recklessness of the strike while the minority condemned the leadership's feeble support for it. Membership fell by two-thirds in a few months, even before the revolutionaries broke away to form the Confédération Générale du Travail Unitaire (CGTU), which aligned itself with the principles of the new communist party.

The reformist social movement begun in 1914 by the role chosen by the CGT within the *Union sacrée* had become entangled with a widespread protest movement in 1917, only for both reform and protest to be defeated in the spring of 1920. The war had opened up the possibility of a lasting integration of workers into the republic, but this had not been achieved. The workers' movement was split apart, torn between a patriotic, republican culture and an independent culture whose roots were given new life by the Bolshevik revolution. Industrial workers remained on the margins of French life. Broken by the failure of 1920, they fell back into the world of industrial suburbs, of small houses cobbled together alongside railway lines, of housing estates built between factories. Concentrated together and separated from the world of the elites, the factory workers of the 1920s did not suffer from unemployment, but saw their work become deskilled through the growth of large-scale industrial production and their wages trail behind inflation. The CGTU and PC sought to recruit from this world, but found only a few, fleeting members: activists joined them only when they wanted to try their luck in a strike, and left immediately afterwards. In contrast, the CGT completed its transformation. It continued its dialogue with the state and it secured the creation of a Conseil National Économique in 1925 as a forum for this discussion. Public services and mining provided most of its membership, which was on the rise once more; it became the trade union of teachers and salaried staff, with few factory hands in its ranks. A new Catholic trade union was formed, the Confédération Française des Travailleurs Chrétiens (CFTC). However, it struggled to create fraternity between employers and their workers, despite the support of the pope. These divisions within the trades union movement reflected some of the divides within the world of the factory worker in France—other divides ran between unionized and non-unionized labour, between native and immigrant workers, between men and women.

Conclusion

On this foundation of general bitterness, anxiety, and frustration, the stabilization of the reduced franc hurt deeply. To the French of 1926, victory tasted of defeat, and the devaluation of their currency was the metaphor for a general reduction of France's power and security. Psychologically, the war only ended in 1926 when hopes for a return to the idealized stability of the prewar era finally vanished. The French were disillusioned, and a social crisis was fermenting.

By then, France lay powerless. Its allies had abandoned it; the franc had devalued; the republican consensus was foundering; new social and political forces were emerging within a traumatized and ageing society. Herriot had tried to rule by the illusory majority delivered by the cartel, until the rout of the franc had exposed this illusion. Poincaré then tried to integrate these depressing realities into a new policy. The revelation of the true state of public finances was critical because the stability of the franc lay at the heart of the republic's social mechanism: it was the sign of the nation's economic and financial power. Its collapse revealed to the French that they had not won the war. It was a war that everyone in Europe had lost.

5

Disaster and renewal: 1926–1958

Disillusioned and exhausted, France needed a period of rest for Poincaré's medicine to work. Instead, it only had the three years from 1926 to 1929, when Poincaré himself led the government. In October 1929 Wall Street crashed, to be followed by the Great Depression. In January 1933 Adolf Hitler became the chancellor of Germany, and Europe's shaky peace was doomed. World War from 1939 to 1945 was succeeded by Cold War from 1948 and by the eruption of powerful independence movements in the French empire, which culminated in the devastating Algerian war of 1954–62. Throughout these years, the French economy continued its shift from small-scale to large-scale production. The losers in this were the independent, self-employed craftsmen, shopkeepers, and peasant farmers, heirs to the nineteenth-century petty bourgeoisie. In their place came salaried employees, both factory hands (*ouvriers*) and managers (*cadres*). This shift, which had been gathering pace since the end of the nineteenth century, was too fast for the liking of the self-employed yet too slow to keep French agriculture and industry internationally competitive.

These external catastrophes and internal economic modernization translated into political life through increasingly bitter conflicts and the rise of extremist parties on both left and right. They destroyed three regimes in these thirty years, as the Third Republic, Vichy regime, and Fourth Republic crumbled amid defeat or the pressures of war. Instability inside these regimes was also severe, as ministries fell with chronic frequency. This profound political instability sprang from the difficulty of finding an institutional formula in harmony with the shift in society. The irrepressible modernization of the economy and hence of society overturned the socio-political compromise made in the early Third Republic because it undermined the very social groups who were the pillars of the republic. This accelerated after 1944 with a comprehensive state-led effort to modernize the French economy. Conflicts and confusion abounded, and hesitant, often contradictory reforms were attempted before a genuine refoundation took place with the birth of the Fifth Republic in 1958.

The economic crisis of the 1920s and 1930s

Poincaré's restoration

The first external catastrophe to strike France was the global depression of the 1930s, which overturned the successful readjustments Poincaré had made to French finances and its economy. In 1926, Poincaré aimed to begin the renewal of France by forcing it to adjust to the realities and constraints produced by the war. Though his government was anchored in the traditions of the wartime *Union sacrée* (it contained six former presidents of the Council of Ministers, plus a strong Radical presence around Herriot), it aimed to build for the future through a policy based on the stabilization of the franc. Poincaré's opening speech as premier was entirely devoted to the financial crisis. From the autumn of 1926, he balanced the budget by a combination of courageous cuts in spending, administrative rationalization, and higher taxes, which hit people on middle incomes especially. He created an independent fund to pay off the public debt, which was solemnly written into the constitution, and rapidly brought the exchange rate back to 122 francs to a pound, thus wiping out the last devaluation. But what was the right exchange rate for the franc? Many argued for a return to the prewar rate of 25 francs to a pound, including banks and the conservative mass-circulation press. Counter-pressures came from industrialists and from the self-interest of a heavily indebted state; these views were reinforced by the problems experienced by the United Kingdom, where sterling was overvalued because it had returned to its prewar exchange rate against gold in April 1925. Poincaré waited till his majority had been confirmed by the elections of 1928, and then passed a law that June which returned the franc to the gold standard at a rate of one franc to

65.5 milligrams of gold, a devaluation of four-fifths. This was the end of Napoleon's *franc de germinal*. It was also the final price of the war, the ultimate sacrifice of France; French power was reduced in monetary terms as it was in everything.

In order to reconcile French society to this readjustment, Herriot, as minister of education, launched his grand project to combine primary and secondary schools in a single system, which would therefore provide free secondary education for all. This project was born out of the fraternity of the trenches: the different social classes had served together in the war and they now wished for their children to share the same education (though this was not achieved until the 1970s). Laws passed in 1928 encouraged the construction of social housing and regulated housing estates. In April 1928, Poincaré himself introduced a major bill on social insurance, for France lagged well behind its European peers in its welfare provisions. Opposition by employers, the peasantry, and the medical establishment forced the government to reduce its scope considerably in order to get the bill passed into law, in April 1930; it was soon supplemented by a law on family allowances in 1932. Overall, Poincaré pursued a policy to reinforce social cohesion, with impressive results. He achieved the old social programme of the Radicals combined with a liberal financial policy—one of the few times that such a centrist policy had been pursued successfully. The reduction in French power was compensated by an increase in social cohesion. But this was only achieved by drawing on the darker side of the *Union sacrée:* Albert Sarraut, Radical minister of the interior, officially excluded the communists from the national community (summed up by the slogan 'Communism is the enemy') for their anti-militarist, anti-colonial, and anti-republican activities. He also repressed the movement for autonomy in Alsace because it challenged the unity of the nation. The exclusion of internal enemies helped the reconstruction of French society.

The illusion of prosperity

The return of the franc to the gold standard and the apparent return of prosperity led to a spectacular inflow of currency and gold. The reserves of the Banque de France soared from eighteen billion francs in 1927 to eighty billion in 1930, and the accumulated budget surpluses were nicknamed 'Chéron's treasure' after the minister of finance. The trade deficit was largely covered by income from reparations, tourism, and capital inflows. Because the reserves of the Banque de France, the budget deficit, and the trade deficit had been three key expressions of France's postwar ills, their health in the late 1920s was taken as proof that France was now an island of prosperity amid a world in turmoil. But the first signs of economic difficulties soon appeared: wholesale prices fell from 1926; the trade deficit soon worsened once the stabilization of the franc had reduced the advantage of a weak exchange rate; output from agriculture exceeded demand. However, these were masked by the budget surplus of five billion francs in 1930, new records for production across the board, and low unemployment—just 1,700 workers drew benefits in 1930. It appeared that sacrifice of the franc had not been in vain, and that the defining feature of the traditional French economy, namely the mass of small, family-run firms and farms, had preserved it from the chimeras of modernity that ravaged Germany and the United States.

This vision was not far from reality: the French economy was initially well protected from the world depression by its archaic structure. It did not depend on foreign investment, and so did not suffer from the withdrawal of American capital after the Wall Street crash; because so few of its industries were funded by debt, it was not affected by the banking crisis. But the new-found stability of the franc was exposed by international currency crises. Until 1930, Poincaré's devaluation had ensured that French products had an advantage in the export market; this advantage was steadily eroded as prices fell internationally. The devaluation of sterling in September 1931 and widespread controls on currency exchange also compromised this stability. In April 1933, the dollar fell from 25 to 18 francs. Now French prices were clearly and persistently above world prices. A new devaluation was out of the question; Poincaré's devaluation had been intended as the final settlement for the war. The franc's exchange rate had to be defended and France formed a gold bloc to protect it, along with Belgium, the Netherlands, and Switzerland, even though they were not France's main trading partners. This bloc fractured in March 1935, when the Belgian franc devalued. French exports fell rapidly from 1933 to 1935, by which time the total volume of trade was just one-third the level achieved in 1929. The trade deficit was reduced by half simply because imports shrank too. The laws on protection passed by Méline in the 1890s were hardened by increased duties on agricultural and industrial goods in 1931 and 1932, supported by other restrictive measures.

The effects of this defence of the franc were devastating. French agricultural goods were generally expensive because most farms were small and fragmented, so productivity was low. Three major crops, wheat, wine, and sugar beet, produced the bulk of income on farms ranging from small vineyards to vast beet-growing estates, so the majority of them were severely hurt when the prices of these crops collapsed at the start of the 1930s. French farming relied on exports because domestic production exceeded domestic demand, but their output had now become too expensive for export, and imported crops were often cheaper than French ones even after customs duties had been added. In industry, the crisis crept from sector to sector. Heavy industry was initially protected by demand from the state, and thus many modern sectors continued to grow. Electrical production increased by 20 per cent during the 1930s, largely thanks to the hydro-electric generators installed on the rivers of the Massif Central and the Rhine. Aluminium, chemicals, and especially oil-refining continued to expand spectacularly. Other sectors, such as car manu-facture and aviation, saw production fall by a third over 1930–2, then recover slowly. But the older, less productive sectors saw their export markets close then disappear, after which foreign competition ate into a shrinking domestic market. These industries—textiles, iron and steel, mining—were also the biggest employers. The loss of profits ruined investment, so ageing factory equipment was not replaced and productivity slipped even further behind foreign rivals. Companies sought refuge in protected markets, where they kept their prices as high as possible while reducing output, and the French empire became a vital captive market for agriculture and for traditional industries.

Because devaluation was politically and morally unthinkable, the sole policy on which most politicians could agree was deflation: to reduce the price of French goods to a competitive level by reducing costs. State expenditure that increased prices and drained consumers' income through taxes was one target, while the budget deficit was another, because it was seen as a machine for printing money, thus inflating prices. When André Tardieu, nicknamed 'the fabulous', succeeded an ailing Poincaré as premier, he attempted to go against this consensus by launching an ambitious 'policy for prosperity' in the autumn of 1929. This was an expensive plan for re-equipment and modernization (to cost five billion francs up to 1932), which would draw on Chéron's treasure to complete electrification, modernize the rail and road networks, develop hydroelectricity, and build the Maginot line to defend France's border with Germany. The state budget also had to fund Poincaré's welfare measures and school programme, a pension for war veterans, and a major increase in civil servants' pay in 1930 . . . all at the same time that the government cut taxes on land and on profits. When prices and output fell after 1930 tax revenues collapsed, and the budget deficit swelled from five billion francs in 1931 and 1932 to twelve billion the next year. Tardieu's expansion could not be sustained, and a policy of deflation followed to reduce the deficit and cut state spending. Finally, Pierre Laval's government of 1935 passed a series of decree-laws to reduce all state spending by 10 per cent; these cuts dragged down prices and wages across the public and private sectors. The constant pressure on prices, wages, and profits produced disastrous social tensions. It managed to stabilize state spending but naturally did not reduce the deficit because the contracting economy produced smaller tax revenues. Nor could French prices fall to the level of world prices because these were themselves also in decline, as governments worldwide followed the paths of protection, devaluation, and deflation. Moreover, other policies contradicted this goal because a number of expensive measures were introduced to stabilize prices in order to rescue peasant farmers, traders, and small businesses. The republic continued to protect these social groups above all, for they were its heart and soul. Strict protectionism and the redirection of Tardieu's modernization plan towards agriculture and public works were substitutes for a policy to combat unemployment. Deflation suffocated the internal market, prolonging the crisis and exacerbating cries for protection. Renewal was postponed.

The economic crisis had two distinct social consequences: it restructured the working class and it weakened the independent middle classes, to the peril of the republic itself. Up to 1933, unemployment affected the fringes rather than the core of the labour force, and thus it had the effect of making the working class more homogenous, stabilizing it and reducing it in size. Immigrants were the first to be laid off, and many of them were sent back to their home countries. Women were next: 330,000 left industrial jobs between 1931 and 1936. The last peasant workers also quit industry for other activities, putting an end to one of the defining features of the nineteenth-century economy, multiple employment. Before 1936 the working population had shrunk by 1,800,000, of whom 1,400,000 were industrial workers, though unemployment remained very low right up to 1933—by when it had reached three million in Britain, six million in Germany, and twelve million in the USA. The factory labour force was reshaped around its core: it was predominantly male, older, more skilled, and more urban than the average worker. But from 1933, the crisis reached this core as well. Unemployment rose from a few tens of thousands to a million by February 1935; aid for people out of work was stretched so thinly that it had to be reduced, and was only given to them for a short period of time. Half the workforce was on short time, often imposed in humiliating conditions. Employers could not afford to invest so they sought to increase returns by reorganizing production using less skilled labour, exemplified by Louis Renault in his new factory at Boulogne-Billancourt, on the edge of Paris. Workers were laid off *en masse* then rehired to do unskilled jobs on lower wages. Less threatened by unemployment but hard hit by the policy of deflation, public-sector workers in the CGT and white-collar employees in the CFTC became much more militant from 1934 onwards. This enabled them to develop a single strategy for all the main unions, including the communists of the CGTU, whose ranks had been severely depleted by the departure of foreign workers. These united, collective conflicts in factories and cities opened a new phase of labour demands in what became known as the 'red suburbs' of industrial zones ringing Paris and other major cities. Local mayors often supported strikers and the committees formed by unemployed workers, and the communist party was victorious in many industrial towns in the local elections of 1935. The middle classes, who were also victims of the crisis, joined the protests because these were made into a campaign against Fascism rather than against property or capitalism. The way to maintain living standards in the 1930s was to have a stable income in nominal terms, but the working and middle classes both had their pay cut. The only social groups who were able to protect their incomes were landowners, landlords, and pensioners on fixed incomes—though these groups had been the chief victims of inflation after the war. Other winners were the big companies who were protected by cartels, and private-sector providers of public services (such as electricity and urban transport); these firms saw their profits and dividends recover from 1934, while the depression endured for others. Retailers and craftsmen, small employers, and farmers faced the worst conditions. Bankruptcies doubled, haunting them with the spectre of proletarian-ization. These groups stood at the crossroads of social promotion in the Third Republic, and their failure meant the failure of the whole social model of the regime. The success of large-scale companies during the Great War and afterwards, and the failure of small ones during the 1930s, restructured French society. The world of paid employees took shape, with factory hands on one side, white-collar workers and public-sector staff on the other. In contrast, the republic's fabled 'little man', the independent trader, craftsman, or peasant farmer, went bankrupt. For a while, though, these divergent groups joined forces to defend themselves in the Popular Front alliance of Radicals, socialists, and communists in the mid-1930s.

The crisis of the political system, 1926–1935

The political system also foundered as Poincaré's successors failed to provide the necessary leadership. Frustration at this failure encour-aged the growth of extremist parties on the far left and far right, who accused the parliamentary system (not without reason) of ineptitude and corruption. Despite, or because of, the successive failures of Clemenceau and Millerand to amend the political system, the demand for reform grew stronger after 1926, and reform of the state was debated for the next thirty years. One common theme was to increase the power of the executive. From the left, one wing of the socialist party, the neo-socialists, saw a strong state as the ideal tool to bring about social transformation. Calls for reform of the regime's institutions and for a directed economy were even heard from the 'young Turks' group inside the Radical party, which was the chief beneficiary of the parliamentary system. Their intervention served as ammunition in the battle for control of the party fought by Herriot and Daladier. From the right, a leading industrialist, Ernest Mercier, advocated a technocratic government freed from parliamentary control; veterans' groups also called for a shift in the balance of power in favour of the executive, though to a lesser degree. Populist and sometimes paramilitary leagues flourished again, as Déroulède's Ligue des Patriotes had during the Dreyfus Affair. They revived in particular when the right lost power at the elections, as in 1924–5 and again in 1932–4. Action Française was also at the height of its influence in 1926. The members of its association and the readers of its newspaper were urban and Catholic; its beliefs remained monarchist, anti-Semitic, and germanophobe, which led it to advocate an alliance with Fascist Italy against Germany. Its activists reigned over Paris's student district, the Latin Quarter. However, it began a slow decline after the papacy condemned Charles Maurras in 1926, to the profit of its newer rivals. These included the Jeunesses Patriotes of Pierre Taittinger, the successors to the Ligue des Patriotes, who clashed violently with the communists before drawing closer to the conventional right-wing parties. Georges Valois's Faisceau was modelled more closely on Mussolini's Fascists. The return of Poincaré in 1926 appeased these militants and their funding from businessmen dried up, until the left's victory in 1932, compounded by the economic crisis and politico-financial scandals, revived their activity and spawned new leagues, such as *Francisme*, which was modelled on Mussolini's Blackshirts, and Solidarité Française. A mixture of rural Fascism and the defence of rural interests created the Comités de Défense Paysanne and their green-shirted militia (motto: 'Pitchforks high!'). The last to be born was the Parti Populaire Français, led by a former communist leader, Jacques Doriot, and based in his working-class stronghold of Saint-Denis, in the northern suburbs of Paris. The most important of these movements was the Croix de Feu, an association of war veterans led by Lieutenant-Colonel François de La Rocque. It expanded through a multitude of affiliated bodies to encompass civic action, grand parades of its members through towns and cities, and covert paramilitary cells. De La Rocque's xenophobia led him to reject the models presented by foreign fascism as well as democracy (too Anglo-American); instead his political programme was marked by traditional themes, nationalism, anti-parliamentarianism, and the organization of society into corporations. When the leagues were banned in June 1936, he founded the Parti Social Français (PSF), the first mass, right-wing, nationalist party in France. This enjoyed a brief success in defence of the middle classes, who felt abandoned by the Radical party.

In the 1980s, the historian Zeev Sternhell provoked a lively debate on the question of Fascism in France. For Sternhell, the seeds of Fascism had first formed in France, with Barrès's national socialist doctrine and Déroulède's league; by the 1920s and 1930s these seeds had germinated into a native French fascism. Almost every French historian denied that there had been any such thing, preferring to see the leagues as a resurgence of the old nationalist right in the fancy dress of foreign Fascism. Membership of these groups was always tiny, they were more conservative than revolutionary, and they lacked the great national frustration born of defeat in war that fuelled Fascism in Germany. Nevertheless, they had a major influence on politics in the 1930s. They were able to mobilize thousands of protesters in the streets, who brought down governments in 1926 and 1934. They expressed extreme sentiments with extreme violence, and the menacing echo of their anti-parliamentarianism, anti-communism, anti-Semitism, and xenophobia penetrated the mainstream press and polluted public debate in the 1930s. This convinced the left that there was a very real Fascist threat inside France, which inspired the coalition that became the Popular Front.

The conventional right was simultaneously weakened by competition from the leagues, contaminated by their hatreds, and supported by complicity with them. The Catholic right evolved differently once it had been freed by the papal condemnation of Action Française, though it was soon faced with a Christian left that developed around Emmanuel Mounier's periodical, *Esprit*. This heir to Marc Sagnier's Sillon movement soon rallied to the Popular Front. Rivalry between right-wing organizations weakened their identity and their appeal to voters, but the left could not exploit this since it faced the same problems. Divisions inside the Radical and socialist parties were compounded by the presence of the communist party on their left. Because the socialists refused to take part in government, they forced the Radicals to rule alone or in alliance with the right. It was not until the summer of 1934 that the Moscow-controlled Communist International (the Comintern) permitted the communist party to become 'the left wing of the republican camp', which made the Popular Front possible. This change of heart was a lesson learnt from the rise of Hitler in Germany: the German communist party had opposed its socialist rivals, and this had prevented them from forming a solid bloc to stop Nazism.

When the left won the elections of 1932, it stumbled once again on the refusal of the socialists to take part in government and on their hostility to the Radicals' conventional economic and social policies. Radical governments were reshuffled regularly, and their reputation was soiled by the exposure of a number of financial scandals where crooked businessmen had been protected by politicians. The Stavisky Affair that broke at the end of 1933 was the worst. Alexandre Stavisky, a Jewish-Ukrainian fraudster, had been under investigation by the police for several years, but his prosecution had been delayed nineteen times thanks to intervention from politicians and lawyers who were also Radicals and freemasons. After this was exposed in the press, he fled Paris and committed suicide in January 1934. Action Française launched a ferocious campaign against his protectors, joined by the other leagues and the major newspapers, which toppled yet another government. The President of the Republic, Albert Lebrun, summoned Daladier to be the next premier because of Daladier's reputation as an incorruptible, determined leader (strongly built and forceful, he was nicknamed the 'bull of the Vaucluse'). The inaugural debate was scheduled for 6 February. The leagues and veterans' associations demonstrated in place de la Concorde, the opposite side of the Seine from the Chamber of Deputies. The demonstration became a riot, and the police and army opened fire. Fifteen people were killed, and about 1,400 were injured. This event revealed a close coordination between the extreme right of the streets, especially the Jeunesses Patriotes, and the right in parliament and in the Paris city council. It also exposed the weakness of France's elites. Though Daladier won a vote of confidence, he was not supported by senior officials, who were afraid that if he stayed in power, it would provoke a civil war. Daladier resigned on 7 February, allowing the right to return to office two years after it had been defeated in the general election.

Lebrun then called on a former President of the Republic, Gaston Doumergue, to replace Daladier. Doumergue proposed a 'truce' in the political fighting and formed a national union ministry which included Herriot, to ensure the votes of Radical deputies, but which was really built around Tardieu on the right. The main project was reform of the state: greater autonomy for the President of the Council of Ministers, parliament to concentrate on legislation and the budget, the President of the Republic empowered to dissolve parliament. But Doumergue hesitated, and his majority fell apart over the budget and the dissolution of the leagues. The Radicals withdrew to form a centrist coalition government, then a purely Radical administration under Laval in May 1935. At the same time the party joined the new Popular Front that vigorously opposed the government's policy over the leagues, deflation and foreign affairs . . . even though the Radicals formed this very government. Its confusion was complete.

The Popular Front

This political dead end, the economic crisis, and the rise of Fascism in Italy and Germany produced an unprecedented alliance that stretched from the centre to the far left, for even the 'republican concentration' of the Dreyfus Affair only won partial support from the socialists. The Popular Front won a sweeping electoral victory in 1936, followed by a tidal wave of strikes. Millions of French citizens voted, struck, and called for renewal. Within weeks of this victory, the outbreak of the Spanish Civil War had sabotaged the chances of achieving this renewal.

The riot of 6 February 1934 was interpreted by the left as an attempted Fascist coup, a Parisian version of Mussolini's march on Rome. A powerful anti-Fascist movement arose from the grass roots, from party and union activists, local associations, and intellectuals, which made its presence felt by a massive political strike and protests on 12 February. The riot also prompted the Comintern to change its strategy because it seemed possible that Fascism might triumph in France as it had in Germany and Italy. The communist party was ordered to moderate itself, adopting the garb of the French revolutionary tradition instead of international Bolshevism. It was encouraged to join forces with other left-wing bodies, and to open its arms to veterans, Catholics, and even the Croix de Feu. This change of tack was duly accepted at the communist party conference of June 1934, and on 27 July it signed a first pact with the socialists. The CGT and CGTU were united once again in 1935. The communist leader Maurice Thorez proposed a broad 'Popular Front' to unite the middle classes with the working classes, and invited the Radicals to join.[1] Daladier, supported by the left wing of the party, became the champion for this alliance within the Radical party, which was sealed by a vast meeting in Paris on 14 July 1935. The Popular Front published its programme in January 1936 under the slogan 'Bread, peace, freedom'. The economic programme was consensual rather than radical. It defined its enemy as a conspiracy of the rich, the 'two hundred families' and their hired Fascist thugs, to oppress workers and small businessmen alike (the phrase came from the 200 major shareholders of the Banque de France, who controlled the bank). Attacks on such a symbolic enemy enabled the Popular Front to hide the essential contradiction of an alliance between Marxists and small businessmen. It had three policies to combat the depression: to organize agricultural markets, to increase the number of jobs by reducing working hours, and to relaunch the economy without devaluing the franc by reflation. At the general elections of 3 May 1936, the left won a clear victory thanks to the votes of the communist party and better electoral discipline, though the Radicals lost support. The socialist party won most seats and so claimed leadership of the government, which Léon Blum presented to parliament on 4 June. Blum, an aesthete, an intellectual, and a Jew, thus became France's first socialist President of the Council of Ministers. He had been brought to socialism by the example of Jaurès, in a quest for human justice rather than by Marxist thinking. As he personified so many of the things that the right hated, he became one of the most vilified men of the Third Republic; despite all the insults, he continued to pursue social justice without seeking retribution against his enemies. Moscow had decided that the communists should support the government but not participate in it, so the novelties of the new administration were the presence of three women (even though women still did not have the vote) and the youth of several ministers (Jean Zay, at education, was 31). The socialists held the economic and social portfolios, and the Radicals held the political ones.

The impact of the Popular Front lay less in its policies than in the vast strike movement that followed the electoral victory of 1936, and in the strong connections between the activities of unions, associations and the government. The strikes of spring 1936 began, as

[1] 'People's Front' is a better translation of the French term *Front populaire*, though it is generally known in English as the 'Popular Front'.

often in France, after May Day and in sectors that were barely unionized. Trade union officials had not expected these strikes, and they were rapidly overwhelmed by their scale. The strikers occupied factories to prevent employers from locking them out, and these sit-ins became festivals, intended both to reclaim workplaces for the workers and to spread the protests. Blum was installed as premier at the height of the strikes, and he immediately contacted the Confédération Générale de la Production Française (CGPF) to propose negotiations between it, the government, and the unions. The result was the Matignon Agreement of 7–8 June. Workers obtained the creation of collective employment contracts, including trade union rights, and pay rises of 7–15 per cent. Blum also announced the main laws that his government passed in the next few days with remarkable speed and unanimous support. Two weeks of paid holidays were announced; though this was not a claim made by the strikers, it had been spreading in practice since 1918, despite resistance by some employers. A minister of leisure was appointed, to the horror of the right—the young Léo Legrange. He gave a special quality to these first paid holidays through cut-price train fares and encouragement for youth hostels. The success of these holidays largely explains the place held by the Popular Front in the collective memory, as well as the preference of French workers for using a reduction in working hours to mean longer holidays rather than a shorter week. Entire sackfuls of postcards saying 'Thanks, Blum!' arrived at the Matignon Palace, the residence of the president of the Council of Ministers. This law was passed very easily (just one vote against it in the Chamber of Deputies and two in the Senate), as was the law on collective bargaining. Yet these laws did not stop the strike movement, which spread to other industries and to white-collar workers as well. At its peak, from 9 to 11 June 1936, there were nearly two million strikers in France, whose sympathizers even included some of the right-wing leagues and the archbishop of Paris. To stop the strikes, Thorez urged strikers to be realistic, using the idea that 'one must know how to end a strike'; the strikers' cry that 'everything was possible' was rejected by the communist leadership. The movement finally ebbed away in the second half of June, ending in Paris first, then the provinces. Its success boosted CGT membership, which rose fivefold, peaking at four and a half million in 1937 for the united CGT and CGTU. Membership of the left-wing parties, especially the communists, also soared, so that one of the chronic weaknesses of French political parties, their small membership base, was cured for a brief moment.

The psychological impact of the strikes was at least as important as the Matignon Agreement. Workers regained confidence in themselves, in their place in society, and in their own workplaces. The sense of inferiority workers felt before June 1936 was captured by Simone Weil, a philosopher with a masochistic streak, who worked in factories for several months over 1934–5, including Renault's Boulogne-Billancourt complex.

Do you now remember how afraid you were, how ashamed you were, how you suffered? There were some workers who did not dare to admit what their wages were, they were so ashamed to earn that little. Those who could not follow the rhythm of work, being too weak or too old, did not dare to admit it. Do you remember how we were obsessed by the rhythm of work? We never made enough; we always needed to stretch ourselves to make a few pieces more, to earn a few *sous* more. When we managed to go a bit faster by pushing ourselves, by exhausting ourselves, the timekeeper increased the pace. So we pushed ourselves again, trying to beat our comrades, getting jealous of each other, and wore ourselves out even more.[2]

The working class was redrawn—or was perhaps at last properly formed—by the crisis. It gained a framework for bargaining; it was now massively unionized and was allied to white-collar workers. It was finally integrated with the nation.

Because the socialists depended on the support of the Radicals, Blum did not believe that he had a mandate from the people for a revolutionary transformation of the economy, and in any case the left had itself been divided on these reforms since the 1920s. As a result, the government's purely economic reforms lacked boldness after this dramatic overture. Eight armament companies were nationalized; the aviation industry was reorganized; the railway companies (heavily in debt) were amalgamated and nationalized as the SNCF; the Banque de France was put under better public control, though it remained private. These reforms came from a desire for modernization more than for state control of the economy. The government's ambitious agricultural programme was wrecked by the Senate, leaving only the wheat office, a body to regulate the wheat market, which had been

---

[2] S. Weil, 'Lettre ouverte à un syndiqué (après juin 1936)', in *La Condition ouvrière* (Paris, 1951), p. 175. This edition also contains her diary of factory life.

hardest hit by falling prices. Educational and cultural reforms were undertaken by Jean Zay, the young Radical minister for education and the arts. His actions covered a wide range of educational and cultural issues, from authors' rights to the status of a scientific researcher, from encouraging young theatre companies to modernizing the procedure for public commissions, from the creation of the Cannes film festival to the creation of the Centre National de la Recherche Scientifique. In schooling, he gave a decisive push to the creation of a single school system once the school leaving age had been raised to 14. He refreshed teaching methods and introduced physical education. Zay's policies sprang from the impressive mobilization of intellectuals and cultural associations that had been prompted by the formation and election of the Popular Front. This exemplified the most remarkable feature of the social experiment of the Popular Front, which was the way that government action was anchored in the social movement, in a debate between the authorities and the people. But this massive social mobilization could only happen once.

The scale of the strike movement and of the Popular Front's electoral victory temporarily stunned its opponents. In parliament, the opposition meekly accepted the government's social reforms, only voting against the law to reduce the working week to forty hours, and it accepted the long-debated dissolution of the right-wing paramilitary leagues. But the political situation changed quickly from the summer of 1936, and for the worse. Throughout the electoral campaign of 1936 and onwards, the violence of the press was shocking, based around anti-communism and anti-Semitism: the strikes were a communist plot; Blum was a French, Jewish Kerensky. This opened a period that Serge Berstein has called a 'pretend confrontation' before the real confrontation of 1940–5, but it was far from bloodless. Roger Salengro, minister of the interior, was slandered so viciously that he committed suicide in November; an extreme right-wing terrorist movement nicknamed the 'Cagoule' perpetrated several bombings and murders in 1937; left-wing demonstrators clashed with police when they protested against a march by de La Rocque's PSF in the Parisian suburb of Clichy in March 1937. The police opened fire, leaving thirteen dead.

Rifts in the Popular Front coalition swiftly appeared, both between parties and inside them. There were three main and related causes to this: the civil war in Spain, the weakness of the franc, and the government's social policy. On 17 July 1936, General Franco led a military rebellion against the republican government in Spain, which was also a Popular Front alliance of socialists and communists. The eruption of a civil war on France's borders, just weeks after the electoral victory of the French Popular Front, traumatized the country. The initial policy of support for the Spanish republicans was met by a torrent of criticism from the right and split the left as well, because it exposed the contradiction between anti-Fascism and pacifism. The communist party advocated a bellicose anti-Fascism, and campaigned for 'cannons for Spain', against the policy of non-intervention defined by Blum on 2 August, and against the pacifist anti-Fascism of those who wanted to avoid the risk of any conflict, who were numerous among the Radicals and the socialists. The perilous international situation meant that France had to rearm, which strained government finances and increased attacks on the franc. Profound contradictions over social policies also resurfaced. As early as August 1936, the CGPF formed a propaganda body to win back the small businesses who were hurt by the reduction in working hours and the rise in pay. The franc was attacked several times on the foreign exchange markets, till it finally devalued on 1 October, despite all promises to the contrary. This outraged public opinion generally, and turned the mainstream press against the government. The independent middle classes, the bulk of the Radicals' voters, felt abandoned, afflicted by rising prices, a new wave of strikes, and the forty-hours law. The combination of economic, social, political, and diplomatic conflicts produced a stormy party conference when the Radicals met in October. Henceforth, the party was torn between its social identity as the representative of the middle classes and its political loyalty to the left-wing alliance. This rift became worse when the economy picked up following the devaluation only for employers to find that they could not increase production because the forty-hours law took effect from December 1936; prices had to rise instead, which then revived demands for wage increases. The Radicals called for conventional, rigorous economic policies, and Blum had to delay further reforms long before he officially declared a 'pause' on 13 February 1937, to the dismay of the CGT, the communists, and much of the socialist party. Blum requested full powers to make financial policy from parliament; the Chamber gave him lukewarm support, and when attacks on the franc began again the Radicals in the Senate overturned his government.

The end of the Popular Front came in stages, but the fall of Blum in 1937 laid down the direction. The Radicals rejected an economic and social policy that favoured employees, which they described as Marxist, and they defended their traditional clientele of the self-employed, small businessmen, and farmers, who now no longer thought of themselves as victims of the depression but as victims of the economic and social policy of the socialist-led government. The Radicals created a 'Committee for the defence of the middle classes' in March 1937 and once again swung into open opposition to the government while still being part of it. The slow evolution of French society lay at the heart of this profound political crisis. After June 1937, even though the Chamber remained unchanged, a Radical government was formed under Camille Chautemps with the moderate Georges Bonnet as minister of finance instead of the socialist Vincent Auriol. Bonnet returned to the policy of deflation to combat deficits in the budget and in the balance of trade. Taxes went up, state spending went down . . . and union militants went on strike in autumn 1937, demanding that the reform movement be restarted. In response, Chautemps formed a new ministry in January 1938 with no socialists in it, which was brought down by the socialists on the financial question in March. Blum returned to office briefly in a ministry that proposed economic expansion as advocated by Keynes's *General Theory of Employment, Interest and Money* (the plan was prepared by a young Pierre Mendès France, making his first entry into government). This government was rapidly despatched by the Senate. The time had come for a realignment around the centre, led by Daladier.

Daladier received almost unanimous support for his ministry on 12 April 1938, which showed how every party wished to make the new government work. Better supported on the right than the left, Daladier aimed to relaunch the economy to meet the needs of rearmament without having to confront the left. He rejected any further reforms, devalued the franc again, and suspended the forty-hours law for the arms industry. On 21 August 1938 he gave a radio broadcast in which he declared: 'France must get back to work'—i.e. abrogate the forty-hours law—because of the international tension caused by Hitler's demands for Czechoslovakian territory. The Munich agreement, which Daladier signed with no illusions about

Hitler's goodwill, made it easy to break with the communist party, which had spared its attacks on Daladier till then in order to combat Fascism. But Munich also stimulated a wave of patriotism that Daladier hoped would carry him through. His minister of finance was Paul Reynaud. Short, energetic, and one of the most intelligent critics of the Popular Front's economic policies, he was likened to a fighting cock compared to Daladier's bull. He announced the suspension of the forty-hours law and an increase in taxes. This provoked the CGT, communists, socialists, and many other organizations linked to the Popular Front to call a general strike for 30 November 1938, to protest against the government's economic measures and the Munich Agreement. But to protest against both sets of policies was contradictory: to argue that Daladier had been weak at Munich when confronted by Germany's new strength meant accepting that France had to become stronger too, which meant ending the forty-hours law. Daladier encouraged employers to move against strikers, requisitioned transport, and threatened sanctions against the unions. The strike was a crushing failure, and was followed by severe repression. The Popular Front was over.

For the next eighteen months, France was ruled by a strange ministry that maintained an apparent respect for the rites and principles of the republic while distorting its institutions. The government increased its powers by habitually issuing decree-laws which bypassed the legislature; the Chamber of Deputies was prorogued even before the war; the President of the Republic was ignored. The government drew its strength from public opinion via the press, buoyed by the success of the economic recovery and by anti-communism, which spread after Munich. Public opinion welcomed Daladier's preparations for war because this seemed to be the only way to avoid war: Germany would not dare to attack France if it was strong. Military spending stimulated the economy, and the industrial mobilization of France was a great success in 1939, both before and after the declaration of war. France produced more cannons and aeroplanes than Germany, thanks to a rigorous financial policy, extending the working week to sixty hours, and the activity of the minister for armaments. But labour relations remained dreadful, and employers had not yet finished taking their revenge. The Nazi–Soviet pact of 1939 made anti-communist feelings more violent than ever, doubled by anti-Semitism and by the fear of war. The left accused the right of preferring Hitler to Stalin, or even to Blum, and of trying to direct Nazi aggression to the east. The right accused the left of disarming France by the forty-hours law and the strikes. Anti-Semitism gained ground on the moderate right and the pacifist left from fear of a war fought out of solidarity with German Jews. Foreign policy was riven by two versions of pacifism: a peace party prepared to make any concession to Hitler and a war party prepared to fight in order to stop Hitler and to rescue peace for the future. Every party except the communists was split along this line, which added to the political confusion.

The fall of France

When Germany invaded Bohemia in March 1939, in contravention of the Munich Agreement, public opinion in France and Britain was shocked, and Daladier followed Britain's lead by guaranteeing the independence of Poland. The western allies began negotiations with the Soviet Union, but these were full of mistrust, and instead Stalin signed the Nazi–Soviet non-aggression pact on 23 August. This gave Hitler the confidence he needed to invade Poland on 3 September, and he was amazed when the allies honoured their pledge to Poland by declaring war on Germany. The French public greeted the war with more resolution than was long believed by postwar historians. Daladier managed to contain pacifism, which was henceforth limited to a silent minority. From the autumn of 1939 the communist party was mercilessly repressed as the internal enemy, since its masters in Moscow had allied to Germany. The mobilization of 4.5 million soldiers was completed without problems, to fight a national war as in 1914. But the Great War had fundamentally changed expectations of how the war would be fought, dictating a defensive strategy (literally) built on the Maginot line. After the rapid defeat of Poland, the morale of the troops and of the interior deteriorated during the long wait of the 'phoney war'. Gathering discontent and the defeat of Finland by the Soviet Union overthrew Daladier on 20 March 1940. Reynaud succeeded him, sounding a more resolute note, but his cabinet was as divided as Daladier's—and Daladier remained as minister of war.

On 10 May 1940 Hitler launched his attack on the Netherlands and Belgium, where he was faced by the best French and British troops, before piercing the French front by an armoured attack through the Ardennes forest that outflanked the Maginot line. In just six days the Germans reached the Channel and the Franco-British armies were trapped at Dunkirk. General Weygand counterattacked without success on the Somme and Aisne rivers. On 10 June, when Italy entered the war alongside Germany, the French government left Paris for Bordeaux, for the third time in seventy years. Undermined by the divisions within his cabinet, Reynaud resigned on 16 June in favour of Marshal Philippe Pétain, France's most prestigious living soldier and vice-president of the Council of Ministers. Pétain was the chief supporter of an armistice that would pass responsibility for the defeat from the army to the politicians; this armistice was requested without delay, under the enemy's guns. It was signed on 22 June 1940 in the same clearing in the woods at Réthondes, in the same field train as the armistice of 11 November 1918—a symbolic revenge for Hitler and the German army. Yet the defeat was clearly military. The high casualty rate testified to the bravery of the troops, and the French army's equipment matched that of the Germans in everything except aeroplanes. The failure came from the military doctrine—Pétain's doctrine—of a continuous defensive front that had been swiftly broken by the Nazi Blitzkrieg. Once again, the memory of 1914 had been overpowering, for the men who had fought in the Great War were now in charge of the army. It was also a strategy that had blatantly compromised France's diplomatic options: because France could not take the offensive, it could not help its allies to the east of Germany, and was unable to save Czechoslovakia or Poland from invasion.

In the face of this rapid military collapse, the solidarity of 1914 could not be recovered. Instead, civil society collapsed, leading to the exodus of eight million Frenchmen, put to flight by fear. The richest left first, driving south to cross the Loire by car; the poorest, women, children, and the elderly followed them in carts, on bicycles, and on foot, in endless lines of refugees that were strafed relentlessly by the Luftwaffe.

The caravan flowed on [...] This was the kingdom of the mattress. One would have thought that France was the land of the mattress, that the mattress was the most precious possession of the French. In many cars, old women lay stretched out, no longer looking outside themselves, and children slept as if they were dead. The lorries were like ships packed with emigrants and their luggage; the passengers were sometimes spread over the pile of bundles, sometimes lined up under the canvas roofs like a row of spectators in the theatre. Through the windows you could see dogs, cats, birds in their cages. A monkey was attached to a radiator [. . .]

The caravan of cars was accompanied by men and women on bicycles and limping along by foot. Their heads seemed to be pulled towards their feet. Some carried a travelling bag, others carried one or two suitcases in their hands. Can you imagine how exhausting this march was, with a suitcase at the end of each arm? Others pushed a pram, filled with children or bundles, the best of their belongings, or they pushed the strangest vehicles built from planks of wood and old bicycle wheels. A woman was sitting on the cover of a tricycle; a man pedalled it. An old cyclist, alone, led his dog on a lead.[3]

In the towns, bishops and mayors, firemen and bakers vanished. The French had been abandoned, and Pétain heard their lament. The military high command, which took power following Pétain's appointment at the climax of an unbelievable defeat, blamed the rank and file, sapped by a corrupt political class, and their treacherous British allies. Crushed by defeat, the mass of Frenchmen accepted this blame, feebly grateful that the old marshal took responsibility for the armistice, and turned with respect to the Germans as the only force left amid the chaos.

Pétain made the most of this emotion to restore order quickly and to secure peace through the armistice. The Vichy regime was founded by the armistice much more than by subsequent constitutional laws. The terms of the armistice were just generous enough to make it acceptable, and forestalled the planned departure of the authorities for North Africa. France was left with its navy, based in Toulon, its empire, and an unoccupied zone covering the country south of the Loire except for the Atlantic coastline; together, these concessions preserved the illusion of a sovereign French power. The armistice disarmed and neutralized France, and extorted huge sums of money to pay the costs of France's own occupation: 400 then 700 million francs a day. It kept 1.6 million French prisoners of war as hostages, and rejoined Alsace and Lorraine to the Third Reich. It required the 'collaboration' of the French administration by article 3 of the armistice and impelled it because two-thirds of the country was 'under the

[3] L. Werth, *33 jours* (Paris, 1994 edn.), pp. 14–15.

rights of the occupying power'. Indeed, collaboration with Germany seemed to be the only realistic option in the summer of 1940. It was widely assumed that Britain would sign a compromise peace to protect its empire, as it obviously could not defeat the Third Reich alone. Recriminations against Britain turned to rancour when British forces sank the French fleet stationed off North Africa to prevent its capture by the enemy. Vichy's aim was to rule France as a sovereign power within Hitler's new European order, and to this end it made great play of its famous aces—the fleet, the empire, and the unoccupied zone. Ultimately it became the author of its own damnation because it sought to prove its independence by pre-empting German demands. This gave Germany an indirect control over the whole country, making it easier for the Nazis to exploit France, and led Vichy to repress Germany's enemies on its behalf. Laval, who entered the government on 26 June 1940, proposed the destruction of parliament and the other republican institutions. Backed by popular support for Pétain, the silence of leading figures, and the fear afflicting political parties and their personnel generally, Laval alternated promises with threats to overcome objections. On 10 July 1940 the Chamber and Senate, sitting together in Vichy, voted the devolution of 'full executive and legislative powers to the government of Marshal Pétain', as well as the power to draft a new constitution. Only eighty deputies and senators voted against this, mostly from the left, to whom one should add the communist representatives who had been banned since 1939 and twenty-seven others who had left Bordeaux to continue the war from North Africa but who had been detained in Morocco. The republican regime had committed suicide amid its own profound crisis as well as defeat in war.

Vichy: the French State in a spa town

Out of the supreme disaster of 1940, Pétain sought renewal by returning to the past instead of pursuing modernization. The new regime styled itself the 'French State', obliterating the hated title of 'republic'. It was a charismatic, authoritarian regime incarnated from start to end by Philippe Pétain. Pétain brought with him the entourage he had built up during the 1930s, which mixed followers of

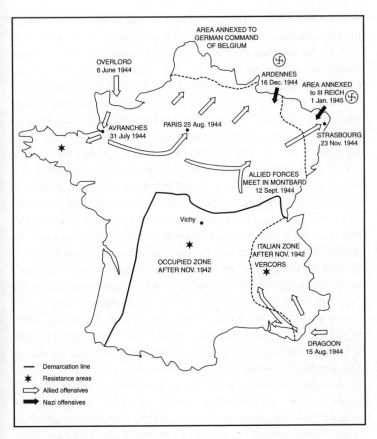

Map 5.1 The occupation and liberation of France.

Maurras (such as Alibert, his first minister of justice), military leaders finally freed from political control (General Weygand and Admiral Darlan), and senior civil servants, many of whom had worked in the private sector as well. If there were some men from the left, the bulk of the regime's personnel came from various elements of the right: the leagues, Catholics, technocrats, and free-market liberals. Revision of the constitution was interrupted in the autumn of 1943, and was never completed. The government behaved like an eccentric army general staff; ministers were appointed, then abruptly dismissed; Pétain's personal doctor took part in discussions. Universal suffrage was abolished for all elections except village councils, but no elections were ever held. The Chamber of Deputies and Senate were forbidden to meet, mayors were appointed, public servants swore a personal oath to the marshal, the powers of the departmental councils were transferred to the prefects, who were themselves cosseted by the central authorities. The leaders of the Popular Front and of the ministries of 1939–40 were put on trial, though the proceedings were suspended when the evidence did not favour Vichy's rulers. Political parties were banned by the Germans and were soon suspended in the southern zone too. The National Council, a consultative body of notables formed in 1941 to plan the new institutions, sketched a France structured around its ancient provinces (departments were to be abolished as artificial creations of the Revolution), though its work was never finished. Pétain united the veterans into a single Légion Française des Combattants, which was to spread the values and the cult of the marshal, and to act as its eyes and ears. However, it failed to become the vehicle for Pétainism as a movement, and merely served as the model for the Service d'Ordre Légionnaire; in January 1943 this became the Militia, an auxiliary political police. The regime's intermediary bodies were a failure, and all that was left to support it was the genuine popularity of Pétain and control of public opinion by censorship, propaganda, and numerous forms of policing. The Aryanization of the press made this easier to achieve . . . and sent the press into decline. The big Parisian newspapers relocated to the south, but they lost readers as they became more conformist, and suffered from shortages of paper; when the Germans occupied the south, they destroyed their own equipment. Radio Vichy met competition from Radio Paris, in the hands of German propagandists, who also financed a more extreme collaborationist press. Soon it was also challenged by French broadcasts from the BBC, which were far more credible.

Pétain's programme, entitled the National Revolution, was a mixture of classic French nationalism flavoured by Catholicism and the army. As a son of peasants, he exalted the land, 'for it does not lie', and contrasted the rural values of an eternal France with false modern and urban values. This vision promoted the workshop against the factory, the village against the city, the notable against the politician, locality (*terroir* again) against cosmopolitanism. Anti-Semitism sprang readily from this, and was rapidly put into action. He tried to restore the old moral order by replacing the Revolution's motto of 'liberty, equality, fraternity' with 'work, family, country', and he re-established inequalities and hierarchies, with the blessing of the Catholic church. The new regime rejected the individualism of the Third Republic in favour of community—the natural communities of family and trade, which collectively formed the nation. This was given form by a law on social organization of professions, the Labour Charter of October 1941, which divided 321 professions into twenty-nine professional families. Within these corporations, employers managed to make their influence felt now they were free from the counterweight of the unions. For businesses, the stakes were access to raw materials and contracts to supply the Germans. The National Revolution's vision of the family was promoted by laws that limited divorce, punished adultery severely, made it a capital offence to carry out an abortion, increased the authority of fathers, and took mothers out of the labour force. Dancing was banned by the French authorities to improve morality, and by the Germans to remove opportunities for sedition. The regime's new order was welcomed beyond the elites it privileged (typified by upper bourgeois Catholic war veterans) for a variety of reasons. Those in authority everywhere relished the return of their power; traditionalist schoolmasters shared its elitism and brisk morality; peasants were flattered by the regime and enriched by the black market. Moreover, the regime's supporters were divided into a minority who backed Pétain and his ideals (*Pétainistes*) and a majority who accepted the need for the Vichy regime but disagreed with its subsequent actions (*maréchalistes*).

The Catholic church played its role in the refoundation of society to the full. Pétain's language at the very start of the regime was inspired by Christian ideas, and indicated that Christian principles would be inherent in public life.

To deprive France of its natural defenders in a time of general disorder is to deliver it to its enemy, is to kill the soul of France—it is also therefore to make its rebirth impossible [. . .] I have therefore decided not to abandon the soil of France and to accept the suffering that will be inflicted on the country and on its children. The rebirth of France will be the fruit of this suffering.[4]

The government restored prayers and religious education in state schools, authorized the religious orders banned in 1901, and gave a

---

[4] P. Pétain, vice-president of the Council of Ministers. Note read to the Council of Ministers on 13 June 1940.

grant to religious schools. Jews, freemasons, and communists were purged from schools; teacher-training colleges ('democracy's wicked seminaries') were closed; lycées charged fees again and reintroduced Latin. The army organized youth work programmes to replace military service and to enrol young men into its ranks. Vichy also wanted to train leaders at a college run by Captain Dunoyer de Segonzac, in Uriage, near Grenoble. He gathered a prestigious team of lecturers around the journalist Hubert Beuve-Méry (who later founded *Le Monde*); its original stance was close to social Christianity, but then grew further away from the government and from the regime, which therefore closed it in January 1943. Many of the 3,000 who attended Uriage became France's modernizers after the war, often via the Resistance.

The regime evolved less from the personalities that Pétain summoned around him than from the demands made by the policy of collaboration. The Germans were initially most concerned to secure French neutrality in their war against Britain, but over time their exactions became more and more severe, finally putting the whole country under strict rule. In Paris the German ambassador, Otto Abetz, animated the little world of collaborationists; it included some former league leaders such as Doriot, while others, such as de La Rocque, were deported to German prison camps. These puppets were used to scare the French state, by the threat that they might replace Vichy as rulers of France. This was a hollow threat, since they had no patriotic authority, which remained Pétain's chief asset. Yet the support given to Pétain by the defeated French of 1940, termed a 'passive Pétainism' by Yves Durand, could not survive four years of restrictions and hardship, still less the policy of collaboration, which was unpopular from the start. After a period when Admiral Darlan ran the government, Laval returned to power in April 1942. Laval was a lawyer, businessman, and politician who believed that anything could be fixed by a deal, and that he was the man to fix it—he had no interest in the national revolution. Rejected by the Third Republic, he saw his chance to take revenge and to run the new regime behind Pétain's front. His belief that he could outwit Hitler cost France dear.

Hostility to the regime grew markedly from 1941, with a social dimension as well as a political one. It sprang above all from the massive and almost universal rejection of the German occupation, which was paradoxically a major reason for the general support for Pétain in the summer of 1940: Pétain and the armistice appeared to be the fastest ways to end the war and therefore end the occupation. Onerous restrictions and shortages then fed resentment (as in the First World War, rationing weighed more on the towns than on the countryside). Once Germany was at war with the USA and Soviet Union as well as Britain, from the end of 1941, it began to wage total war, which meant that it demanded more from France. The terms of the occupation were hardened, requisitions of goods and labour increased, and repression became more severe in order to force cooperation. The Vichy government made its collaboration ever closer, despite the occupation of the southern zone of France in November 1942 in response to the Allied landings in North Africa. This completed the rupture in public opinion. In a moment, Vichy had lost its three aces: the empire was lost to it, the southern zone was occupied, and the navy sank itself in Toulon harbour to avoid capture by the Germans. 1942 was the 'bisection' of the war, in Pierre Laborie's phrase. From then on the regime rapidly became more totalitarian, more repressive, more anti-Semitic, more in thrall to Germany. Its disintegration in 1944 was increasingly bloody. Vichy's private army, the Militia, ran amok alongside the German forces in their fight against the Resistance, and murdered a number of Third Republican politicians, including Jean Zay. When the Allies landed in Normandy on 6 June 1944, in Operation Overlord, Resistance groups across the country followed the call to rise up, only to find themselves fighting the German army for weeks with meagre equipment, notably on the Vercors plateau. Thousands of Resistance fighters were killed and thousands more civilians were massacred in reprisals by the German forces and their Vichy partners. The Allies then landed on the Mediterranean coast on 15 August 1944 in Operation Dragoon, driving north to meet the armies from Normandy at Montbard. In August 1944 the retreating Germans took with them Pétain, Laval, and the debris of the French state, jumbled up with the Parisian collaborationists who thought that their hour had finally, belatedly, come.

Nationalism and race

Vichy's vision of the restored French nation rejected the republican ideal of citizenship in favour of an exclusive and racially defined nationalism. From the summer of 1940, without pressure from Germany, the government attacked three of the four horsemen of the 'anti-France' so often denounced before the war: freemasons, foreigners, and Jews. Only Protestants escaped the onslaught, though they were never supporters of the regime. In August 1940, free-masons' lodges were closed and civil servants who were masons were dismissed. The status of foreigners had worsened sharply on the eve of war, against a backdrop of anti-Semitism and the chilly reception granted to refugees from the Spanish Civil War. Now they were threatened by a law on denaturalization passed in July 1940, while German and Austrian Jews were returned to the Third Reich by a secret clause in the armistice treaty. Up to 1942, Vichy developed its own anti-Semitic policy, needing no inspiration from Nazism for this. The initial measures, such as the law on denaturalization, were covertly anti-Semitic, until a statute of 3 October 1940 created an inferior category of citizens on racial grounds. This excluded them from positions of authority and influence, sacking 3,500 civil ser-vants, and opened the way to a series of further measures, beginning with the 'Aryanization' (more bluntly, theft) of Jewish property in the occupied zone: over 40,000 companies were seized in total: the full list of them and an exact evaluation was not made until the year 2000. Pétain simply had the usual anti-Semitism of a Catholic army officer and Laval was completely indifferent to the subject, so they left Jewish policy to the fanatics in their entourage, initially led by Raphaël Alibert. The regime blamed Jews for the defeat, by starting the war and by leaving France unprepared for it; this guilt was extended to Bolshevism, which anti-Semites saw as a Jewish creation, and to the republic, which they believed had been taken over by Jews.

In reality, there was no single Jewish community but 150,000 French Jews who were fiercely patriotic and loyal to the republic, and a similar number of foreign Jews from eastern Europe, many of whom were organized in bodies close to the Marxist left and to Zionism. In March 1941, Vichy created the Commissariat Général aux Questions Juives to deal with this population. This was initially run by Xavier Vallat, a much-decorated and much-injured veteran of the Great War who had become a deputy and a follower of Maurras. Vallat was replaced in May 1942 by Darquier de Pellepoix, a thuggish member of the leagues who had served as a Paris city councillor. On 2 June 1941 Vallat published a second statute that was much stricter in both its racial and religious definitions; it set out measures to conduct a census of the Jewish population and to exclude it from the national community. Foreign Jews were rounded up in concentration camps in both the occupied and non-occupied zones. Everything changed in the spring of 1942, when Vichy made itself more clearly complicit in the Final Solution then being planned by the Nazis. In an effort to show that his government was still sovereign, Laval bartered French Jews for foreign ones and offered the active support of the French police alongside the Gestapo in operations against the Resistance, by the Oberg-Bousquet accords of August 1942. He insisted that children under 16 be deported as well—the Germans were prepared to leave them behind in France. Seventy-nine convoys deported 76,000 Jews from France: 26,300 Poles, 24,000 French, 7,000 Germans; 10,000 aged under 18, 2,000 aged under 6. After the war, 2,500 returned. The worst year was 1942, when forty-three convoys deported 43,000 Jews, all to Auschwitz. The most brutal operation became known as 'la rafle de Vel'd'Hiv': the arrest of 12,884 stateless Jews on 16 and 17 July 1942, who were held in a cycling stadium, the Vélodrome d'Hiver; they were then moved to a camp at Drancy, just north of Paris, which was the point of departure for the extermination camps. The Vichy regime was guilty of abetting the Holocaust at every stage within the borders of France. However, the behaviour of the French people changed significantly. Their initial passivity (which applied generally, not just to the fate of Jews) was replaced by sympathy in 1942. After this had emerged spontaneously, the churches, Catholic and Protestant, developed it further, with the result that three-quarters of French Jews were saved.

Resistance and liberation: renewal from the ashes

A profound urge for renewal emerged out of the repression of Vichy and the debris of war, yet the nature of this renewal was far from obvious in 1944. The communists had been redeemed by their major role in the Resistance and they aimed to make the most of it, whereas the Allies were intent on keeping France within the western bloc; many prewar politicians wished to restore the republic, with some modification, in contrast to members of the Resistance, who wanted a profound transformation of the country and its institutions. Perhaps the most resolute of all these, de Gaulle intended to restore the central state as the supreme authority internally and to restore France as a major power internationally.

The postwar aims of the Resistance were influenced both by its social composition and by a 'spirit of the Resistance' that formed in its ranks. A sociological approach to the Resistance must be made cautiously: the first resisters, and often the leaders of movements and their networks, were generally bourgeois who had broken ranks with their peers. The best example of this is de Gaulle himself. But the bulk of resisters were young, skilled men from the middle and working classes. This social profile is explained partly by politics: as Vichy's social programme promoted peasants and craftsmen, so the Resistance was manned by workers and the salaried middle classes. Once the communist party had rallied to the Resistance after Germany invaded the Soviet Union in 1941, it brought its working-class membership with it. Young men predominated both because of the military nature of the Resistance and because they faced deportation to Germany as forced labourers from February 1943 if they stayed behind. While the Resistance was very small in size, with just 400,000 recognized members, it depended on the support of the rest of the population. This support was widespread, though variable. The earliest recruits aside, joining the Resistance meant accepting a system of values, a spirit which was both revolutionary and reformist, and which fuelled social renewal after the war. The Resistance emerged from the shadows with the Allied landings of June 1944, taking extreme risks to ensure that it held a political and social role at the vanguard of the nation. As Vichy's French state vanished, an alternative state appeared simultaneously, which had been defined in secret by a handful of its leaders. As these men were mostly drawn from the middle classes and bourgeoisie, the French elites were still drawn from the same social classes after the war as before; however, these elites were rejuvenated and their values were profoundly refreshed.

De Gaulle's emergence as the leader of the Free French and of the Resistance owed much to Churchill, who made him head of the Free French for want of anyone better, and even more to de Gaulle's belief in himself. De Gaulle was a career army officer, as befitted the son of a bourgeois Catholic family. Between the wars he advocated a mobile, professional army equipped with tanks, instead of Pétain's doctrine of static defence, and his counterattack against German forces in 1940 was one of the few highlights of the French defence. It also won him his only prewar political appointment, as under-secretary of state for war in Reynaud's government. He flew to England in June 1940, from where he broadcast his now famous call for resistance on 18 June, in which he was barely more tender towards the Third Republic than Pétain was, even if de Gaulle did blame the defeat on the military command. The Free French were initially a military structure that he steadily turned into a political one. He formalized his power in October 1940 by creating a Conseil de Défense de l'Empire, which brought together the military leaders and colonial governors who had rallied to the Free French. In September 1941 he established the Comité National Français as the government in exile. While he condemned the anti-Semitic and xenophobic policies of Vichy, he was no less harsh on the republican abdication of power, and he wielded an absolute authority over the Free French. This alienated the democrats, who were ill-disposed to trust an army general anyway. Support for de Gaulle rose with military successes and with his broadcasts on the BBC, which gave encouragement to the republicans and especially to the Resistance inside France. It was above all the actions of Jean Moulin, a brilliant and courageous young prefect acting as de Gaulle's exclusive representative in occupied France, that rallied politicians to de Gaulle from the spring of 1942, including the communists and the heads of the Resistance. Through control over their funding and equipment, Moulin secured the creation of a unified Secret Army, followed by the creation of the Conseil National de la Résistance (CNR) in May 1943. The arrest of Moulin the next month threatened the Resistance with catastrophe, but he died without revealing its secrets under torture by the Gestapo. The CNR gathered together representatives of the main resistance movements, political forces, and trade unions, and it recognized the authority of de Gaulle. This legitimacy was a major asset in the contest between de Gaulle and General Giraud, whom the Americans made leader of the French in North Africa after their landings there in November 1942. De Gaulle steadily confined Giraud to military matters and in June 1943 presided at the first meeting of the Comité Français de Libération Nationale (CFLN) in Algiers, henceforth capital of Free France and of the liberated empire. Inside France, a new administration and a military rising were carefully prepared to accompany the liberation, in order to establish the legitimacy of the CFLN, which became the Provisional Government of the French Republic in June 1944.

For de Gaulle, the goal of liberation was to re-establish French power at home and abroad. Domestically, this was to be achieved by restoring the authority of the central state, which meant containing the autonomous, decentralized Resistance once it had shown that the French had substantially liberated themselves, and replacing Allied forces with French administration as soon as possible. General Leclerc was therefore despatched with his army to Paris to receive the German surrender on 25 August 1944 alongside the insurgent Parisians. De Gaulle moved into the ministry of war, which he had left in June 1940, and forbade the CNR to proclaim a new republic because de Gaulle maintained that he himself embodied continuity with the old one: Vichy had been an aberration, not a legitimate regime. De Gaulle swiftly integrated the Resistance leaders into the regular army; he also demobilized the patriotic militias led by the communist resistance in return for allowing Maurice Thorez to return from exile in the USSR, where he had fled to in 1940. During the autumn of 1944, he personally asserted the authority of the prefects over the colonels of the Resistance, causing some tension and bitterness in the process, as these prefects had dutifully served Pétain. This same logic lay behind the postwar trials, which were harder on journalists and writers than on Vichy's civil servants. Pétain's defence of Verdun in the Great War saved him from the firing squad that claimed the life of Laval.

Though the country's torments were much less than those of eastern Europe, France was ravaged by the end of the fighting, which lasted until 20 March 1945. The human losses were below those of the Great War, with 210,000 lost in combat, 250,000 who had died in Germany, and 150,000 civilian deaths; of these, 60,000 were killed by bombing and 30,000 had been executed. But unlike the Great War, almost every part of the country had been damaged, and several towns had to be rebuilt in part or in whole, both near the coast, such as Le Havre and Caen, and inland, such as Orléans. There was no national market because the road and rail networks, goods trains and lorries had all been destroyed. There was no coal; industrial production was one-third that of 1929; wholesale prices were three times those of 1938; the value of francs in circulation had gone up fivefold; government revenues only covered 30 per cent of spending, and exports covered less than 20 per cent of imports. An obsession with food, fuel, housing, and other necessities took some of the shine off the liberation, along with the settling of scores with collaborators. Even so, liberation was celebrated with the largest public dances that France had ever known.

The Fourth Republic, 1944–1958

The postwar period was not only an opportunity for renewal; it was physically necessary to reconstruct the country and politically necessary to start again. The spirit of the Resistance fed into a self-conscious attempt to modernize France, in the start of what Jean Fourastié later termed the *trente glorieuses*, the thirty years of economic advance that lasted from the end of the war to the oil crisis of 1973. Yet, as after the First World War, there were also strong forces at work to preserve traditions and existing interests. The image of the republic had been improved by its vilification under Vichy, and initially there was a consensus among all parties save the communists that the empire should be preserved. De Gaulle especially had liberated France in order to restore its greatness, not to liberate the rest of the world. By the end of the Fourth Republic, renewal was limited— or rather, uneven. Economic and social modernization only affected specific sectors, in keeping with the general ambiguity of the Fourth Republic. It was attached to the old political model of the republican tradition, to the empire, and to protection behind customs barriers. At the same time the Fourth Republic modernized the structures of the labour force and of the economy, and launched the project of European unity. These modern and defensive impulses alternated and conflicted up to 1958, pitting the innovative France of Pierre Mendès France against the conservative France of Antoine Pinay and Pierre Poujade.

At the liberation, the communist party, the CGT, and the provisional government launched the 'battle for production' without delay, under the slogan 'Roll up our sleeves!' This drive to increase production was inseparable from the drive for modernization, which was the major (and sometimes the only) theme in French economic history for the next thirty years. Modernization did not only concern machinery and equipment; it involved the very structure of society and the economy, which were jointly blamed for the defeat of 1940. The aim was not just to repair the damage done by the war but to effect a total reconstruction. Employers were blamed for France's backwardness and denigrated for their complicity with Vichy and the Nazis, so the government took charge instead. State direction was both ideological (liberal capitalism was damned as a failure by the communists and the Christian democrats) and technical (because the scale of the work to be done was so vast). The programme of the CNR set out its principles and aims, and was rapidly put into motion. The public sector expanded greatly. Energy became the responsibility of huge public companies (Éléctricité de France, Gaz de France, Charbon de France). The four largest retail banks and the Banque de France were nationalized, as were the thirty-four leading insurance companies, but not the smaller banks nor merchant banks. The state took over maritime transport and founded Air France. Outside these sectors, there were only a few more nationalizations as a punishment for collaboration with the Nazis, such as Berliet (a truck manufacturer) and especially Renault, whose owners were jailed.

Planning for state direction was entrusted to Jean Monnet, in charge of a team of young technocrats in the new Commissariat du Plan. The first five-year plan, for 'modernization and equipment', was launched in January 1947. It laid down ambitious targets for production and gave priority to the equipment needed to make consumer goods; it was financed by the resources of the French government and the American Marshall Plan, which gave $1.6 billion towards it. Inflation was a major problem during the early years of the first plan. It exceeded 50 per cent a year until 1948, and aggravated labour relations from 1947 because rising prices forced workers to demand increased pay, which in turn forced up prices in a vicious circle. Inflation also rapidly wiped away the debts of the state and of private companies, though it thereby wiped away assets and savings as well. Inflation was balanced by three devaluations between 1945 and 1949, until it was reduced by government measures in 1948 and even more by the arrival of the massive Marshall Plan credits. The pivotal year 1949 marked the end of reconstruction and the beginning of expansion: it saw the end of shortages and rationing, and production recovered to the same level as 1939.

The liberation was also a key moment in the modernization of the labour force. Trade unions participated fully in the battle for production: the old-established CGT (again reunified and again dominated by the communists, with five million members in 1945) and CFTC (with 700,000 members) plus the new Confédération Générale des Cadres and the Confédération Générale Agricole. The CGT and the communist party influenced the 1946 law on the status of public servants, which gave them substantial protection. Employers initially accepted these reforms, then in 1946 they founded a new Conseil National du Patronat Français (CNPF). This took a highly defensive position, rejecting both the government's plan and any form of Keynesian policy. Unions and employers' organizations co-managed the new social security programme, created by decrees of December 1944 and October 1945. This integrated the old forms of social insurance into a new, universal protection for all employees—nine million workers and their families. Only family policy remained apart, under pressure from the new Catholic-inspired Mouvement Républicain Populaire (MRP). State benefits were substantial, and by 1949 benefit payments accounted for 12 per cent of all household income. But this social reconstruction soon collided with the Cold War, which ruptured the support given by the unions. In October 1947 the CGT led strikes to break France away from the western bloc (membership of which was a prerequisite for Marshall Aid); this forced the non-communist fraction to break away, under the command of the inexhaustible Léon Jouhaux, to form the CGT Force Ouvrière union in April 1948. This division led to a rapid drop in union membership, and unity only reappeared spasmodically, to campaign for a minimum wage, for a moving scale of pay, and to preserve the status of public servants. With union solidarity broken, the state abandoned its role as arbiter and the CNPF rejected social dialogue. Once again, employers negotiated with the state and resumed secret payments to the political parties that favoured them. On balance, the renewal of labour relations was at best half-achieved.

Political renewal was also limited. The first limitation was de Gaulle's insistence on continuity and on the power of the central state, keeping France firmly on the path laid down by the monarchy, the Revolution, and Napoleon. The provisional government was recognized by a consultative assembly and governed without real parliamentary control, while the parties that had supplied most of the

Third Republic's governments were swept away. But the Resistance failed to transform itself into a political movement from fear that the communists would dominate it, and only yielded a small centre-left party, the Union Démocratique et Socialiste de la Résistance (UDSR). Three major movements dominated the CNR, which became known as tripartism: the old communist party, the SFIO, and the new Mouvement Républicain Populaire (MRP). The communist party had considerable strength at the liberation, as it was the backbone of a multitude of Resistance bodies and possessed a vast network of printing presses. Its entry into government, for the first time in France, gave its rhetoric a split personality, as it had to maintain both the verve of militants and the responsible tones of a party of government. The SFIO leadership rejected ideological renewal and rapprochement with the new Christian democrat currents as proposed by Léon Blum, leading the Christian democrats to form the MRP, led by Georges Bidault, a Resistance leader believed to be close to de Gaulle and a former president of the CNR. Although it was Catholic, the MRP could support the republic and work with the SFIO and PC because its leaders and principles were associated with the Resistance, not Vichy.

In October 1945, after the return to France of prisoners of war and deportees, elections were held in which women voted for the first time. The MRP won the votes of many women: as the left had feared under the Third Republic, they voted for a Catholic party—but they also voted for the republic and for the left. De Gaulle put forward a double referendum that rejected a return to the Third Republic (approved by 96 per cent of those voting) and also limited the powers of this assembly; it was to draw up a new constitution within seven months and it could not overthrow the government. However, this personal success for de Gaulle was tarnished the very same day when three-quarters of the electorate voted for the three major left-wing parties; the Marxist parties (communist and socialist) had a majority, while the centre and right were humbled.

The tortuous debate on France's new institutions lasted until the end of 1946, and was of interest to politicians far more than to the general public. The Marxist left supported a regime based around an assembly, against the MRP's advocacy of the liberal concept of a balance of power between executive and legislative. De Gaulle, unsurprisingly, wanted to make the executive pre-eminent, and he resigned abruptly on 20 January 1946 when it became clear that this would not happen, declaring that 'the exclusive regime of the parties has reappeared'. The three leading parties then signed an alliance to form a government. But the first proposed constitution was rejected by a referendum on 5 May 1946 (by 53 per cent votes against), and when a second constituent assembly was elected straightaway, the MRP overtook both the PC and SFIO, who began a long decline. The new tripartite government was led by Bidault, and it redrafted the first proposal. The assembly remained as the leading body, elected by universal suffrage and proportional representation, but it was counterbalanced by a consultative upper chamber and by a President of the Republic elected by the assembly, with the traditional powers of this role. The constituent assembly aimed to reduce instability by defining a ministerial crisis strictly, with a motion of censure required to overthrow a government. This proposal was approved by a referendum, though it only gained the votes of a little more than a third of the total electorate. For all the counterweights, the Fourth Republic was still a parliamentary regime. The head of the government was still harried by debates in the Chamber, and the clauses about a motion of censure became redundant because governments were toppled by parties simply withdrawing their support from a coalition. The head of the government could only dissolve parliament under very precise conditions, so could not discipline parties with the threat of an election.

Constitutional details aside, events developed in such a way that instability was even worse under the Fourth Republic than under the Third. In May 1947, the communist ministers were evicted from the government as the Cold War developed, which ended tripartism and increased dependence on coalitions; this brought back some of the debris of the past and reinforced the role played by the heads of parties, who became the real powers in the regime. On the other wing, de Gaulle had rejected the nature of the institutions still being developed in a speech at Bayeux in June 1946. The Cold War encouraged his criticism of the regime, and he founded the Rassemblement du Peuple Français (RPF) in April 1947. This rapidly gained hundreds of thousands of members and had considerable success in the local elections of autumn 1947; it then demanded a national election in order to reform the nascent republic. The President of the Council of Ministers was appointed by the President of the Republic, but the holder of this office, Paul Ramadier, increased the power of parliament by putting his cabinet forward for approval by the deputies as well, which then became a tradition. Proportional representation fragmented the political landscape, and the extreme difficulties that confronted the country compounded this by splitting parties internally as well. Ministerial crises were both frequent (twenty-five governments in eleven years) and long (they lasted a month on average). So the rejection of the Third Republic in 1944–5 turned out to have been premature. Even the customs of the Third Republic flowed back: the second chamber gained the title of Senate, then the right to debate government policy and to pass motions of no confidence; the motion of censure was abandoned and motions of confidence were abused. The Fourth Republic interpreted national sovereignty as parliamentary sovereignty, and then reduced this to partisan politics. Petty calculations and personal conflicts carried the day. The modernization of France's institutions did not take place.

By the end of 1947, the regime relied on the 'third force' of the MRP, SFIO, and what was left of the Radicals, which governed until 1952. Both the government and public opinion slipped to the right as the Cold War took shape, but this did not hold the coalitions together. Six out of eight ministries fell on economic and social questions that divided free-market liberals from supporters of the planned economy. The third force pursued a vigorous defence of democracy against communism, mercilessly breaking communist-led strikes in the autumns of 1947 and 1948. The regime's achievements in foreign policy were substantial. Its policy was resolutely based around the Atlantic Alliance, accepting Marshall Aid and helping to create NATO. It also began the construction of European unity, in order to allow for the redevelopment and rearmament of West Germany that the USA required for the Cold War. The foundations of this were laid by the Monnet–Schumann plan for the European Coal and Steel Community and the Pléven plan for the European Defence Community (EDC). The final factor uniting the coalitions was a common colonial policy, which was to maintain the empire in full.

In the elections of 1951, the third force was reinforced by ingenious legislation which topped up proportional representation with extra seats for the majority parties. This benefited the Radicals and moderates (the centre-right) most of all, and a party of about 100 Gaullists added their voices to the moderates. The President of the Republic,

Vincent Auriol, saw that a more stable coalition could now be produced without the socialists, and the shift to the right continued. He appointed Antoine Pinay as President of the Council of Ministers in March 1952. Pinay, a small businessman from the depths of the country, had voted to give full powers to Pétain in 1940, and had been a member of Vichy's National Council. He conducted an orthodox financial policy to restore confidence in the franc, aided by favourable international economic conditions, and a tight labour policy, which provoked a burst of strikes in the summer of 1953. This 'little man in a grey hat' became a hero for those who had lost by modernization—the independents who formed another France from the worlds of employees and public servants. They felt that they had been abandoned since 1944, threatened by economic and social modernization as they had been in the 1930s, with the additional menace of colonial conflicts that threatened both their image of France and their protected markets. It was the accumulation of these conflicts that finished the centre-right majority, after interminable wrangling about the EDC. The colonial conflict in Indochina reached a peak in the summer of 1954, when French forces enticed the nationalist Viet Minh army to engage in a pitched battle instead of guerrilla warfare, around an airstrip at Dien Bien Phu. The plan backfired, French forces were routed on 7 May, and the government collapsed a few weeks later. The pitiless critic of this failed colonial policy was Pierre Mendès France.

Mendès France was the leading figure of the new France in the middle of the 1950s, in contrast to the traditionalist Pinay. His career was by then already long and brilliant. He had qualified as a barrister at 19, completed a noted thesis on the financial policy of Poincaré when he was 21, and was the youngest deputy in the country at his election in 1932 (as one of the Radicals' young Turks). He was the author of the Keynesian plan proposed by Blum's second ministry; he escaped from Vichy's prisons to become an airman for the Free French; at the Liberation, he resigned from the economics ministry of the provisional government because de Gaulle had not supported his rigorous financial policies. He was once again elected as a deputy, though he also served as an expert at the International Monetary Fund and as professor of political economy at the newly created École Nationale d'Administration (ENA). He was supported by young left-wing journalists at *L'Express*, the first French news magazine, in which they invented *mendésisme* and declared that Mendès was the man to whom France should turn. When he was appointed premier after the fall of Dien Bien Phu, he put a detailed policy to the Chamber in the form of a contract, point by point, together with a timetable for its execution. He also rejected the convention that the Chamber had a vote on his nomination. In one month, he signed an agreement in Geneva to end the French presence in Indochina and opened negotiations with Tunisia that took it to independence. After the Chamber rejected the proposed EDC (an issue on which Mendès did not stake his majority), he accepted the restoration of full sovereignty to West Germany and its rearmament within NATO. He also made minor adjustments to the constitution by re-establishing the legislative powers of the Senate. Finally, he launched a vast programme of Keynesian economic and social modernization, to encourage research and improve the country's infrastructure, with the aim of rapidly developing the French economy. Much of this policy is encapsulated by the term *aménagement du territoire*, which covers regional policy, urban development, and infrastructure such as roads and railways.

Mendès France explained his policy to the French people directly, over the radio on Saturday evenings. His popularity was real but ambiguous. The image of 'PMF' in the media was largely created by *L'Express* using modern publicity methods, and while the magazine was generally hostile to the regime of the Fourth Republic, Mendès himself remained a stalwart republican even though he had voted against the constitution.[5] Every one of his major decisions swelled the ranks of his opponents. The MRP never forgave him for the loss of Indochina or the failure of the EDC; the communists and many socialists condemned the rearmament of West Germany; the right rejected his economic policy. Political anti-Semitism played a part too: opponents of the Fourth Republic attacked it through Mendès, who was Jewish, as they had once attacked the Third Republic through Blum. On 6 February 1955, his government was overthrown by the developing Algerian crisis, which liberated the forces of *mendésisme*. From here on, PMF represented the promise of a rebirth of the left in the eyes of a younger generation, especially among those in the

---

[5] The use of initials instead of the full name of an organization, such as 'CGT', began around 1900. PMF was the first Frenchman to be generally known by his initials.

universities and in business. *Mendésisme* prepared the way for an alliance of the non-communist left which was finally realized by the reformed socialist party under Mitterrand (the Parti Socialiste, or PS) some twenty years later—but it also opened the road for what became the Gaullist method of rule, namely a personalized, active executive that relied directly on public opinion.

The right, too, was changing. In 1953, a publisher and bookseller from the south of France named Pierre Poujade began an anti-tax crusade of retailers and craftsmen; these groups were threatened by the end of shortages and by the modernization of distribution methods, both of which gave the upper hand in production and retailing to large-scale manufacturers and shops. Poujade was a gifted demagogue, a civilian General Boulanger who expressed the bitterness of the old order through a populist electoral campaign to 'ditch the deputies'. When his ministry fell in November 1955, the outgoing premier Edgar Faure dissolved the Chamber without hesitation (thus breaking the ban on this that had cowed ministers since the fall of MacMahon) in order to hold elections before *mendésisme* and *poujadisme* could take shape. Faure led a centre-right coalition against a centre-left coalition directed by Mendès France. The two coalitions were neck-and-neck, but the success of Poujade, with fifty deputies from rural France, gave the advantage to Mendès France. The President of the Republic followed the convention of nominating the leader of the largest party in the Chamber as head of the government, and this was the socialist Guy Mollet, for Mendès France led the smaller Radical party. The government kept its promises on social policy by introducing a third week of paid holidays, a car tax to fund aid for pensioners, and an agreement on healthcare. It also revitalized European policy by negotiating the Treaty of Rome to found the European Economic Community, in March 1957 granted independence to Morocco and Tunisia, and passed a framework law for sub-Saharan Africa. But these achievements were swamped by the Algerian war, which had come to dominate everything by 1957.

The crisis of French power

Throughout these three decades, developments inside mainland France were repeatedly disrupted by conflicts that originated outside its borders. This also challenged the country's self-image and sense of identity because they revealed that France was no longer a great power in command of its own destiny, as it had been for most of the nineteenth century. Under the two Napoleons, France had been able to redraw the map of Europe; under the early Third Republic it had conquered vast areas of Africa and Asia. The collapse of French power in Europe and across its empire led to new, and contradictory, directions in foreign policy, on one hand rebuilding its position in Europe and the world through partnerships in the North Atlantic alliance and the European community, and on the other rebuilding France as an independent world power.

In the aftermath of the First World War, there were two main arenas in which France could restore its power: its relationship with Germany and its empire. Its German policy was a story of successive, and cumulative, failures. When Poincaré returned as premier in 1926 he abandoned his policy of 1922, which had been to maintain French superiority over Germany through a strict interpretation of the Treaty of Versailles. He instructed Briand to continue the foreign policy begun by Herriot in 1924, namely a policy of détente both with Germany and with France's allies, and of collective security through the League of Nations. It became clear that collective security would not protect France when Germany withdrew from the Conference on Disarmament and the League of Nations in 1934. Louis Barthou, the foreign minister in 1934, drew the lesson that bilateral alliances were needed instead, and therefore opened negotiations with the Soviet Union, bringing it into the League of Nations. He was trying to build a Mediterranean pact when he was assassinated in Marseille in October 1934, alongside the king of Yugoslavia (the real target of the assassin). Yet these were piecemeal efforts to patch together alliances where they could be found, and they did not amount to a coherent system in the manner of Delcassé's diplomacy. Over the next four years France's position in relation to Germany worsened drastically as Hitler overturned the Versailles treaty clause by clause. Barthou's successor, Laval, negotiated a very loose pact of assistance with Moscow and drew close to Mussolini, leaving the latter free to act in Ethiopia in 1936. France's weak sanctions against Italy were enough to push Mussolini into Hitler's embrace without saving Ethiopia—though even these sanctions were vigorously opposed by the right. Germany itself remilitarized the Rhineland in March 1936 without provoking resistance from France: the country was diplomatically isolated (Britain did not protest either) and was in the middle of an election campaign under a caretaker premier. The military high command insisted that France could not risk challenging Hitler without a full mobilization, which the interim government did not dare to order. This meekness was born of the fear of conflict created by the Great War, from a misunderstanding of Hitler as being no different from any previous German leader, and from the internal paralysis of French politics by early 1936. The Rhineland reoccupation handed Germany a profound military and psychological victory. When the civil war erupted in Spain, Blum had to renounce his original policy of support for the Spanish republican government because of British opposition and because the socialist party, Popular Front coalition, and public opinion generally were severely divided on the issue. Anti-Fascism and pacifism separated. France showed the same paralysis in the face of the Anschluss of March 1938, when Austria and Germany were united. During the Czechoslovakian crisis that subsequently broke out, when Hitler made claims on Czechoslovakian territory, Daladier followed the British policy of compromise and appeasement, and yielded to German pressure at Munich. Czechoslovakia was abandoned, and France was left to gauge its impotence. It had the protection neither of Versailles, nor of collective security, nor of robust alliances.

The humiliation of Munich began to turn opinion round in both France and Britain. Italy's wild claims on Tunisia, Nice, Corsica, and Savoy, and Germany's dissection of Czechoslovakia in spring 1939 enabled Daladier to draw on a new-found resolution. The two allies gave a guarantee to protect Poland, which was clearly marked as the next victim of Nazi expansion. Instead of helping it, this guarantee doomed Poland because Hitler did not believe that Britain and France would honour it, while Stalin did. This allowed Stalin to sign the Nazi–Soviet non-aggression pact, leaving the western allies to fight Hitler while he watched (equally, Britain and France had been half-heartedly negotiating with Stalin in the hope that the Soviet Union would do their fighting for them). With this pact signed in August 1939, Hitler invaded Poland on 3 September, initiating the Second World War.

Defeat in 1940 and the subsequent armistice took French power to its lowest level since Waterloo. At first Vichy wished to become neutral in Germany's war against Britain, in order to nurture the national revolution at home. But a policy of collaboration grew following a meeting between Pétain and Hitler at Montoire, in October 1940. Pétain believed that he could improve France's position by negotiating with a conqueror who held the country at his mercy, and who forced France to give up more and more in order to prove its loyalty and independence, without ever giving the slightest reward. France counted for nothing.

The revival of French power after the war was of primordial importance for de Gaulle: in his words, 'France cannot be France without greatness'. The foreign policy he set out after the Second World War was little different from that pursued immediately after the First. The question of Germany, 'the central problem in the universe' since Bismarck, lay at the heart of his policy. In order to counter Germany and at the same time throw off the Anglo-American tutelage that had been so irksome during and after the war (he had not been invited to the summits of Teheran, Yalta, or Potsdam), de Gaulle revived the traditional system of an alliance with Germany's eastern neighbour by signing a pact with the Soviet Union in December 1944. He hoped that the USSR would support his policy of dissecting Germany, amputating the Rhineland and the Saar basin, and putting the Ruhr under international control. De Gaulle's evident legitimacy as French leader was strengthened by Churchill's support, fearful that the USA might withdraw from Europe again, as it had done after 1919. This enabled de Gaulle to win several flattering prerogatives: France received the German and Japanese surrenders, gained a permanent seat on the United Nations' Security Council, and took over one of the four occupation zones into which Germany was divided. This allowed France to block the reunification of Germany, which was the Anglo-American strategy, as relations between East and West deteriorated. France had thus regained some power, but as yet only the power to make a nuisance of itself.

This strategy towards Germany and France's western allies was reversed by the Prague coup of spring 1948, when the USSR brutally installed its puppets as the rulers of Czechoslovakia. No longer led by de Gaulle, France chose to depend on the USA instead of pursuing an independent line: economic and financial dependence came from the Marshall Plan and military dependence came through NATO. In June 1948, the French zone of Germany joined the Anglo-American bi-zone, and in 1949 France supported the creation of a sovereign West German state. The acceptance of German restoration was the result of the decision to align with the USA, and it simultaneously generated a new European policy. When the outbreak of the Korean War made the Cold War hot, it became imperative that West Germany should first be rebuilt and then be rearmed, in order to share the burden of defending western Europe against the USSR. This imperative produced the Monnet–Schumann plan and the Pléven plan. The logic behind this process was to find a way to restore German power—the bane of France for the past eighty years—that would be acceptable to the French people. The heatedness of the debates on the EDC showed how deeply divided opinion was. Despite this, European construction arose from the logic of this dual North Atlantic and Franco-German policy; it gained a real, positive momentum of its own when the Common Market was launched in March 1957, by the Treaty of Rome. At the depths of French dependence and weakness, just months after the disaster of the Anglo-French invasion of Suez and when decolonization had just begun, France laid the foundations for a realistic renewal of its power, taking Europe for its partner instead of the empire.

The end of empire

France awoke to the role that its empire could play in the restoration of its power after the First World War: until then, it had only really been of interest to the colonial lobbies who encouraged colonization and profited from it. The Colonial Exposition of 1931, held in the Bois de Vincennes outside Paris, was the moment when the mass of the population came face to face with the exotic fruits of its empire. Yet all the plans for developing the empire fell short of their goals, and instead it became a prop for struggling French industries. The Second World War increased the importance of empire excessively: possession of the empire was one of Vichy's main justifications for its sovereignty up to 1942, after which it switched to the Gaullist camp; thus it was the colonies that liberated their colonizer. Since France had lost its other sources of power by 1945 and its German policy had met a dead end, the empire became the key device to make France a great power again under its new name, the French Union—at the very moment that the winds of decolonization began to blow. The Fourth Republic refreshed the laws governing its colonies and promoted the myth of a free association that veiled the old colonial practices still in force. In Indochina, the retreating Japanese army gave way to Ho Chi Minh, who proclaimed the Democratic Republic of Vietnam. General Leclerc attempted to reconquer the country backed by negotiations, until the latter were sabotaged by the high commissioner in Indochina and the colonial lobby. By the end of 1946, guerrilla warfare had begun; by 1950 Chinese support for the Viet Minh and the Korean War turned this into a full-scale war fought as part of the Cold War. The USA had opposed French efforts to retain Indochina in 1945 because it was opposed to European imperialism; by 1950, it supported the French because the Viet Minh were communist. Washington paid 45 per cent of the costs of the war, making France its dependant once again. The decisive battle of Dien Bien Phu was lost just as negotiations, forced on France by the USA, began in Geneva. While the army was humiliated, the mass of the population was indifferent.

French policy towards its African colonies shifted rapidly after 1944. The activities of the well-developed nationalist parties in the protectorates of Morocco and Tunisia were severely repressed immediately after the war, until Mendès France promised to respect their autonomous status. Edgar Faure then ceded their independence, which was achieved in March 1956. The Fourth Republic also passed a framework law that granted internal autonomy to the remaining African colonies within the French Union. The Fourth Republic was set on the path of decolonization by consent when the Algerian war exploded.

For the French people, Algeria was not a colony but three departments of France, an integral part of the 'one and indivisible' republic. It sent deputies and senators to Paris like every other department, though only French citizens had a vote, and it was administered by a governor-general rather than a prefect. Its population comprised a million French citizens and eight million Muslims who held an inferior status. Long-standing grievances about the treatment of

Muslims and their lack of rights were fuelled by the physical hardships endured by the indigenous population during the Second World War, and by rapid population growth, especially in the cities. A warning sign of the troubles ahead came on VE Day itself, 8 May 1945, when a demonstration calling for equal rights turned into a massacre of settlers, in the small town of Sétif. French forces—and armed settlers—suppressed the rising at the cost of around 3,000 Algerian deaths. De Gaulle's provisional government and the Fourth Republic were no friends of the settlers (known as *colons* or *pieds noirs*) because they had been solidly behind Vichy, and a modest reform was made in 1947 by the creation of a new assembly that contained 120 members from both the French and Muslim communities. It was not enough: the assembly was largely powerless, and the elections were shamelessly rigged. The elimination of the old Arab aristocracy and the Muslim middle classes meant that the moderates who were elected had few followers. Most nationalists drew the lesson that peaceful reform would never come, and that violence was the only road to independence. The examples of the French Resistance and even more of the Viet Minh influenced their decision to rebel.

In order to create a united nationalist movement, the young leaders of Algerian nationalism took inspiration from the Geneva Accords and proclaimed the Front de Libération Nationale (FLN). They marked its creation with a series of seventy terrorist attacks in 1954 on the night of 31 October–1 November, while the settlers celebrated the festival of All Saints. Mendès France and his minister of the interior, François Mitterrand, refused to negotiate, but they did announce some reforms and named the Gaullist and ethnographer Jacques Soustelle as governor. In August 1955, the FLN provoked deliberately cruel massacres near the town of Constantine, in order to force the French and Muslim communities apart and to overturn the reforms. In reply to the murder of over 100 Europeans and Algerians opposed to the rebels, a savage repression killed between 1,000 and 3,000 Muslims. A political crisis ensued in Paris, until Mollet formed a coalition ministry in February 1956. He gave way to pressure from activists in Algiers and defined his policy as 'cease-fire, elections, negotiations', which demanded the surrender of the FLN as a pre-requisite to further developments. The Chamber of Deputies and Senate awarded special powers to the government, and by the summer of 1956 there were 400,000 soldiers in Algeria, mostly conscripts.

Mollet was haunted by the ghost of appeasement and the spectre of Munich, which pushed him into ordering the invasion of Suez, in the belief that this would cut the rear bases of the Algerian nationalists. Failure was complete, and the international community intervened. After the bombardment of a Tunisian village which killed sixty-nine people, including several children, the government was overthrown. The ministerial crisis lasted for several weeks, until the MRP leader Pierre Pflimlin, who was reputedly in favour of negotiations with the FLN, was due to be appointed as premier on 13 May 1958. This provoked rioting in Algiers by the settlers, who stormed the government buildings and made Generals Salan and Massu the heads of a Committee of Public Safety (resurrecting the name of the committee that had led the French Revolution in 1793–4). The army did not respond to the civilian government, and instead threatened to mount its own coup in Paris and to summon de Gaulle. Paratroops from Algeria landed in Corsica and took power there, to show that this was no empty threat.

The failure of successive governments to end the Algerian war from 1954 onwards had prompted more and more people to say that they needed de Gaulle to emerge from his self-imposed retirement, to save France once again. He himself had been cautiously communicating with the leaders of the Fourth Republic, notably Mollet, to reassure and negotiate with them. Summoned to Paris by the President of the Republic, de Gaulle was made the last President of the Council of Ministers of the Fourth Republic on 1 June; on the 2nd he was voted full powers, and on the 3rd his government was accorded the power to draft a new constitution. The Fourth Republic was no more.

Conclusion

Thus thirty years of crises reached their climax. The crisis of the Fourth Republic and the Algerian war was arguably more profound than Vichy had been. Although the fall of France and four years' occupation had been bloodier and more extreme, Vichy had been born and had died through foreign invasion; this disaster had to be resolved by France itself. At stake lay the power and identity of

France, and these two were inseparable. Despite the evolution of social structures to the advantage of salaried employees, the protection of the old independent groups lived on in the framework of empire and protectionism. France constantly obstructed world trade agreements in the name of protecting vital national interests, slowing down the rate at which its economy opened up and at which it could develop. The respective weight of different branches of industry and the size of companies changed little. There were indeed two Frances, which became ever more visible in the country's geography; in 1947 Jean-François Gravier published a profoundly influential book, *Paris et le désert français*, which set the basis for the policy of *aménagement du territoire* for the next thirty years. Modernization of the economy and society, the regime's institutions, and its foreign and colonial policies were unfinished business.

The crisis of 13 May ended ninety years of the parliamentary republic. The Vichy interlude had delayed political modernization by giving a stay of execution to the old republican, parliamentary tradition. It is easy to match the coalitions of the third force with those of republican concentration, the republican front with the Cartel des Gauches, Pinay with Poincaré. This culture had protected the social groups that supported it, made up of independent 'little men'. But the Fourth Republic had poor foundations to deal with the gigantic problems that destabilized, divided, and finally destroyed it. In its lifetime, it had created some innovations in technical parliamentary matters and had accelerated the rise to power of the top civil servants, henceforth moulded by the École Nationale d'Administration, whose power was reinforced by ministerial instability. The double crisis of French society and politics paralysed its power. France was dependent in turn on Britain, Germany, and the United States between the 1930s and 1950s. The retreat to the empire, which became France's biggest trading partner, was another expression of this decline. In these areas, the Fourth Republic was ravaged by powerful forces of change that the Fifth Republic harnessed. The Fifth Republic abandoned confrontation with Germany in favour of European construction. It accepted dependence on the western military alliance but decided to develop its own nuclear weaponry. Finally, having refused any possibility of decolonization, it agreed to it. It fell to the new regime to absorb all of these obstacles and these changes, and to mould a new politics from them.

6

A new republic, a new France: 1958–2002

The Algerian war was the final convulsion in the long crisis that started in the late 1920s. Out of it came the Fifth Republic, which transformed France's political system, accelerated economic changes that overturned traditional social structures, and revived its foreign standing with *élat* . It founded a new model for the republic in harmony with its era, just as the Third Republic had done in its time, and created a new role for France on the world's stage. This time it rested on the salaried middle classes, which had now become the dominant social class in the country. Yet France has not reached the end of its history, for there have been two distinct versions of the Fifth Republic, before and after 1974. The same forces of economic modernization and social transformation that renewed France went on to upset the balance of the regime by the 1970s, and the social effects of the economic recession that began in 1974 cracked de Gaulle's elegant construction. They accelerated the transformations already in progress, and added the impact of long-term mass unemployment, which produced problems that have destabilized the political system. The behaviour of the regime evolved rapidly as well. De Gaulle's monarchical republic became a double act of president and prime minister under Pompidou; power passed from one party to another with the elections of Giscard d'Estaing and Mitterrand. The alternation of power between left and right since 1981 has also produced the practice of 'cohabitation' between presidents and prime ministers from opposing parties. In international relations, the end of the Cold War and the development of the European Union also transformed global politics, and pushed France back into the wings once more.

A new regime

The Fifth Republic was founded in three months in 1958 and was completed in 1962. The National Assembly gave de Gaulle full powers to rule and then went on holiday; the main political parties maintained their presence by membership of the government (except for the communists), even if key posts were occupied by technical specialists, not politicians. Government business was prepared by the office of the President of the Council of Ministers, which was headed by Georges Pompidou. For the first time, the new constitution was drawn up by the government instead of a constituent assembly; the only limit on it was to maintain a parliamentary system, which taxed the lawyers directed by Michel Debré, the minister of justice, as they sought to marry this with de Gaulle's wish for a strong president and a weak parliament.

The President of the Republic was first chosen by an electoral college. He had the power to go over the head of parliament to the people by calling referenda; he could also dissolve parliament and rule with full powers for six months, in the case of a grave emergency. These powers were designed to overcome both the chronic instability of the Third and Fourth Republics and their inability to handle sudden emergencies such as 1940 or the Algerian war. The assembly was elected for five years by the first-past-the-post system, in order to produce clear majorities instead of coalitions. Its control over the executive was dismantled: its ability to force impromptu debates on government policy (interpellations) was abolished, sessions were cut back, and the agenda was fixed by the government, which became almost the only body able to propose legislation. Motions of censure and votes of confidence had to be passed by an absolute majority of all deputies, not just a majority of those voting. The goverment was given a power of veto and procedural rules that allowed it to cut debates short and limit amendments to its bills; a new Constitutional Council was created to check that laws were in keeping with the constitution. Ministers gave up their seats in parliament for the time that they served in government. All this shifted power from the Assembly to the President of the Republic, yet at the same time the government was given a vital role because the constitution stated that it 'determines and leads the nation's policy' and because it had to have the support of a majority in parliament. This introduced the risk of a dual leadership in this hybrid regime, half-presidential and half-parliamentary.

The constitution was unveiled on 4 September, the anniversary of the declaration of the Third Republic. It was supported by all the parties except the PC and the Union des Forces Démocratiques, a party created for the occasion by leading left-wing unionists and politicians, including Mendès France and Mitterrand. The electorate approved this massively, with 80 per cent of votes in favour—even a third of PC voters therefore approved of it. The first legislative elections in December threw out the sitting candidates, notably the leading lights of the Fourth Republic, and savaged the left. The communist party collapsed from 150 seats to just ten. A new Gaullist party, the Union pour la Nouvelle République (UNR), was created a few days before the elections, and proceeded to win 42 per cent of the vote. Together with its allies, it held two-thirds of the seats. On 21 December, de Gaulle was elected president by 78 per cent of the electoral college. He made Debré the head of a government which replaced the socialist ministers with UNR deputies and technocrats (the head of government was now known as the prime minister rather than as the President of the Council of Ministers). De Gaulle could now set to work rebuilding the greatness of France.

The liberation of Algeria from France—and of France from Algeria

The creation of a new regime was only one of the reasons that de Gaulle had been recalled in 1958. The other was to end the Algerian war. In 1944, de Gaulle believed that the empire formed one of the main sources of French greatness, but whatever his initial intention had been in 1958, he soon opted for a progressive decolonization. While Algerian nationalists fought to gain independence from France, de Gaulle realized that the cost of the war in terms of men, money, and international isolation meant that France needed to be liberated from Algeria. He had no emotional ties to Algeria (unusually for a career soldier, he had never served in North Africa), and took a purely pragmatic view of the situation. Although French forces defeated the FLN in the 'battle of Algiers' in 1957 and by 1959 had beaten the FLN across most of Algeria, the war had driven such a deep divide between the French authorities, settlers, and Algerians that no political settlement could be achieved. Elections were held for a single chamber of Europeans and Muslims, which gained no legitimacy in Algerian eyes, and a bold plan for economic and social development was drawn up, which remained on paper because it failed to attract investment. France could at best hope to occupy the country indefinitely, at tremendous cost, or let it go. In September 1959, de Gaulle spoke of self-determination for Algeria and for the first time envisaged its secession; when this was followed a few weeks later by the recall of General Massu, the hero of the battle of Algiers, this provoked the *colons* to put up barricades in Algiers in defiance; it took the authorities a week to dismantle them. De Gaulle's policy was vindicated in January 1961 by a triumphant referendum in France on the autonomy of Algeria, which enabled him to define decolonization 'as our interest and therefore as our policy'. Four former generals seized power in Algiers, supported by professional soldiers such as the Foreign Legion's parachute regiment, determined not to lose Algeria after all their sacrifices (and after defeat in Indochina), but the conscript rank and file were won over by a moving radio broadcast from de Gaulle and they abandoned the rebellious generals. Diehard partisans of French Algeria turned to terrorism by forming the Organisation Armée Secrète (OAS), and violence spread to mainland France. Atrocities worsened, infecting both France and Algeria. Nationalist fighters (*fellaghas*) mixed guerrilla warfare with terrorism and torture; the French army tortured the nationalists to break their cells; the OAS used terrorism against both Algerians and the French authorities, even attempting to assassinate de Gaulle for what they saw as his betrayal. The cycle of revenge can be summarized in a single story, that of Mohamed Badache, an Algerian living in Paris who was stopped by two policemen in October 1961.

'Shall we take him?'
'Yes, let's take him.'
'OK, get in. We're going to the police station.'
They went a long way in the darkness. About half past midnight, the side-car stopped on a bridge above the Seine. Mohamed Badache thought of the stories he had heard recently about drownings. The driver said, 'Let's go on.' 'If you want to kill me, do it here,' said the Algerian. The two policemen

laughed. 'No, no, we're only taking you to Vincennes.' Perhaps they were afraid that he might cry out. One of them put handcuffs on him and fastened them very tightly. The side-car drove off, then stopped in the Meudon forest. The policemen got him out. One of them stood in front of him and said, 'My brother was killed in Algeria by the *fellaghas*. The good must pay for the bad.'[1]

The policemen then strangled Badache, who managed to save his life by slipping two fingers between their rope and his neck.

Above the violence, negotiations continued with difficulty. On 18 March 1962 the Évian Accords recognized the independence of Algeria, and this was approved by 90 per cent of the French electorate in a second referendum. When France finally withdrew, around 700,000 *colons* and some loyalist Algerians fled to France, with a few more emigrating elsewhere, nursing bitter grievances against it and against Algerians, fuelling support for the far right in future decades (a number of National Front strongholds are towns in the south where many *colons* settled). The Algerians who had fought for them, the *harkis*, were abandoned in order to limit immigration; it is estimated that between 30,000 and 150,000 *harkis* and other Algerians loyal to France, along with any Europeans who had dared to stay behind, were killed by the victorious FLN. The furious violence of the OAS in the last few months of the war had finished any chance for Europeans to remain after Algeria gained its independence on 3 July 1962. With the war settled, de Gaulle announced: 'Henceforth France has its hands free.'

---

[1] J.-L. Einaudi, *La Bataille de Paris* (Paris, 1991), p. 90. A couple of nights later, on 17 October 1961, the FLN organized a demonstration by Algerians in Paris in protest against a curfew imposed on them. The city's police turned on them, murdering between 100 and 200 protesters. The events of this night were only fully exposed in 1991 by Einaudi. The official in charge of the Parisian police force at this time was Maurice Papon, who was revealed in the 1980s to have been active in the deportation of Jews and the fight against the Resistance as an official under Vichy, and in the torture of nationalists in Algeria before his promotion to be prefect of Paris.

The many faces of the Fifth Republic

The Gaullist monarchy

For more than forty years the Fifth Republic has presented the façade of a single, continuous regime. In reality, the practice of politics has taken several forms in that time, by different readings of the constitution and by different arrangements between the same institutions. The first change was to move from the dominance of one man, de Gaulle, to a diarchy of rule by president and prime minister under Pompidou and Giscard d'Estaing. This shifted from a diarchy where both president and prime minister are from the same party to cohabitation, which itself has varied between the different combinations of president and prime minister.

The long-drawn-out settlement of the Algerian question enabled de Gaulle to tailor the institutional system to his liking. It led to the creation of what his lieutenant Jacques Chaban-Delmas called the 'reserved domain' of major questions of national interest, including foreign policy, which were to be decided by the president alone without regard to the prime minister. It also led to the subordination of the government to the president. De Gaulle summarized the formula as 'the essential and the contingent': the president made the decisions and the government implemented them. He exercised his political authority in many ways. For example, there were no more debates in the Council of Ministers, and Antoine Pinay was summarily dismissed as a minister when he confessed his opposition to de Gaulle's Algerian policy. De Gaulle ruled by decree during the week of the barricades, and for six months after the generals' coup he ruled without parliament, as article 16 of the constitution allowed—even though the coup had quickly collapsed. The UNR, which was formed to provide 'the General's foot soldiers', was his obedient political instrument. Press conferences were carefully stage-managed and referenda were used to bypass parliamentary majorities, showing that power had changed hands.

In April 1962 de Gaulle sacked Debré as his prime minister and replaced him with a cultivated technocrat, an academic and banker who had served in de Gaulle's personal office but who held no elected office, Georges Pompidou. In the wake of a series of terrorist attacks by the OAS, de Gaulle proposed a referendum on the election of the President of the Republic by direct universal suffrage. Parliament voted against the government—only for de Gaulle to defend the latter and dissolve the former. In historical terms, this was 16 May 1877 once again: de Gaulle had republican culture and history against him as well as every constitutional lawyer and non-Gaullist politician. Yet de Gaulle won where MacMahon and Millerand had failed; he became the successor to the Napoleons when he was re-elected as president in 1965 by the direct will of the French people. The referendum of October 1962 completed the foundation of the regime when it was approved with 62 per cent of the population voting in favour. Beyond the conservative bastions of the east and west, the 'yes' votes came from the big, dynamic cities of the north: Gaullism broke the traditional left/right divide. In the legislative elections of November, the Gaullists defeated a *cartel des non*, an alliance of opponents of the referendum. The traditional, non-Gaullist right was wiped out, as the traditional left had been in 1958. De Gaulle confirmed the appointment of Pompidou as his prime minister. Henceforth the Fifth Republic was a presidential regime; in de Gaulle's words, 'the head of state, elected by the nation, is the source and possessor of authority'. This interpretation of the constitution was reinforced by the renewal of Gaullist majorities in 1967 and 1968. Parliament served merely to record the president's decisions, and the old party system lay in ruins. Yet the victory of the president was too complete for its own good, for the eclipse of parties and parliament did not mean that political tensions had been erased as well, only that they had to be expressed elsewhere—notably in the street.

The UNR became the party of government, as the Radicals had been in the Third Republic. It won votes with increasing success (32 per cent in 1962, 38 per cent in 1967, 46 per cent in 1968), and though it had trouble acting as a right-wing party because partisanship ran counter to Gaullism's culture of unity, the collapse of the traditional right and the UNR's predilection for authority pushed it in that direction. (Hence the contrasting views of Maurice Duverger, for whom Gaullism is a version of centrism, and René Rémond, for whom it is a variant of the right. Similar arguments apply to the two Napoleons.) The previously numerous centrist factions generically known as the 'independents' were reduced to the Independent Republican party led by the young minister of the economy and finance, Valéry Giscard d'Estaing, who had rallied to Gaullism. Despite their name, they were dependent on the UNR for their survival. The communist party remained loyal to Stalinism even as the Soviet Union renounced it; it fell back to 20 per cent of the vote, concentrated on its strongholds of the working-class red suburbs. It remained a force for opposition, but not for government. The SFIO was equally stuck. Its membership was ageing, controlled by the immovable Guy Mollet. Caught between its support for the government's Algerian policy and opposition to its constitutional and economic aims, it shrank to around sixty deputies. The political reconstruction of the left took place in two ways. Ideologically, renewal came from small clubs and committees born from opposition to the Algerian War and the means that the French army used to wage it. These means—retaliation, torture, and terror—provoked a profound moral crisis on the left and in Catholic circles, which fuelled campaigns similar to the Dreyfus Affair, mobilizing opinion through petitions, manifestos, and pamphlets. The Parti Socialiste Unifié (PSU) emerged from these groups in 1960. It united the dissidents and rejects from various left-wing parties, who were few in number but high in talent (such as Mendès France and Michel Rocard) and in new ideas. The PSU had platforms in the form of the student union UNEF, the trade union CFDT, and a magazine, *Le Nouvel Observateur*, which became required reading for left-wing intellectuals. These debates reached their peak in 1966 at a conference in Grenoble that defined a modern socialism, freed at long last from the fear that the communist party might overtake it from the left.

Since the presidency had become the axis around which the political system revolved, political parties had to change their structure so that they could fight presidential election campaigns. For the first campaign, in 1965, Gaston Defferre and the news magazine *L'Express* attempted to group together all the non-communist opponents of the Gaullists, from the SFIO to the MRP (recycling the 'third force'). Building this coalition was slow work, and Defferre was overtaken by François Mitterrand, who drew on the tradition of republican solidarity to form an alliance on the left that included the communists and excluded the Christian democratic centrists (recycling the *Cartel des Gauches*). The result of this was the Fédération de la Gauche Démocrate et Socialiste, formed in September 1965. The Christian democrats were stripped of leaders such as Bidault and

Soustelle, who had been condemned as supporters of the OAS; renewed and rejuvenated, the MRP led the political centre around the candidacy of Jean Lecanuet, who stood for a 'liberal, Atlantic and European' presidency and who reformed the MRP as the Centre Démocrate in 1966 on the back of this campaign.

In the presidential campaign of 1965, the main issue was the fair division of the fruits of economic and social progress. Television played a role in the election for the first time, for until then most people did not have a set, and state control of broadcasting meant that the opposition had been kept off the airwaves anyway. Viewers now saw the fresh faces of de Gaulle's opponents, with the surprising result that Mitterrand, the left's sole candidate, forced de Gaulle into the second round of voting, which de Gaulle duly won with 54.5 per cent of votes cast. The opposition was encouraged by this, and began to prepare their campaign for the parliamentary elections of 1967. Pompidou ensured that the right's candidates did not compete with each other, and managed to win a slight majority. The crisis of May 1968 (discussed later in this chapter) and the social fears that it generated had contradictory political effects. Its immediate effect was to hand de Gaulle a massive victory after he dissolved the assembly on 30 May, producing another 'incomparable chamber' to match that of Louis XVIII in 1815, more royalist than the king, more Gaullist than de Gaulle. But this conservative assembly did not understand de Gaulle's intentions to implement reforms based on the lessons that he had drawn from May's turmoil. Although Pompidou had been the bulwark of the regime in May and the architect of the June elections, de Gaulle replaced him with the austere Maurice Couve de Murville, the minister of foreign affairs, in order to reassert the presidential nature of the regime and the disposable nature of prime ministers. This began a formula repeated by most presidents since de Gaulle (including Pompidou himself), where an independent, reforming prime minister is replaced by one of the president's creatures, often without any charisma of his or her own. De Gaulle then opened up two areas for reform: the university system, and a major regional and political reform that would replace the Senate by a consultative chamber drawn from local authorities and socio-professional bodies. This project was put to the people in another referendum, and it inspired opposition well beyond the usual suspects, this time including the influential notables of the Senate and Giscard d'Estaing (who had been dismissed from the government in 1967). On 27 April 1969, 53 per cent of voters rejected the reforms, and de Gaulle resigned as president immediately. He died in November 1970.

Diarchy: Pompidou and Giscard

The ten years of Gaullist rule had enabled the institutions of the Fifth Republic to take root, and to evolve. When the regime's founder departed, commentators expected a thorough transformation in the way the state worked, as so much had seemed to depend on a unique personality. The regime did change, but not so profoundly; successive presidents donned de Gaulle's crown until Chirac lost it in 1997. The Fifth Republic had created a new model for the republic, without philosophical roots or specific historical precedents—only the Second Empire was akin to it. Its political culture emphasized the republic in the classical sense understood by de Gaulle, namely the *res publica*, the public sphere, the secular, impartial state that guaranteed the nation's stability and power, led by its president. The salaried middle classes sought its protection in their desires for increased consumption and social promotion. The state met their demands by orchestrating economic growth, distributing the wealth it produced and democratizing education—the main instrument of social advancement. The political and social systems of the country were thus bound together inseparably, and it was this unity that formed a new republican model. The Fifth Republic supported the values of the salaried middle classes as the Third had supported those of the independent middle classes.

This unity of the republic and its dominant social class has been the main reason for the survival of the regime's institutions and for the continuity of political life. The transition from de Gaulle to Pompidou was remarkably easy. Supported by the Gaullist parliamentary majority and by Giscard's party, Pompidou won over some centrists as well in exchange for a promise to relaunch France's European policy. The left had still not recovered from the shock of defeat in June 1968, and Pompidou won the second round of voting easily, winning 58 per cent of votes against the centrist candidate Alain Poher, on a slogan of 'change within continuity'. Often compared to Guizot, Pompidou believed that prosperity produced grandeur and therefore he defined his role in an original way by directing foreign policy on the one hand and by setting the strategic priorities for state-led industrial development on the other. Changes in government were limited to the prime minister, with the appointment of Jacques Chaban-Delmas, a loyal Gaullist from the Second World War and a reformer who wished to turn the 'blocked society' that had produced the events of May 1968 into a 'new society, prosperous, young, generous and free'. The two main instruments of this unblocking were liberalization (of television news, the rights of parliament, regional decentralization, and autonomy for the management of state-owned companies), and partnership (by the expansion of collective agreements, encouraging social dialogue, and the right to continued training and education). Though Pompidou himself scarcely believed in this approach, and the conservative majority in parliament had even less faith in it, this double-headed executive reached a peak of popularity, delivering electoral victories despite almost constant strikes and demonstrations. Despite this, diehard Gaullists connived with Pompidou against a popular and independent prime minister, and although the National Assembly continued to support him, Chaban-Delmas was dismissed in July 1972 amid a scandal caused by the publication of his tax returns in the press. Pompidou appointed an austere conservative Gaullist, Pierre Messmer, to head a ministry whose sole purpose was to fight the legislative elections of 1973. The left had by this time rebuilt itself: Mollet had finally been ousted by the SFIO in 1969, and Mitterrand's splinter group rejoined it at the 1971 party congress to form the new Parti Socialiste (PS). Supported by the big socialist federations of the Nord and the Bouches du Rhône, and the left wing of the party (led by Pierre Mauroy, Gaston Defferre, and Jean-Pierre Chevènement respectively), Mitterrand was elected as leader of the socialists the very day that he joined them. He made the party into an instrument for the conquest of power, to be achieved first by the unity of the left and secondly by a shift in the balance of power within the left at the expense of the communists (who had begun a belated, hesitant de-Stalinization in 1968). The PS and PC signed a common programme in June 1972, in which Mitterrand agreed to a vast programme of nationalization in exchange for which the PC accepted French membership of NATO, the development of the European Economic Community (EEC), and political pluralism.

The 1973 legislative elections were very close, and the vote of the right was squeezed by the left as its realignment paid off. But the government seemed unable to take advantage of its victory to relaunch its domestic policy, nor was it able to seize the initiative at a very delicate point in international affairs, when Egypt and Israel fought the Yom Kippur War in October 1973. The reason for this only became clear when the death of Pompidou was announced on 2 April 1974, and the French people learnt that he had been ill for some time. The resulting presidential elections of 1974 were the first where an avalanche of candidates put themselves forward, though many never made it to the first round of voting. Of the twelve who made it that far, Mitterrand was, unsurprisingly, the left's single candidate, while the right was divided between Chaban-Delmas and Giscard d'Estaing, who had similar positions as reformists. Giscard won through to the second round thanks to the defection (or treason) of forty-three Gaullist deputies led by Jacques Chirac, Messmer's minister of the interior, and to his superior media appeal. In the second round, Giscard defeated Mitterrand by a mere 420,000 votes, with just 12.5 per cent of the electorate abstaining. The old political and geographical divides between left and right, which Gaullism had effaced, also reappeared clearly.

Giscard d'Estaing, the first non-Gaullist President of the Fifth Republic, was the political heir to the Orléanist and liberal right allied to business interests of previous regimes. He was also the physical heir to these circles both through his own family and by his marriage to a granddaughter of the ironmaster Eugène Schneider. Hostile to ideology, Giscard wanted to build a consensus around the political centre in a middle-class society. He cultivated a relaxed image in office, dining in the houses of unknown, modest French families. He invented government departments to develop his vision of a new France, even though the election had revived the traditional division between left and right. Chirac was rewarded for his support when he was appointed prime minister, aged 41, with the task of controlling the Gaullist deputies in parliament and reconciling them to their weak presence in government (just four ministers out of fifteen, even though they made up most of the right's parliamentary majority). Giscard's personal office was filled with young liberal *énarques* (graduates of the ENA), who supervised the government's actions. This set the stage for several hard battles before the president could put forward an ambitious reform programme, against the opposition of the conservatives. Among his political reforms, Giscard cut the age of civil and political majority to 18, gave members of parliament the power to ask the Constitutional Council to check that new laws were constitutional (previously only the government had this right), and created privately owned radio and television channels. The most difficult battles were over divorce and the legalization of abortion. The law of 1884 had permitted divorce if one party was at fault, not by mutual consent; this became legal in 1975. The right to abortion had been one of the main demands of feminists since the late 1960s; the defence of the proposal by Simone Veil brought her into the front ranks of politicians. It met fierce opposition from the Catholic church, doctors, and two-thirds of government deputies, and only became law thanks to the votes of the opposition. More ambitious structural reforms (such as a general value-added tax and a revision of company law) remained blocked. The theoretical and practical need for educational reform was clear: sociologists highlighted the social dimension to inequalities in the school system, which obstructed the republican goal of advancement through education, and every spring saw protests by university students and lycée pupils against failings in the system. At last, the Haby law established a single system for secondary education between the ages of 11 and 16, as had been advocated since 1918.

These reforms were too much for the Gaullists to bear. They opposed Giscard's policies as social democracy, as the policies of the opposition, just as they had harrassed Chaban-Delmas. After poor local election results in 1976, Chirac called for a return to right-wing policies and early elections to the National Assembly, to cut short the left's preparations for the elections due in 1978. He resigned abruptly in August 1976, the first time a prime minister had resigned instead of being dismissed in the Fifth Republic. From one perspective, his replacement by Raymond Barre showed that economic and social questions would dominate governments' agendas in future; it also re-emphasized the president's power to appoint a man from outside the political mainstream, as Pompidou had been—though Barre was not a Giscardian loyalist. Chirac was re-elected as deputy in his Corrèze stronghold, and refounded the Gaullist party as the Rassemblement pour la République (RPR) in December 1976 (the UNR had become the UDR in 1968). In reply, Giscard federated the different centrist and liberal factions into the Union pour la Démocratie Française (UDF) on the eve of the elections.

The battle raged between the two parties of the right, notably at the local elections of 1977, when Paris was allowed to elect its mayor: since the Commune of 1871, it had been the only municipality banned from doing this. Chirac won the mayorship against Giscard's candidate. Outside Paris, the left won two-thirds of the big cities, with the socialists clearly ahead of the communists. This prompted the PC to scupper plans to revive the common programme of 1972, with the result that the left was once again divided on the eve of the elections. The left won the first round of voting in March 1978, only to fall behind at the second round in terms of seats won. On the right, victory came from the UDF alone because the RPR fell away. It was now the turn of the right to be re-balanced. The next battles were over the first direct elections to the European Parliament. Chirac launched his platform in December 1978 in stridently Gaullist tones, but to no avail—the UDF largely won the European elections.

From 1974 onwards, economic difficulties had become the main factor in social and political life. France was immediately exposed to the global recession that began that year because its borders were now open (in contrast to 1929), and eventually realized that it could not pursue policies that ran counter to those of its partners. French economic policy was initially out of step with other western states because it was committed to the measures agreed in 1968, and so could not counter the inflationary surge of the late 1960s by restrictive fiscal policies; instead, the franc was devalued in August 1969 in order to counter inflation. The resulting rapid growth further fed the ambitions of the 'new society'. Giscard d'Estaing, in control of economic policy as the minister of finance before his presidency, attempted to fine-tune the economy by alternating quick bursts of stop/go policies, putting on the brakes between bursts of growth in January 1971, December 1972, and December 1973. The oil crisis of October 1973, when oil prices quadrupled after the Yom Kippur War began, came as a severe shock, both by the sharp rise in prices that it caused and by the sharp drop in production in debt-laden industries. Giscard's plan of June 1974, when he was president, made the recession worse, and rising unemployment henceforth became the main symptom of the economic crisis, along with steep inflation and growing instability of exchange rates. Faced by constant strikes to fight redundancies, the prime minister, Jacques Chirac, announced a plan to restart the economy. Growth remained above 3 per cent but it was erratic and did not lower unemployment, which reached a million in November 1976. Just as the tail-end of the baby boom joined the labour market, they found companies shutting down or cutting their workforces in order to restore profitability. The franc was forced out of the European monetary snake (this required members to limit fluctuations in the value of their currency within an upper and lower bound). Raymond Barre was made prime minister by Giscard, who praised him as 'the best economist in France', and this appointment ushered in a better understanding of the crisis. Barre's first target was to reduce inflation, and he began by blocking pay and price rises, supported by long-term measures to redress the budget and state spending. Given the unpopularity of these measures, it was a surprise when he won the 1978 legislative elections; this enabled him to return to market economics by the abandonment of price controls, the end of public-sector subsidies, and strong encouragement for savings. These policies were soon derailed by a sharp rise in American interest rates which forced France to tighten its monetary policy too, in order to hold its place in the European Monetary System (the EMS was the successor to the snake; France had joined it March 1979). A second oil crisis in 1979 was made worse by the strength of the dollar, which doubled its value against the franc. The old industrial sectors, which were major employers, were swept away by the recession.

The end of Giscard's presidency was devoted to fighting these problems in the economy, which had now lasted for the whole of his term of office. The election of 1981 was an open race: both the right and left were divided. In the event, the war fought between the UDF and RPR damaged the right much more than the war between the PC and PS. Giscard eliminated Chirac in the first round, but found himself the target of attacks by both Mitterrand and Chirac. On the left, the rift with the communists won floating voters over to Mitterrand because he was no longer seen to be in debt to the PC. On 10 May 1981, Mitterrand was elected as President of the Republic.

Alternation: the pendulum swings from right to left . . . and back again

The switch from right to left was a substantial shock in a country that had been ruled by the right for the whole of the Fifth Republic, twenty-three years. Explosions of joy around the place de la Bastille in Paris, a left-wing district as well as a symbol of the Revolution, were countered by the suspension of trading on the stock exchange as prices tumbled. Mitterrand went in solemn ceremony to the Panthéon to place a rose on the tombs of Victor Schoelcher (who abolished slavery in French territories), Jean Jaurès (to represent socialism and pacifism), and Jean Moulin (martyr of the Resistance). His first prime minister was the deputy mayor of Lille, Pierre Mauroy, whose blunt speech contrasted with the smoother tones of his predecessors, and the whole government had a refreshing noisiness to it. Mitterrand then dissolved the Assembly in order to win a majority for Mauroy's ministry; the left won the legislative elections easily thanks to the high level of abstention among dismayed right-wing voters. The PS held a majority on its own, with twice as many votes (38 per cent against 16 per cent) and five times as many deputies as the PC. Mitterrand could afford to include four communists in Mauroy's ministry now that he did not have to rely on them.

France's institutions were profoundly reformed under Mitterrand. The Defferre law on decentralization transferred powers that had been the preserve of the prefects for nearly two centuries to local authorities. The death penalty, legislation on state security, and special tribunals were abolished by Raymond Badinter, the minister of justice and one of the country's leading lawyers. Numerous measures were taken to democratize the republic: reforms of hospitals, of the relationship between landlord and tenant, of television and radio, of the universities, of the ENA. Finally a major bill to abolish private schools and to unify education within the secular state system was unveiled in December 1982. In economic policy, the new administration nationalized the five best-performing groups in French industry, the two largest financial companies, and thirty-six banks. State planning had returned. Workers' rights were strengthened; the minimum wage was raised; family allowances and the minimum old age pension were boosted by 25 per cent. The government aimed to distribute jobs better by cutting the working week to thirty-nine hours, giving workers a fifth week of paid holidays, and reducing the age of retirement to 60.

The government rapidly found itself under fire from two sides, just as the Popular Front had been in 1936. On one side, socialist and communist militants demanded further reforms, while on the other there was strong resistance from every interest group that felt threatened by the government. The rump parliamentary right tried to draw these malcontents together by energetic opposition to legislation. Opinion polls, by-elections, and local elections in 1982 and 1983 showed that the popularity of the left was crumbling rapidly, along with its whole economic policy. Its expansionist policies forced the franc to be devalued by 8.5 per cent, still within the framework of the EMS, yet even after this the main beneficiaries were German companies that exported goods to France; the trade and budget deficits worsened, inflation picked up speed again, and the left's natural supporters, workers and trade unionists, were being thrown out of work. The government attempted to correct this by a second devaluation in June 1982, accompanied by some budget cuts, followed by a third devaluation in January 1983—but despite these measures its whole policy was now in question. France could either recover the freedom to follow the policy it wished and quit the EMS (which ran the risk that France might enter a long decline if there were no external constraints on the economy), or reaffirm its commitment to Europe and to modernization. The electoral failure of the socialists in the local elections of March 1983 prompted the government to opt for the second course. It proceeded to adopt a more rigorous, conventional economic policy that effectively condemned the long tradition of socialist economics.

This change of direction undermined the government fatally, though its downfall actually came from opposition to its educational programme. Despite considerable efforts to reconcile the ardour of the secular camp and the supporters of Catholic schools, who were close to the right-wing opposition, politicians on the right could not resist the chance to exploit the issue. Demonstrations in favour of private schools were remarkably successful. The European elections of June 1984 produced a sensational result: abstentions were high, the PS fell to 20 per cent of the vote—and the National Front surged forward to take 11 per cent of the votes cast. It has remained an essential part of French political life up to the present. The following

Sunday, a million people gathered in Paris to demonstrate in favour of independent schools. Mitterrand withdrew the proposal to abolish them, and accepted the resignation of Mauroy's ministry in July. Since the 1920s, the main division between left and right in France had been their support for socialist or capitalist economics. In the early 1980s, France found that it could not stand alone against the global trend towards free market economics, and at a stroke this fundamental division was largely erased. Conquering the economic crisis became the primary goal of political life, and at every election since then the voters have punished governments for failing to do this, giving victory to the opposition. The growing tide of abstentions and protest votes for the extreme right and the extreme left are other signs of disarray and dismay.

The new ministry was led by Laurent Fabius, a brilliant technocrat aged just 38. It was made up of Mitterrand loyalists, with no communists in it. The declared aim was no longer 'to change life' but 'to modernize and unite', in other words to appease. Reforms were minor, or by agreement; for example the school system was told to educate 80 per cent of a year group to the level of the baccalaureate by 2000. Appeasement took time to work, while nationalist disorders in New Caledonia and the *Rainbow Warrior* affair tarnished the image of the prime minister (in July 1985, a journalist was killed when the French secret services planted a bomb that sank a Greenpeace ship protesting against French nuclear tests in the Pacific). Support for the PS slowly crept back up, so the government switched the voting system to proportional representation to limit any damage in the 1986 legislative elections. The RPR–UDF coalition narrowly won, and the socialists had a good result with 215 seats. But proportional representation also let the National Front into parliament, with thirty-five deputies.

Alternation and cohabitation: Mitterrand and Chirac

With Mitterrand still president and the right in control of the National Assembly, the first period of cohabitation began. As there were just two years to run before the 1988 presidential elections, much of this first cohabitation was a long prelude to the campaign proper. This time the ideologists were on the right, in the new parliamentary majority. As head of the largest party, Chirac was prime minister again, this time pursuing free market economic policies (termed 'ultra-liberal' in France) after the examples of the USA and UK. Almost twenty groups were privatized, though they were protected from full-blooded stock market capitalism because large blocks of equity were sold to selected companies that formed a hard core of friendly shareholders. The government also freed prices totally, lifted foreign-exchange controls, cut taxes, and abolished the tax on wealth. Companies were encouraged to take on more staff through greater flexibility in the organization of labour and by measures to simplify redundancy—strict controls on dismissals had meant that firms hesitated to expand their workforces if they could not cut them again when the business cycle turned down. The results of these policies were mixed. Growth slowly accelerated and stopped unemployment from rising for a year, but severe pressure on the franc and on the country's trade deficit forced two further devaluations. Their achievements were not enough to carry the day against massive strikes and demonstrations opposing reform in December 1986, against the disquiet these reforms created within the majority itself, against Mitterrand's tactical undermining of his prime minister, and against the demagogy of the National Front.

The presidential election of 1988 brought no surprises. Chirac's pre-election hyperactivity contrasted with 'the tranquil force' of the president, who recovered his popularity as Chirac lost his. Chirac emerged as the right's front-runner from the first round, narrowly ahead of Raymond Barre and harried by the National Front leader, Jean-Marie Le Pen. Mitterrand won the second round of elections on 8 May 1988 with over 54 per cent of the votes cast. In keeping with the 'united France' proclaimed by Mitterrand, the new government led by Michel Rocard included centrists as well as socialists. The Assembly was dissolved for new elections in June 1988, held under the first-past-the-post system once again, and the PS emerged without an overall majority. The centrists proved unwilling to enter a coalition, despite the success of the 'Rocard method' in rapidly defusing tensions in New Caledonia. Rocard attacked several fundamental issues facing the country, though this approach was often difficult to 'communicate' to public opinion. Protest movements continued, though this time the most serious was the sudden—but henceforth endemic—eruption of violence in the outer suburbs, the *banlieues*. Rocard's achievements were considerable: he launched an attack on poverty at its base by restoring the minimum income (to be funded by a tax on wealth), and on social imbalances, by creating a new social welfare tax and by discussion of pension reforms; in addition, the civil service was overhauled and a new plan for the universities was launched. The Rocard method appeased the right/left divide as well, to the outrage of elements within the PS itself, which were encouraged by Mitterrand. These disagreements exploded at the 1990 party congress and repelled voters, who abstained massively (63 per cent did not vote on the referendum on New Caledonia) or voted for extremists. After the Gulf War, which had briefly united opinion behind the executive, Rocard was dismissed mid-term, as Pompidou and Chaban-Delmas had been.

This dismissal was the start of a profound crisis in the PS that did much to discredit Mitterrand's second presidency. Against the background of a weakening economy, the government of Edith Cresson was a disaster. The appointment of a woman as prime minister might have pleased public opinion; the appointment of a former mistress of the president did not. The brutal authority of her decisions and the crudeness of her tone alienated the public as much as it did the politicians who had to work with her. The PS was engaged in a civil war between supporters of Rocard and of Fabius—the prize was to succeed Mitterrand as the left's presidential candidate. It was finally hit by a series of scandals that involved both fraudulent personal enrichment and illegal party financing. One of the perennial problems of political parties in France, low levels of membership, had raised its head again. Both the PS and the RPR had used illegal methods to raise funds for their campaigns in the absence of adequate income from membership fees. The PS slumped to 18 per cent of the vote at local elections in March 1992. Pierre Bérégovoy, who had embodied the policy of a strong franc for nearly ten years, became prime minister in an effort to stave off disaster in the legislative elections of 1993. The public's rejection of state authority largely explains the narrow success of the referendum on the Maastricht Treaty (passed by 51 per cent of the vote) even when opinion polls showed that 70 per cent of the population favoured European integration. The 1993 elections duly punished the socialists, who were reduced to sixty seats, with twenty-four falling to the communists; haunted by growing accusations of corruption in Mitterrand's entourage and the electoral defeat, Bérégovoy committed suicide a month after the elections. Though the right only won 40 per cent of the vote, it had a crushing majority with 485 deputies. Chirac was reluctant to repeat the misadventure of his previous cohabitation, and nominated his 'friend for thirty years' Édouard Balladur, a former minister of the economy, to be prime minister.

Cohabitation in 1993 to 1995 was very different because Mitterrand would not stand at the next election, having admitted that he had been ill since 1981. In principle, Balladur was not a candidate either, being Chirac's loyal henchman. With no personal rivalry at stake, this second cohabitation was much more harmonious than the first. The government was more centrist and less dogmatic than in 1986, relations between the president and prime minister were courteous, and Balladur was for a long time popular. However, his policy was much the same as Chirac's had been, balancing the budget, cutting social spending, and restricting immigration through the Pasqua laws (these limited immigration by family members, the rights of asylum, and access to French nationality). The government pursued free market economic policies, launched a new round of privatizations, and favoured private education. Balladur appeared calm and resolute throughout events such as the ERM (Exchange Rate Mechanism) crisis in the summer of 1993 (when sterling was forced out) or the final phase of GATT negotiations that autumn. Increasingly, right-wing politicians reckoned that he would be a better candidate than Chirac for the presidency in 1995, and he was the natural candidate for the centrist and liberal strands within the right. He eventually put his name forward as a candidate, to the horror of Chirac's supporters, only to be overtaken in the first round of voting by Chirac, who had risen in the polls on the theme of 'social fracture'. Le Pen polled 15 per cent of the vote (and was the winner in seven departments) and another 5 per cent went to Philippe de Villiers, of the Catholic, traditionalist, nationalist right. The real surprise of the election was the performance of Lionel Jospin, the socialist candidate, who put himself forward after Jacques Delors had declined to enter the contest. Jospin won the first round of voting and only narrowly lost the second round to Chirac.

Alain Juppé was appointed as the head of a government that ruled in opposition to the promises made by Chirac during the campaign. Having based his election campaign on the theme of social exclusion, Chirac declared that the best way to fight exclusion was through economic growth, and he pursued rigid free market policies to achieve this. The government rapidly lost popularity: a plan to increase employment was to be financed by higher taxes and corruption scandals hit the RPR as they had hit the PS before, even threatening Chirac himself. In November 1995 the government put forward proposals to cut public spending by reform of the health system, whose finances are in a perpetual crisis, and by a freeze on the wages of public sector workers. These proposals were met by a strike of railway workers that spread rapidly from 24 November onwards. By early December it had become a general strike, supported by massive demonstrations marching to the cry of 'Tous ensemble, tous!' ('All together'), previously used by supporters of the multi-ethnic French soccer team. This strike movement brought together unemployed workers and strikers for the first time, to the joy of sociologists. It was a protest by French society against a technocratic, arrogant central authority and against the constraints imposed by Brussels and the financial markets—constraints that impelled governments to increase taxes, decrease job security, and make constant appeals to people to tighten their belts and work harder. The authorities retreated in the face of these massive protests, and Juppé lost his majority soon afterwards. Since then, every profession that has felt itself threatened by reform has repeated this mobilization, taken to the streets, and won its case: teachers, doctors and nurses, policemen, and even—for the first time ever—gendarmes in uniform.

Although he already had a majority in the National Assembly, the Senate and across most of local government, Chirac gambled by calling new legislative elections in 1997 while the socialists were still in disarray, in order to reassert his authority and secure a majority that would last until the end of his presidency, thus avoiding the cohabitations that had blighted Mitterrand's reign. This dissolution at the whim of the president was alien to French political culture and the electorate punished Chirac's decision alongside Juppé's ministry. The right had its worst result since 1958, and the presence of far-right candidates in the second round helped to split the vote further (seventy-eight constituencies saw a three-way battle between left, conventional right, and the far right in the second round). This gave victory to a 'plural left', a flexible alliance of socialists, communists, and ecologists, led by Jospin. Far from guaranteeing that he would avoid cohabitation for the rest of his presidency, Chirac condemned himself to it for a full five years. For the first time, the President of the Fifth Republic was subordinate to his prime minister.

A former Trotskyist and *énarque*, Jospin joined the PS in 1971 and had become its number two by 1979, before replacing Mitterrand as head of the party in 1981. He had served as minister of education under Rocard, when he had kept his distance from the decline of Mitterrand and his coterie. He was able to plan his action as prime minister over the full length of the legislature, in contrast to earlier cohabitations that only lasted two years before presidential elections took place; and his approach owed more to Rocard's experience than to the other socialist ministries. The reduction of unemployment was the priority for his economic policy: to achieve this, 250,000 jobs were created for young people and the working week was reduced to thirty-five hours. Together with a favourable international economic climate, unemployment fell by more than a million, the first substantial reduction for thirty years. The public sector retreated in the 1990s: taxes were cut, telecommunications were opened to competition, and Renault was privatized. Renault's Boulogne-Billancourt factory, stronghold and icon of the French factory worker, was closed. Stimulated by the opening of world markets, the consolidation of companies accelerated again—this time often alongside European partners—and elevated some French firms to the front rank of global businesses, such as Bouygues, Total Fina Elf, or Vivendi Universal.

Other notable reforms included the Pacte Civil de Solidarité (PACS), a civil union that gave rights to unmarried couples including homosexuals, the establishment of male–female equality among electoral candidates, and the reduction of the presidential term to five years. These changes, combined with Jospin's style of government, without charisma but also without demagogy, succeeded in maintaining his popularity throughout his term, and made him the favourite for the presidential rematch with Chirac in 2002 right up to the start of the election campaign. Jospin did alienate some groups, especially in the countryside. Hunters transformed themselves into a political force to oppose European regulations (which placed restrictions on the season for shooting wild and migratory birds), and they had a remarkable success in the European elections of 1999 when they outscored the communists. Farmers, accused of pollution and even of poisoning during the BSE crisis, opposed any reform of the Common Agricultural Policy (CAP), and here they were supported by Chirac, eager to adopt the pose of a countryman. José Bové, leader of the Confédération Paysanne since 1987, became the hero of anti-globalization campaigners by his destruction of a McDonald's building site on 12 August 1999. Surprisingly, the other group offended by Jospin were schoolteachers, who are traditionally loyal to the socialists. They were roughly treated by Jospin's minister of education, Claude Allègre, a volcanic vulcanologist who was finally chased from office by demonstrations in the autumn of 1999.

The successive failures of governments to combat the long economic and social crisis explain the massive and repeated swings from left to right and back again that have characterized French political life since the middle of the 1980s. These swings have made cohabitation into the dominant form of political life, though it is entirely against the spirit of the Fifth Republic set out by de Gaulle. Governments that have tried to enact major economic reforms from either the left or the right (as with Mauroy in 1981–3, Chirac in 1986–8, and Juppé in 1995) have found themselves blocked by the failure of these policies, massive demonstrations in the street, and rejection at the polls. The future of the regime itself has now come into question.

Economic modernization and social transformation

The years of plenty

France prospered as never before during the second half of the *trente glorieuses*, from 1960 to 1974, under the direction of the state. The economy grew by 5.8 per cent a year in real terms, even faster than West Germany. Since 1974, growth has been slow and intermittent, and it has generated severe imbalances—most seriously, society has been destabilized by mass unemployment.

The foundations for this new phase of economic development were laid out in December 1958 (the Pinay–Rueff plan), and its main device was the opening of French borders to trade, breaking with the protectionism established by Méline almost a century before. A new franc was introduced, worth 100 old francs, which was used to mask a devaluation of 17 per cent in the value of the currency; the indexation of prices was ended; the budget was balanced; and France's commitment to the Common Market was reaffirmed. Customs duties were steadily lowered from 1959 onwards, until by 1968 they had been abolished within the EEC and lowered by 90 per cent for trade with OECE (now OECD) countries. Foreign investment in France rose fivefold. Exports rose from 10 per cent to 17 per cent of GDP by 1970; 55 per cent of this was now with France's European partners, compared to 10 per cent in 1958. The franc zone of the former empire counted for only 5 per cent of trade.

State planning and the substantial public sector (170 companies generating 15 per cent of GDP) were ideal instruments for de Gaulle, who shared Napoleon's urge to direct the economy like an army on manoeuvres. The state orchestrated a dramatic series of mergers in order to build national champions in each branch of industry, so that these giants could use their domestic oligopoly as a springboard for conquering European markets. Consolidation tripled; investment rose by 8 per cent a year, reaching 25 per cent of GDP at the end of the 1960s. The state restructured old industries such as iron and steel making in 1966, encouraged high-technology companies to merge as well, and organized the transition from coal power to oil power. The number of industrial workers rose to 8.5 million in 1974, or 40 per cent of all employees in the secondary sector; even more significant was the increase in productivity as new factories were built using new machinery with a better organization of labour, and were staffed by better-qualified workers. These improvements cost money, which firms could not afford out of their own profits. They therefore borrowed heavily from 1965 onwards, increasing the capital employed per worker in order to compensate for substantial increases in labour costs. Success was not universal. While the motor industry boomed (four companies built 2.7 million vehicles in 1970), the chemicals industry was split between the giant multinational Rhône-Poulenc and a mass of struggling small companies; construction and textiles were still dominated by small firms.

Agriculture underwent its own industrialization, and achieved even higher productivity gains than industry. The first reason for this was that the rural exodus speeded up, with 100,000 farmers and labourers migrating each year; their number fell from six million in 1946 to just two million by 1974. Secondly, mechanization became universal, and the number of tractors in use rose from 120,000 to 1.3 million over the same period. The massive use of fertilizers and industrial fodder for livestock also contributed to the increase in productivity per head. The state oversaw this agrarian transformation by promoting the recomposition of farms, where owners swapped scattered parcels of land in order to consolidate their farms in single units. It supported farm credit (a monopoly of the Crédit Agricole bank) and agronomic research, organized the market for the chief crops, and guaranteed their prices. This model was extended across the EEC in 1962, in the form of the CAP, to the great benefit of French agricultural exports. In parallel, the Debré law of 1960 and Pisani law of 1962 helped to reform agrarian structures and land rights, and rejuvenated the workforce. These developments rested on the support of a new generation of farm unionists committed to reform, largely recruited from a Catholic movement, the Jeunesse Agricole Chrétienne. While industry and agriculture made great productivity gains, the largest number of new jobs came in the service sector. By 1974 half the labour force was employed in the tertiary sector, which generated three-quarters of all new jobs, especially in banking, telecommunications, and public administration. A side effect of this was the greater feminization of the workforce: women were employed in the service sector much more often than in industry or agriculture.

Rapid growth also produced some serious imbalances. Inflation was higher in France than elsewhere, and the rigour of the Pinay–Rueff plan could not be sustained without reining in growth. The government's wage policy softened in 1961, and the budget went into deficit because of the state's numerous commitments. De Gaulle asked his minister of finance, Giscard d'Estaing, to stabilize the economy, which he did from 1963 through a free-market plan that increased prices but slowed growth as well. Inflation led to conflict over wage claims, but it also aided investment by reducing the value of debts held by companies and by the state. The speed of transformation also upset social stability. Despite help for consolidating farms, and the consent of farm unions in the rural exodus, the 'end of the peasantry' (to use a phrase of the sociologist H. Mendras) was accompanied by violent demonstrations, which have become a recurring event in France since the first road blocks in 1960 and the occupation of the sub-prefecture of Morlaix, in Brittany, the next year. The closure of small shops fed a renewed burst of *poujadisme* and protests against taxation in the late 1960s.

The French were on the move in the 1960s, altering the social geography of France around an axis running between Le Havre and Marseille. The bulk of the population and of industry was concentrated on the north-east side of this line, while rural areas south-west of it were emptied, especially of young people. In response, the government created DATAR (Délégation à l'Aménagement du Territoire) in 1963 to nurture regional centres such as Toulouse and Bordeaux as counterweights to the Parisian region, to foster industrialization in the west of the country, and to redevelop the old mining towns of the north-east. Three distinct regional profiles have emerged. To the south-west of the Le Havre–Marseille line lies 'peasants' France', where farmers are significantly over-represented in the workforce (7 per cent of the workforce was in agriculture in 1992, compared to 4 per cent nationally). The north-east side of the line splits into two, a 'workers' France' and a 'professionals' France'. The 'workers' France' is formed of the industrial areas of the north around Lille, the east, and the Parisian region, where 34 per cent of the workforce are in industry. Paris itself falls into the 'professionals' France', along with the south-eastern corner. Here engineers, professionals, and intellectuals are most numerous (18 per cent of the workforce), for example around Lyon, Grenoble, and the Côte d'Azur's new technological centre, Sophia-Antipolis.

The speed of the economic transformation and the extent of the changes that it wrought in society were so great that Mendras has described this as 'a second French revolution'. Certainly the country's demographic profile was revolutionized. The population reached 50 million in 1969 thanks to strong natural growth (at a rate of over 300,000 yearly) and immigration (a net gain of 100,000 to 150,000 people annually, plus the *pieds-noirs* in 1962). The birth rate had shot up after the Second World War and it remained high during the 1960s as the postwar baby-boomers themselves had children. The death rate fell rapidly (from 16 to 11 per 1,000), and increased life expectancy soon translated into an ageing population. The size of the labour force had remained stable around 20 million for most of the twentieth century, until the children born after the war reached working age around 1965. Their entry into the active labour force was delayed by an unprecedented expansion of students in secondary and higher

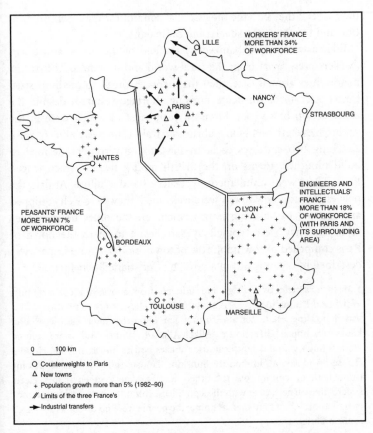

WORKERS' FRANCE
MORE THAN 34%
OF WORKFORCE

LILLE

NANCY

STRASBOURG

PARIS

NANTES

ENGINEERS AND
INTELLECTUALS'
FRANCE
MORE THAN 18%
OF WORKFORCE
(WITH PARIS AND
ITS SURROUNDING
AREA)

PEASANTS' FRANCE
MORE THAN 7%
OF WORKFORCE

LYON

BORDEAUX

TOULOUSE

MARSEILLE

0   100 km

O Counterweights to Paris
△ New towns
+ Population growth more than 5% (1982–90)
// Limits of the three France's
➤ Industrial transfers

Map 6.1 Changes in the social geography of France since the 1960s.

education. The numbers of the former soared from 400,000 in 1949 to 2.1 million by 1970, while the latter group rose from 130,000 to 600,000 in the same period. This explosion went well beyond the increase generated by their higher birth rate. It stemmed from a powerful social demand for education that far exceeded the expectations of the authorities, who responded with hastily and shoddily built facilities and a massive recruitment of teachers, but without adapting the educational system. Another social revolution began in the summer of 1963, when the cult radio show *Salut les Copains* organized a series of surprise pop concerts in Paris, in place de la Nation. The teenager had arrived. Wearing jeans and miniskirts, teenagers now formed a social group distinct from either children or their elders; they became the essential conduit for mass communication and the target for advertising campaigns.

France was truly urbanized by the end of the 1960s, and town-dwellers grew apart from the rural world and its values. At first, the major cities grew in size, then the increase spread to medium-sized towns after 1970. An acute housing shortage resulted, despite the construction of 500,000 homes a year, most of which were in the suburbs, exacerbated by the abrupt arrival of the *pieds-noirs* in 1962, clutching two suitcases each. In 1965, the government decided to build nine new towns on the British model, five of which ringed Paris. These were simultaneously a success and a failure. At first, the new estates and new towns were welcomed: they were well equipped and seemed to be a big improvement on the older housing they replaced. They were typified by Sarcelles, a town to the north of Paris composed of row upon row of tower blocks, whose impact was described by a young girl in a novel by Christiane Rochefort.

You reach Sarcelles by a bridge, and suddenly, from above, you see everything. Wow! And I thought I lived in a tower block! These really were towers! This was a housing estate for the future! For kilometre after kilometre after kilometre, house after house. Alike. Aligned. White. Still more houses. Houses houses houses houses houses houses houses houses houses. Houses. Houses. And sky: an immensity. Sunshine. Houses full of sunshine, passing through them, coming out the other side. Enormous green spaces, clean, superb, like carpets, each with the sign 'Please mind the grass', which seemed to have more effect here than at home; the people were no doubt as advanced as the architecture [. . .]

Coming home, our estate seemed poor to me, behind the times; a real antique. We were already yesterday, things moved quickly, quickly. Even the blocks opposite, the big ones, didn't look like anything much. A dozen miserable shacks on a small patch of ground. I surely wouldn't cry for them any more.[2]

But before long 'Sarcellitis' spread through these developments—a term coined for the loneliness and depression of the inhabitants of soulless housing estates. They were disliked for their monotony and for the long commuter journeys into Paris that they necessitated even before the urban crisis of the 1990s developed. They fuelled nostalgia for a house and garden in the countryside, for life in peasants' France.

At the heart of this new society, the middle classes were profoundly

[2] Christiane Rochefort, *Les Petits Enfants du siècle* (Paris, 1961), pp. 124–6.

remodelled by a final collapse in the numbers of independent peasant-farmers, shopkeepers, and small businessmen, and the irrepressible rise of the employee. The role model for the employee was the senior manager, who thus fixed the pattern of consumption for the whole group. As with the middle classes at the start of the twentieth century, their variety disguised a deep unity. They formed a distinct economic class through their position as employees, and a distinct social class because they were conscious of belonging to the same group. They were aware of the fragility of their social status, with the potential to rise and fall a long way from their current position. Collectively, they sought to achieve social promotion by imitating the bourgeoisie and by the patronage of the state, for it fell to the state to satisfy their needs by organizing the (limited) democratization of education and by ensuring greater prosperity through economic growth. This was the new social compact that underpinned the regime.

The world of the factory worker was also at its peak. In comparison with the great generation of workers of the 1940s and 1950s, workers' groups fragmented, largely because of the increased number of women and immigrants in the labour force. Though the working week was one of the longest in the developed world, the increase in wages (indexed to prices from 1952) opened up mass consumption to workers, and the gap in living standards between workers and other social groups narrowed. This variety in the workforce added another layer of division in the trade union movement, on top of the rifts caused by the Cold War and the heavy burden of union history. These divisions affected pay bargaining because rival unions attempted to outdo one another in the settlements they secured for their members. The CGT, with between 1.5 and 2 million members, was still influenced by the communist party; it orchestrated a major strike in 1963, which turned into the last stand of French miners. In 1964, the previously Catholic CFTC became the Confédération Française Démocratique du Travail, as the majority of its members were now non-Christian. It took on a new, revolutionary tone, supporting members in their industrial disputes, and preaching workers' control of companies. Overall union membership remained low, and the weak control of union leaders was revealed in May 1968.

The great motor of French society in the 1960s was access to consumption. The share of income devoted to food fell significantly, in favour of spending on housing, home improvements, cars, health, hygiene, culture, and leisure. By 1975, 90 per cent of households had a refrigerator, 70 per cent had a washing machine, television, and car, and 62 per cent went away on holiday. These widespread and considerable improvements were not always perceived as such because contemporaries' attention was largely fixed on the high levels of inequality that still existed in income and even more in wealth. The argument was over a more equal distribution of the country's wealth. Transfer payments, which redistributed income through taxation and welfare benefits, rose from 15 to 20 per cent of national income, which was not enough for some and too much for others.

May '68

The events of May 1968 inaugurated the long-drawn-out crisis of the final quarter of the twentieth century in France. May '68 was the French version of a general crisis of western societies, a rebellion against the rigid values of the Cold War world, against authority, against the drive to increase production that had been an obsession in the postwar years. Student unrest was grave in France because of the rapid increase in student numbers and the inadequacies of both the system of higher education and its facilities. Left-wing groups proliferated after the end of the Algerian War, drawing their inspiration variously from the USSR, China, or the Third World—and always from the war in Vietnam. The first incidents broke out in March 1968 in Nanterre, a new university created in 1963 in the middle of a shanty town to the north-west of Paris in order to ease the pressure on the old Sorbonne. The closure of Nanterre brought the protest movement back into Paris. On 3 May the Sorbonne was occupied and the first barricades went up. A cycle of provocation and repression began, which worsened each night and which won public opinion over to the students' side.

On 13 May, a general strike was declared in support of the protestors, and the baton passed from students to workers through a series of vast union demonstrations. The strike movement grew from the base upwards and was soon out of the control of the trade unions, as in May 1936. By 22 May, seven million workers were on strike and another three million were prevented from working. The country was paralysed; no trains or other public transport ran; there were no television broadcasts. Every sector was affected, from doctors to the Cannes film festival. The main demands made by workers revealed a desire for recognition and greater responsibility, a rejection of hierarchies and of the disciplines of the assembly line, echoing the demands of 1936. The strikers described their utopia of workers' power in a thousand ways while the CGT attempted to translate everything into pay rises. It banned access to factories, which forced Georges Pompidou, then prime minister, to negotiate the Grenelle agreement of 27 May: this gave a rise of 35 per cent in the minimum wage, of 10 per cent on all pay, and some other concessions—which were promptly rejected by strikers everywhere. De Gaulle then intervened by dissolving the Assembly and reframed the social crisis in terms of a political crisis of authority, just at a time when a large part of public opinion had become tired of the strikes and anxious for their own futures. The strike movement began to crumble and work resumed progressively during June—as in 1936.

French historiography is divided on the meaning of May 1968. It agrees that it was a rejection of authority, in the form of both organized factory labour and the paternal figure of de Gaulle. The rebelliousness of students and teenagers coincided with the frustration of workers, and together they ripped a hole in the moral fabric of the country. The relationship between citizens and state, men and women, parents and children, teachers and pupils, priests and parishioners, managers and employees were changed enormously. May '68 also heralded the economic crisis by rejecting the forms of economic growth that had driven the *trente glorieuses* and the alienation caused by mass consumption. More concretely, May '68 prepared the way for the economic crisis by forcing companies to over-invest and rack up excessive debts in their efforts to compensate for the sharp rise in the cost of labour.

The decline of physical labour and the rise of the manager

The social changes wrought by economic growth were sharpened further by the recession that began in 1974, and aggravated by the impact of high and long-lasting unemployment. The major social phenomenon was the collapse of the traditional working class from 40 per cent of the workforce in 1974 to just 25 per cent by 2002, with a million jobs lost in the 1980s alone. The demise of the old industrial sectors was compounded by restructuring elsewhere, which replaced skilled workers with a smaller number of technicians, and by the transfer of jobs to the tertiary sector. Social identities based around factories and factory communities were severely weakened, which in turn hurt trade unions: membership fell by two-thirds, more so among industrial workers than among state employees. The crisis was made worse by divisions between union leaders, who were split by party political ties (vindicating in a small way the suspicions of the CGT back in 1895). In their place, local committees sprang up, who fought the most intransigent strikes. The new opportunities for negotiation created by the government and the emergence of a new generation of union leaders could not prevent this.

The 'winners' of these socio-economic trends were the managers, engineers, liberal professions, and intellectual occupations, whose numbers doubled from 1.5 to 3 million in the twenty-five years after 1975. More than ever they defined a common culture and pattern of consumption for the whole of the middle classes. The latest variant, born with the new millennium, is the *bo-bo* (bourgeois-bohemian), the current target of sophisticated marketing campaigns. If a business or industry can capture this group as its customer, the rest will follow. Beyond them, the bulk of the middle classes are composed of intermediary professions and employees, for what remains of the independent sector is being squeezed ever smaller. Despite the democratization of higher education, the elites have been able to reinforce their position. Their wealth is now more liquid than it used to be when it was tied up in land, and they have used this to their advantage. They have protected their social reproduction through the selective *grandes écoles* which bypass the mass university education system, through the use of favours and influence (*piston*) to give one another a helping hand, and through codes of behaviour taught from an early age that foster a distinct social identity and friendships with 'people like us', to use an equivalent English phrase.

Geographical mobility also increased after 1974. The rural exodus left the central massifs of France deserted, and depopulated a band drawn diagonally across the country from the north-east to the south-west. The old industrial regions of the north-east and the Parisian region, previously magnets for internal immigration, began to lose inhabitants, while the south-east and Côte d'Azur gained the most. Urban expansion slowed down in favour of 'rurbanization', townspeople moving into the countryside, which extended the grip of the big cities further into their hinterland. While the construction of new housing has slowed, the existing housing stock is now better equipped and more spacious than ever before, and 55 per cent of householders own their home (though this is still below the average for the EU, and owner-occupation is 68 per cent in the UK). Yet this has also been accompanied by a real urban crisis, fuelled both by the physical degradation of the big housing developments that surround many cities and by the human cost of social and family breakdown. In the countryside, the rural exodus gathered pace when reforms to the CAP in 1984 and 1992 cut support prices and closed down the least profitable and most indebted farms. Even prosperous ones were jeopardized by price fluctuations and BSE. These problems weakened the authority of the traditional agricultural unions and led to the rise of the Confédération Paysanne, and the proliferation of violent protests.

Alongside a fall in the birth rate, the population began to age significantly thanks to greater life expectancy, and this now poses questions about how to fund the generous state pension; this is run as a pay-as-you-go system, where today's workers fund today's pensioners rather than building up capital to fund their own retirement. Several expert committees have examined the difficulty of maintaining this system in future decades, as the number of workers falls and the number of pensioners rises. The first steps towards correcting it were taken by the Balladur government, which extended to forty the number of years needed for private sector workers to qualify for a maximum pension. The problem remains acute, especially as today's pensioners enjoy a better standard of living than today's workers (although there are major inequalities between pensioners). Proposals to create private pension funds are suspected of preparing the way for a weakening of the pay-as-you-go system, which is widely defended as one of the fundamental expressions of social solidarity.

The social revolution

If 1974 is the key date for the transformation of the economy, 1968 is the key for the transformation of manners and morals. These changes were reinforced by the malaise of the economy, and set into law with more or less of a delay. Feminism was reborn in the 1970s, built on a surge in the number of women entering higher education and in female employment: women had made up a third of the workforce in 1965, about the same level as in 1900. By 1999 they made up 45 per cent of it, rising to 50 per cent in a couple of towns. The women's liberation movement led the charge for women generally; it was especially influential on the non-communist left, and reached a mass audience through the leading women's magazines such as *Elle* and *Marie-Claire*. The main points of conflict lay in the right to contraception and abortion: free contraception was provided from 1974; abortion was provisionally legalized the next year and definitively legalized in 1979. Pressure from the women's liberation movement led to a series of laws to ensure equality, the most recent of which was a law for the municipal elections of 2001 that required electoral lists to contain equal numbers of men and women, because women are severely under-represented in elected positions. The condition of women has also been transformed by a crisis in the family. The rate of marriage has halved since its peak in 1963–4; the average age at marriage has risen, as has the number of divorces, from 30,200 in 1960 to 110,800 in 1993. Cohabitation has become the normal preliminary to marriage instead of a rarity: only 10 per cent of marriages began with cohabitation in 1965, compared to 90 per cent in 1995. It also became more of an alternative to marriage, to judge from the illegitimacy rates: by 2000, 43 per cent of all babies and 55 per cent of all first babies were born outside marriage. The number of re-formed families has risen sharply, as has the number of single-parent families, which are usually headed by a woman. While these trends apply to men as well as to women, and represent liberation from the constraints of the traditional family for both sexes, figures show that it is easier for a man to form a new relationship after divorce or widowhood than for a woman, and that single-parent familes have much higher rates of unemployment and isolation. Moreover, while female workers are nearly as numerous as male ones, inequality remains high in terms of promotion, pay, and unemployment.

Unemployment passed the symbolic barrier of 10 per cent in 1993, at the same time that it broke the three million mark. It became the most important social question, overwhelming all others in public debate. There are several aspects to it. It led to an increase in inequality, after a long period when this had been falling. After 1993, it struck the middle classes and managers, who had been safe from it until then, and especially those aged over 50. It took young people longer to get their first job, which was itself increasingly precarious. Unemployment thus struck at the keystone of the regime, which was to assure social promotion and increased income. The anxiety of the middle classes that this has produced is a vital political issue within the Fifth Republic. Worse still, unemployment promotes social exclusion, though it is not the sole cause or symptom of it. An analysis of recipients of the minimum income has revealed the diverse elements of a new poverty that combines unemployment, the collapse of family ties, isolation, and housing problems. This has been especially severe amongst young men, more and more of whom have become homeless.

The number of foreigners has stabilized since the start of the crisis at around 3.5 million. This population, increasingly from North Africa, is now more stable and family-based than in the 1960s, when it was largely composed of single, male migrant workers; but it is also more concentrated in specific neighbourhoods, and it has found it harder to join mainstream society because it has been the principal victim of unemployment. The birth rate of immigrants has rapidly fallen into line with the average from higher initial levels, which can be seen as one indicator of assimilation. This has not stopped the National Front from making immigration its main campaign issue, and blaming it for all the ills of French society. The National Front was founded in 1972 and has been led since then by Jean-Marie Le Pen, a former paratrooper, *poujadiste* deputy, and supporter of French Algeria with a talent for demagogy. His electoral breakthrough between 1984 and 1986 illuminated once again how easily simplistic and xenophobic slogans win substantial support during prolonged economic crises, as they had in the 1880s and 1930s. As before, the appeal of the far right contaminated both the conventional right and the popular classes, under severe pressure from social and economic difficulties. The leitmotifs of Le Pen's campaigns have been the appearance of new forms of insecurity and an obsession with Islam. New forms of poverty and exclusion now rub shoulders with the most ostentatious forms of wealth and consumption, leading to violent frustration. From the start of the 1980s and even more in the later 1990s, this has led to disorder around the big cities, often linked to drug trafficking, sometimes escalating into riots across housing estates.

The slogans of the National Front have caught the attention of the media, public opinion, and finally the whole of the body politic. It wins support from people's anxieties about economic pressures and social breakdown, and their contempt for the political system. It adds one more ingredient to this mixture, which separates it from other fringe parties: anxiety about French identity, which it translates into the simple language of race. While it cannot win an election nationally, and while the party itself might not outlive Le Pen, its appeal will not go away as long as these four factors remain.

The politics of grandeur

De Gaulle's foreign policy rested on 'a certain idea of France', a France 'which is not itself unless it is in the front rank'. This vision owed more to Barrès than Maurras: it was a republican nationalism that accepted the Revolution, not a traditional royalist nationalism. Around France stood a world composed of nation-states, each the fruit of its own history, for de Gaulle had little faith in supranational constructions, be they global organizations like the UN or regional ones like the EEC. He also rejected the division of the world by the Soviet–American condominium that he dated from the wartime Yalta summit—to which he had not been invited—and which had been reinforced by the humiliation of Britain and France over their landings at the Suez Canal in 1956. This policy was maintained into the 1990s despite changes of context and of presidents, and even survived the switch from rule by the right to the left in 1981 (although later presidents avoided the excesses that sometimes sprang from de Gaulle's oratory). Foreign policy remains the preserve of the president, at the heart of the 'reserved domain', and it has hardly been touched by cohabitation.

Anti-Americanism: half a century of neurosis

The central problem with the policy of grandeur is that it rapidly turned into a neurotic hostility to the USA, and has been trapped in this ever since. Since 1947 France has been confronted by American domination, and its bid to reclaim its own sovereignty has been made by opposition to the USA. When de Gaulle returned to power in 1958, the western alliance was weakening. The communist menace had largely faded, and the new strategic doctrine of a graduated response developed by the Kennedy administration left western Europe outside the shelter of America's nuclear deterrent; this was highlighted by the restrained response of the USA to the construction of the Berlin Wall in 1961. When Britain gained nuclear weaponry, this unbalanced the Atlantic Alliance further. From September 1958, de Gaulle began to withdraw France from the integrated military command of NATO after his proposal for a directorate composed of the USA, France, and Britain was rejected by Eisenhower. This withdrawal was completed in 1966 by the closure of American and Canadian bases. But France stayed within NATO, took part in international manoeuvres, and was a loyal political ally (though more so over Cuba than Indochina). French independence was bolstered by the deployment of its own nuclear force in 1960, with a strategy termed 'deterrence against all comers', from the weak to the strong, and the army was reorganized around the nuclear arsenal.

This desire for autonomy can be found in every domain where France appeared to be dependent on the USA. It made de Gaulle contemptuous of the way that America allowed its trade deficit to undermine the value of the dollar, the world's reference currency, which he saw as neglecting its global responsibilities. France's reserves of dollars were systematically sold for gold. Investments by American firms were limited and supervised. The implicit aim of state-backed technological projects was to re-establish economic independence, through projects such as Concorde, enriched uranium for nuclear power stations, a special protocol for colour television, and the 'Calcul' plan to develop a French information technology industry. De Gaulle was a constant critic of American intervention in Indochina and in Latin America, which he toured triumphantly in 1964. The anti-American speech that he made in Phnom Penh in 1966 was well received across the Third World, but he went too far when he cried out 'Long live free Quebec!' in Canada in 1967, provoking concern both in France and abroad.

Anti-Americanism also implied friendship with the eastern bloc. For de Gaulle, Marxism was merely a veneer laid over the Russian nation, and he developed warm relations with its leaders from 1963 onwards. This did not prevent him from denouncing Soviet domination when he toured Poland and Romania as well, to great acclaim in those countries. He also wished to open up a sphere of international activity for France that would be in keeping with its rank. Paradoxically, this was first developed through the construction of the EEC, which de Gaulle wanted to be a confederation of nations under French influence. This was the motive of the Fouchet plan that he put to his partners in the Common Market in 1961 (and which was rejected by the supporters of federalism) and of his opposition to the entry of the United Kingdom to the EEC: Britain was too close to the USA and would rival France within Europe. In 1965, when the European Commission in Brussels attempted to extend its powers, he left France's chair at all European meetings empty for six months, until it gave up its claims.

Because the EEC had not proved fertile ground, de Gaulle decided to nurture the Franco-German relationship instead. The choice of Germany as partner was imperative: the long-standing conflict between these two great countries had accelerated the decline of Europe, and only their friendship could reverse this. West Germany had recovered its economic strength by 1958 but remained weak diplomatically, which made it the ideal ally for de Gaulle. De Gaulle and Chancellor Adenauer had much in common: their age, their personal authority, and their Catholic faith; both were concerned at the consequences of an American withdrawal from Europe. Between 1958 and 1963, they met fifteen times and exchanged forty letters. The alliance was sealed by the Élysée Treaty of January 1963, which organized bilateral activity with two summits a year, and closer cultural and military links. Public opinion was more enthusiastic about these new relations than diplomats and specialists because the latter were aware of the numerous contradictions it masked, particularly regarding the USA and the USSR. West Germany depended absolutely on the USA for its security, while France wished to find a counterbalance to it. France hoped to find this in the USSR, while West Germany saw the USSR as an obstacle in its efforts to hold a dialogue with the Soviet zone of Germany, which had by then become the German Democratic Republic. These contradictions meant that the alliance was becalmed after the retirement of Adenauer in 1963, when Willy Brandt pursued a policy of *Ostpolitik*, opening relations with the east and thereby displacing France as the bridge between eastern and western Europe. When the Franco-German tandem was later revived, it propelled European construction forward once again.

The success of decolonization and of his denunciation of Soviet–American domination led de Gaulle to woo the Third World, though he only found suitors in Africa and the Arab world. A pro-Arab policy was made possible by the end of the Algerian War; it distanced France from Israel and hence from Israel's chief sponsor, the USA. It is difficult to assess the results of France's African policy because it was run semi-clandestinely by Jacques Foccart from de Gaulle to Chirac, mixing official policy with covert action. From 1958 the African colonies (except Guinea) chose membership of the 'Community', an association based on the Defferre law of 1956. At the end of 1959 they chose independence, which was rapidly agreed. After this, French policy aimed to maintain the stability of states' borders and governments, and to maintain French military bases in them; the ultimate goals were to protect French investments and secure votes for France at the United Nations. This amounted to a prototype for neo-colonialism. Africa remained dependent on its former masters, as the second largest market for French goods and a supplier of raw materials on terms favourable to France.

The most striking feature of French foreign policy was how long its main principles stayed in place, lasting at least up to the Gulf War and the collapse of the Soviet Union. It only altered in its details, depending on the personal views of successive presidents and changes in circumstance; the fundamental choices remained unchanged as if they were the only possible ones, a legacy inherited from the past that could not be disowned. But as time passed, the vanity behind this attempt to hold a place in the front rank of world powers became more obvious.

The main change was in European policy. The industrial imperative at the heart of Pompidou's rule meant that the economy had to be more open and more committed to European development in order to increase exports; this opening was necessary politically when Pompidou required the support of centrists in parliament. He supported Britain's entry to the EEC at a price: the CAP became permanent and the European monetary snake was established. This restored the leadership of Europe to France, giving it extra weight against the USA. However, this was undermined by the low turnout of the electorate in a referendum on expanding the EEC, by the collapse of cooperation over international monetary policy, and by increased tensions with the USA when Nixon and Kissinger sought to extract trade concessions from Europe in return for continued American military protection. Pompidou's successor, Giscard d'Estaing, was deeply committed to European construction. He revived the Franco-German partnership, and his friendship with Helmut Schmidt enabled them to create the European Monetary System (EMS) in 1979. Yet the EEC was still primarily run by cooperation between governments, and although the European parliament was henceforth directly elected by its citizens, it did not receive increased powers. Mitterrand's decision to abandon his socialist policies of 1981–3 for a more orthodox, free-market approach in order to stay within the EMS was one decisive moment in French policy, followed by another during the French presidency of 1984, when Mitterrand supported the proposal that the European Commission should be answerable to the European parliament in Strasbourg, and secured the nomination of Jacques Delors as head of this commission. Through his friendship with Helmut Kohl, the Single European Act of 1986 was passed. This prepared the way for a single market and a common foreign policy, and replaced the need for unanimity with majority voting in the Council of Ministers (the body of government ministers from each country). German unification pushed Mitterrand to accelerate European unification, to bind Germany into the western bloc. This resulted in the Maastricht Treaty of February 1992, which agreed to introduce a single currency after a period of economic and monetary convergence, and to create a common citizenship and foreign and defence policies. The European Community was renamed the European Union. Yet the collapse of Yugoslavia soon revealed how weak the EU was diplomatically. Faced by British hesitation and German eagerness to recognize the seceding republics of Croatia and Slovenia, France could not persuade the EU to intervene and had to watch responsibility pass to the UN and NATO instead. Weakness and self-doubt became inseparable. The Maastricht Treaty was only barely ratified by a referendum in September 1992, which highlighted the new divisions between partisans of French sovereignty and of Europe. As president, Jacques Chirac stood by the main objective, the creation of the single currency. The euro came into effect on 1 January 1999 and successfully entered circulation on 1 January 2002. In contrast, progress towards other objectives (notably expansion of the EU to the east, airily promised by Chirac, and reform of its institutions) has become enmired for the lack of a positive dialogue with its partners, and especially Germany.

Anti-Americanism is the best example of how French foreign policy was frozen by de Gaulle. This attitude was further hardened by Pompidou when he rejected the agreements on nuclear arms that came out of the Soviet–American détente, for he feared that American power would become even more assertive once it was freed from the burden of the Vietnam War. This attitude evidently could not stop the abandonment of the Bretton Woods agreement on exchange rates and the rise in the dollar after 1971. Giscard d'Estaing was not instinctively anti-American, being the first non-Gaullist president; and though he oversaw a series of conflicts with the USA about new technologies, he supported the policy of floating currencies freely and increased collaboration with NATO, even for nuclear weaponry. He also formalized the G7, after a summit at Rambouillet in 1975. When the Cold War worsened again, in the late 1970s, French policy turned back to a Gaullist suspicion of America and indulgence towards the east, until Mitterrand corrected this to some extent. He supported NATO over the deployment of nuclear missiles in Europe, then opposed Reagan's 'Star Wars' missile defence plan because it would leave Europe unprotected. The Gulf War was a crucial test. France joined the allied coalition in the hope that it could have an influence in the conduct of the conflict, at the risk of ruining its carefully nurtured influence in the Arab world. Similarly, after the collapse of the Soviet bloc it returned to the NATO fold in order to have some influence inside the alliance. The crisis of 11 September 2001 showed how difficult it was to make its voice heard: France again chose to be a model ally diplomatically, but it lacked the military capacity to contribute on the battlefield and therefore lacked the ability to be a real counterweight to American unilateralism.

Since the collapse of the Soviet bloc, France has not found an effective way to make its voice heard on the world stage. At the start of the 1970s Pompidou began regular bilateral talks with the USSR, which were kept separate from talks to reduce nuclear arms. He supported the Soviet proposal to create the Conference on Security and Cooperation in Europe, on the condition that it would cover human rights as well. Giscard d'Estaing pursued this relationship during both the détente of the early 1970s and the subsequent chill in east/west relations, but his meeting with Brezhnev in Warsaw soon after the Soviet occupation of Afghanistan appeared to condone the invasion, and this weighed against him in the presidential elections of 1981. Mitterrand was more reticent: he waited three years before he visited Moscow, when he proceeded to criticize human rights violations by the Soviet Union. Relations between the two countries only improved after Gorbachev took power. Once the eastern bloc began to crumble, France was keen to maintain stability and often appeared slow to respond both to the liberation of eastern Europe and to the dissolution of the USSR.

An alternative sphere of influence lay in the Arab world: France supported Arab states against Israel, especially during the Yom Kippur War of 1973 and by the sale of arms to Colonel Qaddafi's Libya. The oil crisis led Giscard d'Estaing to champion north/south cooperation, and Paris hosted a conference on this in 1975 (which broke up two years later in disagreement). He also persuaded Europe to back the Palestinian cause—with at least one eye on the big industrial contracts to be won from oil-rich Arab states. Mitterrand's visit to Israel in March 1982 was the first by a French head of state, though he was no more obliging to his hosts than he was to be in Moscow: he expressed his support for a Palestinian state in front of the Knesset, and committed France to the protection of Palestinians living in Lebanon at the end of that summer. Arms sales to Arab countries increased, especially to Iraq in its war against Iran, with a side effect in the form of terrorist attacks on France between 1982 and 1986. Once again, French support for the Gulf War coalition reduced the distinctiveness of French policy in the region.

The last great spheres of influence were Africa and Latin America. France became more openly interventionist in the 1970s, in Zaire, Mauritania, Chad, and finally in the Central African Republic, where the relationship between Giscard and the emperor-dictator Bokassa became a major scandal at the end of Giscard's presidency. As a socialist, Mitterrand supported Third World development and anti-imperialism, and for a few months this focused on Latin America through backing for the Sandinistas in Nicaragua. This was partly inspired by the example of Chile, where Allende's socialist rule had been overthrown by the army; it was also—yet again—a policy that indirectly opposed America. But these attitudes did not last long in either Latin America or Africa. France returned to realpolitik in 1983 when it despatched 3,000 men to Chad, to counter a rebellious ex-president who had Libyan backing. The results of Mitterrand's African policy were damning: it culminated in the abandonment of the Central African franc in 1994 (the common currency for several former French colonies, linked to the French franc) and the Rwandan genocide of 1994.

What remains of the policy of grandeur? French policy had been directed against the Soviet–American division of the world that flowed from the Yalta summit, yet paradoxically the end of the Cold War, the 'end of Yalta', stripped France of the ability to maintain a unique position in the western bloc. Even if its powers, be they economic, diplomatic, or nuclear, are undiminished, it has yet to adapt its policy and change its attitude to the new world order. This uncertainty about France's place in the world plays an important part in the crisis of identity that currently plagues the French, because this crisis is especially acute when confronted with the foreign, whether this takes the form of immigration or globalization. One of the reasons to strive for greatness was to restore energy and pride in the hearts of French citizens after the calamity of 1940 and the loss of empire. Today France needs to find a new way to understand its position in the world—and to understand itself.

Conclusion

The normalization of France?

By the end of the nineteenth century, new methods of communication had changed France from a honeycomb of local communities into a single cell, a single Hexagon. Though France had long existed as a nation, and though there was still great diversity, roads, rivers, and railways had created a single economy; newspapers and the telegraph spread a common culture; French had became the standard language through universal schooling. By the end of the twentieth century, this process had been repeated on a global level. International air transport makes it as quick to travel across the world as it was to travel from Paris to Marseille 100 years ago. The French economy is inextricably linked with the European and global economies through the EU, the WTO, and international financial markets. Cinema, satellite television, spectator sports, and the internet have spread a common culture; English has become the standard language of the global community. Once again, this does not mean homogenization: every country in the EU is manifestly different from its neighbours, but they now have more in common than ever before.

The history of France over the past 200 years can be told as the story of its integration with the western world, and this integration was vital to the process of squaring the Hexagon. For France to learn to live with itself, it had to have some of its irregularities knocked off, to become a country like any other. This conclusion reviews the development of France through this perspective, following the main themes pursued in this book, namely politics, society, economy, religion, and France's relations with the rest of the world. In brief, has France been normalized?

The end result of 200 years of empires, monarchies, and republics is that France today is a democracy. Since this is now the common condition of the western world, including most states of eastern

Europe and the former Soviet Union, this is indeed a story of normalization, though one where most other countries have had to catch up
with France. Its democratic precocity, with the Revolution of 1789,
universal male suffrage in 1848, and the installation of a long-lasting
republic in 1870, also help to explain why the reaction against democracy was strong in France. The bloody experiences of both revolution and counter-revolution account for the need to avoid rule by
either far left or far right. This has been achieved either by a parliamentary system dominated by coalitions, as under the Third and
Fourth Republics, or by authoritarian figures ruling above parties
(though with an inevitable bias to the right), namely Napoleon I,
Napoleon III, and Charles de Gaulle. These rulers were another
unique aspect of French political history, and it is to be hoped that
this exceptionalism has passed away too, since they only emerged
from national and international crises.

Yet democracy in France has not finally 'come into harbour' with
the Fifth Republic. Its institutions have undergone constant change as
the balance of power in its double-headed executive has swung from
president to prime minister. The monarchy of de Gaulle was followed
by a diarchy with Pompidou, Giscard d'Estaing, and early Mitterrand,
where the president and prime minister were from the same party;
since 1986, cohabitation has altered this diarchy. More gravely, the
Fifth Republic has not overcome the twin ills diagnosed by Maurice
Duverger in 1967, of democracy without the people and of rule by the
centre. Political parties are unstable (the two centre-right parties,
Chirac's new UMP and the older UDF, are both coalitions in themselves); they have relatively few members; their weak finances invite
bribery; the electorate feels little loyalty to them and switches votes
from one party to another, or abstains, or votes for extremists; political battles are fought in the streets instead of in parliament. Alternation between left and right and the cohabitations produced by it are
the latest versions of rule by the centre. Two brief periods of marked
left- and right-wing government both collapsed in a couple of years,
in 1981–3 and 1986–8, with the result that France returned to rule
by the centre-left or centre-right. In sum, while France is now a
democracy like its peers, it has not escaped from the burden of its
own history and the Fifth Republic does not represent a definitive
settlement. The elections of 2002 have restored the power of the
president to that intended by de Gaulle, but this stability will only be

temporary, and Chirac needs to use this moment to reform the Republic, not to assume that all is now well again.

The pre-eminent oddity of French society from 1800 to 1945 was its low birth rate, an exception that affected many other aspects of society and the economy. This changed in 1945 with a boom in marriages and births, and a higher birth rate was sustained throughout the 1950s and 1960s thanks to a high rate of marriage and younger average age at marriage. The French birth rate caught up with its peers. From 1972 onwards, marriage became less common and couples married later, but the number of births stayed high because the children of the postwar baby boom were themselves having babies. By 2001, although the birth rate had dropped again in line with its European peers, the total number of births outstripped deaths by nearly 250,000; in Germany and Sweden, deaths now outnumber births.

Other evolutions in the French family are familiar across the West. The communal household, containing more than one married couple, has almost disappeared (just 0.6 per cent of the population in 1999). The family has mostly ceased to be a unit of production and its economic identity is primarily as a unit of consumption. Divorce and cohabitation are increasing; more and more children are born outside marriage or grow up in single-parent families. While these developments are general in the West, Jospin's government moved ahead of most countries by recognizing the legal rights of unmarried couples through the Pacte Civil de Solidarité in November 1999. A couple living together can gain additional legal rights and protection without marrying, in return for certain duties, notably to care for one another 'mutually and materially'. This is valid for both heterosexual and homosexual couples. By the end of September 2001, 43,800 PACS had been signed, though official statistics do not yet indicate what proportion of these were between single-sex couples and what proportion between women and men. Social reforms such as the PACS and policies on crime and immigration now mark the distinction between the left and right of politics most clearly, since the battles over the Republic, religion, and the economy have largely been settled.

France has long been a country of immigration, and the presence both of large numbers of immigrants and of xenophobia are in themselves neither new nor limited to France. The census of 1999 recorded 4.3 million immigrants, which is about the same proportion of the population as in 1975; over a third of them have gained French citizenship. There is a significant difference between the countries that currently contribute most immigrants and those who did so in the past. Over half of the migrant population comes from just five countries: Algeria, Portugal, Morocco, Italy, and Spain (in decreasing order). The four countries that currently send most people to France are all non-European, Muslim states: Algeria and Morocco, followed after a gap by Turkey and Tunisia. Together these countries contribute about 20,000 to 25,000 migrants to France each year, or about 35 to 45 per cent of the annual total. In France, the onus has for a long time been on immigrants to assimilate rather than on their hosts to become multicultural; this has been possible in the long run for those coming from the three European Catholic countries listed above, but has been much harder for the North African and Muslim communities. Many immigrants have largely been excluded from mainstream society as a result. In addition, there is now a large *Beur* population in France, people born in France of North African descent (the word is probably back-slang for *Arabe*), many of whom feel at home neither in France nor North Africa, and whose lack of integration is only increased by the xenophobia of their neighbours. Paradoxically, immigration is now having a profound impact precisely because of this exclusion, through violence and crime in the outer suburbs and through the enduring presence of the National Front.

Immigration links into another area of French exceptionalism, namely religion. The Separation of Church and State in 1905 rigorously excluded religious observance from the public domain; for example, crucifixes are banned from state schools, hospitals, and law courts. The quarrel between the state and Catholicism has been resolved for the most part, but it has produced fierce debates with regard to Islam. In 1989, disputes arose when Muslim girls wore headscarves to state schools, since these were religious symbols. By 1994, the courts and government had decided that 'ostentatious' religious signs could be banned from schools, but 'discreet' signs should be allowed as expressions of personal beliefs, which were to be protected in the name of freedom of conscience. French society is not necessarily racist, but the state is necessarily secular, and this may cause further problems with the largest single element in its immigrant community, for there are now three million Muslims in France (compared to 300,000 Jews in 1940). Though this need not create a problem, the principle of the secular state creates a potential for trouble either from Muslim fundamentalists, who refuse to accept this principle, or from the far right, who use it to argue that immigrants should be expelled.

The French economy in the nineteenth and early twentieth centuries was marked by six characteristics: a slow growth rate; multiple employment; the high participation rate of women in the labour force; the coexistence of a mass of small firms and a handful of industrial giants; an even balance between primary, secondary, and tertiary sectors; and, frequently, state intervention in the economy. By the end of the twentieth century, only the high participation rate of women remained as an exception, by then approaching 50 per cent.

Multiple employment was the first of these distinguishing features to go, killed off by the depression of the 1930s. The mass of small firms and farms were also squeezed between the wars, and especially in the 1930s, but were granted a respite under Vichy. From 1944 their decline was more or less continuous, both during the economic boom that lasted until 1974 and during the bust that followed it. By the 1990s, the distribution of employees by size of company put France almost exactly on the average for the European Union. Small companies still abound, but they no longer represent an unusually large share of the economy. The distribution of the labour force by size of company is shown in Table C.1. Compared to France, Britain and Germany have predominantly more employees in large companies that employ more than 250 people, while Italy has substantially more people working in companies with fewer than ten staff.

The distribution of workers between sectors changed little under the Third Republic, and substantially altered only with the Fifth Republic. Industrial employment surged forward while the number of people working in agriculture declined steadily, until the crisis of 1974 heralded the demise of old industries such as mining, iron and steel, and textiles, and forced restructuring among the survivors. Reforms to the Common Agricultural Policy in the 1980s accelerated the flight from the land, till only a small percentage of all workers remained there. Employment in the service sector has risen instead, in line with European economies in general. State intervention in the economy had only been favoured intermittently in the nineteenth century, and its heyday came after 1945. After 1968, and especially

Table C.1 Distribution of the workforce by size of enterprise, 1996/7

Country	% of employees in each band (no. of employees)					
	0	1–9	10–49	50–249	250+	Total employees (million)
France	11.1	22.9	18.9	14.4	32.7	16.2
Germany	4.0	24.0	20.1	11.2	40.6	28.9
Italy	13.2	34.8	20.3	11.4	20.3	14.2
UK	11.6	16.9	14.1	11.8	45.5	21.9
Total European Union	10.0	24.4	18.8	13.1	33.8	111.8

Source: Eurostat, *Enterprises in Europe*, 6th edn. Note that all data are for 1996 except Germany, which refers to 1997.

after 1974, the government became more concerned with managing the economy rather than with transforming it, until the socialist victory of 1981. Mitterrand then attempted to create a socialist, state-directed economy, an experiment that rapidly failed. Since 1983, state intervention has been abandoned in favour of European integration and world trade. French economic policy can now only differ from the EU norm at the margins, and not at all for monetary and exchange rate policy since the franc was swapped for the euro. The success of the 'thirty glorious years' of economic transformation also solved the problem of slow economic growth, through the success of state planning, European reconstruction fuelled by Marshall Aid, and the baby boom. In the late 1990s the performance of the French economy was generally respectable in comparison to the twenty years after 1974, though nowhere near the level of 1944–74. A handful of French companies have emerged as global players, though this is not necessarily compatible with French exceptionalism. When Jean-Marie Messier's Vivendi bought Universal Studios of the USA, it was hailed as a triumph of French business over Hollywood. In the event, it was a triumph for commercialism over cultural exceptionalism because Vivendi's support for independent films, provided through its subsidiary Canal Plus, has declined in favour of big-budget films intended to beat the Americans at their own game. This story is far from over, since Vivendi Universal made the largest corporate loss in French history in 2001 and Messier was forced to resign in July 2002.

The final theme of this book has been the relationship between France and the rest of the world. Throughout the nineteenth century, France was one of the world's great powers, and certainly Europe's greatest power when the Napoleonic empire was at its peak; after the emasculation of the 1930s to 1950s, de Gaulle rebuilt its lost prestige and found a new role for it. Today France is becoming normalized in the sense that it is only one country amongst many in the EU, the UN, or NATO, and lacks exceptional diplomatic influence or military strength. Only the USA now stands without equal.

There are two dimensions to this loss of power, within Europe and across the world. The EEC and related bodies were intended to apply French policy to all their members and to project France's voice beyond Europe. But France is now one country out of fifteen in the EU, with more queuing to join; the powers of the European Commission have expanded; and now the European Central Bank sets monetary policy. European integration remains popular in France, not least because it has bound Germany into a peaceful relationship, but this may change if the powers of national governments are further reduced, if the European Union passes regulations disliked in France (such as restrictions on the season for hunting wild birds), if the ECB's policies do not suit France, and if the CAP is overhauled. By May 2002, France was bottom of the European Commission's league table for the implementation of Single Market directives, and top of the league for proceedings taken by the EC for infringements against such directives (the UK was in the top half for implementation and in the middle for infringements). Every phase of EU expansion has reduced French influence and changed its character. The addition of eastern European countries can only extend this still further.

Globally, de Gaulle restored French power through its military capacity (especially nuclear arms), its relationship with the USSR, and its influence in the Arab world and in Africa. This construction now lies in disarray. The atomic powers no longer form a club of five states based around Cold War rivalries. Its global military capacity enabled France to participate in the Gulf War under American direction, but significant military action without American logistics and intelligence is now beyond any member of NATO. The collapse of the

Soviet Union terminated any Franco-Soviet relations; French support for the US during the Gulf War and retaliation against the Taleban and al-Qaeda after 11 September have jeopardized its Arab policy; genocide in Rwanda discredited French policy in central Africa. France has yet to come to terms with the normalization of its international power.

France's sense of national identity has partly been shaped by its position in the world and by its rivalry with other major powers. From 1800 to 1945 its main rivals were Germany and the UK, for control of Europe and of empire. These antagonisms have now largely been settled, by the development of the EU and the loss of overseas empires. Since 1945 the USA has been the dominant power in the West, and has provided an antagonist against which France could define itself. Since 1989 the USA has been the dominant power in the world, and French governments have repeatedly chosen to side with it, but this has not brought the returns that France had hoped for. For example, Chirac offered to rejoin NATO's full military command in return for French command of NATO's Mediterranean fleet, which was inevitably rejected by Bill Clinton: the US fleet in Naples would remain under US control (how did Chirac imagine it might be otherwise?). The resurgence of American unilateralism under George W. Bush has now made it even harder for France to resolve its neurosis about America.

Today . . . and tomorrow?

France today is a dynamic, prosperous country. It is a leader in technology and engineering; its cities and countryside are prime tourist destinations; its health system is rated the best in the world by the OECD and its life expectancy is one of the best in Europe; the Institut Pasteur has continued the pioneering work of Louis Pasteur by its work today on HIV; its cultural life remains vibrant; its rugby and football teams are (intermittently) among the best in the world. Its wealth is high, measured by income per head, and its quality of life is also high in other ways, whether in the traditionally high standards of its food and quality goods or in the new opportunities opened up by the thirty-five-hour week. There is evidently much that is right, or even outstanding, about France, so one should not paint too black a picture.

Yet there are fundamental and interlocking problems within the Fifth Republic. There is a mismatch between the structures of the regime and contemporary society; there is a social crisis around insecurity and the fears that it engenders; and there is a political crisis produced by the failure of governments and public authorities to tackle the social crisis. Woven through these threads is a conflict between xenophobia and immigration. Without predicting another revolution, mass protests on the scale of 1995 or even 1968 are quite possible, perhaps with an added racial dimension.

The crisis of the regime comes from the way that society has changed in the decades since the foundation of the Fifth Republic. The Republic was built on three pillars: authority, economic growth, and consensus between social partners. Authority was needed to tackle the Algerian War, for the Fourth Republic could only provide paralysis. Although no politician since de Gaulle has been able to match his personal authority, the crisis of authority does not lie in a lack of leadership. Instead, it comes from a rejection of authority itself. This rejection burst forth in May 1968, and has been present ever since: a detailed survey of Catholic priests found that their standing had never been the same since 1968 because they no longer commanded automatic respect by virtue of their office. The citizens of France are all *dreyfusards* now in their rejection of authority. When the Fifth Republic was founded, there was a consensus around the goal of economic growth, and the rewards of this justified the regime. For fifteen years, growth was delivered and the population was handsomely paid for its efforts. Since the oil crisis of 1973, the state has not been able to guarantee material rewards and social advancement through economic growth, and has thus failed to deliver that part of the bargain. Since 1983, when Mitterrand abandoned state-directed socialism for integration in the European and world economies, the state has acknowledged its limitations, though governments are still primarily judged on their stewardship of the economy. The Green movement has eroded this pillar still further by questioning the virtue of ever-rising GDP if it means that the quality of life and of the environment falls as a result. The third pillar was a consensus between the social partners as represented by mass organizations. This suited the 1950s and 1960s, when companies consolidated and trade union membership was high, and as employees replaced the self-employed who had underpinned the Third Republic. Once again, the 1973 crisis cut away this pillar. The number of industrial workers has slumped, taking trade union membership with it—the old heavy industries like coal and steel were formed of large companies with unionized labour forces. Newer industries, whether high technology or services, are dominated by smaller companies and are less organized and less unionized. The other social partners, the employers, are much less cooperative too, and their federation has threatened to quit many negotiations when it has not liked their drift.

In the build-up to the 2002 presidential election, there were many suggestions for reforming the institutions of the Fifth Republic. The new president has a five-year term to run alongside the five-year term of the National Assembly, instead of the seven-year term that produced cohabitation; this is intended to reinforce the executive. The 2002 elections secured a president and parliament from the same camp, but the electorate could some time in the future choose a left-wing president and a right-wing parliament (or vice versa), either because the margins either way are wafer-thin, or if the president is chosen by personality not party, or if the electorate deliberately chooses to hamstring the executive. Other proposed reforms would increase the decentralization begun by Mitterrand in the hope that local participation will get round the loss of authority by the central state and the weakness of the large-scale national organizations it has traditionally used as its partners. This has gone furthest in Corsica, which is an exceptional case. Ironically, Napoleon's centralized regime may have begun to unravel in his own birthplace. Will there be any further reforms in this direction?

The social crisis revolves around insecurity, whose underlying source is unemployment. This has hurt several groups. One is the white-collar, managerial class, whose members never expected to lose their jobs, although they are not usually unemployed for long. The other three social groups have all suffered long-term unemployment. The first comprises manual workers in coal, steel and textiles laid off in the north-eastern region of France, where finding a new job was extremely hard because whole towns were in depression. Secondly, young workers are trapped by a lack of experience that keeps them out of a job, which in turn means that they cannot gain experience.

Thirdly, immigrant or foreign workers are liable to unemployment from a combination of factors: many are young and lack experience; others came to France to work in the old industries; many find themselves shut out of new jobs because of a lack of qualifications or because of prejudice.

The 1995 presidential elections picked up on the plight of the unemployed and the problems that went with it, under the umbrella term of social exclusion. In the electoral campaign, both sides promised to tackle it by a combination of welfare measures and job creation. After his electoral victory, Chirac turned away from welfare measures to free-market policies designed to boost the economy, on the grounds that the best way to tackle unemployment was through economic expansion. After Jospin became prime minister in 1997 he passed legislation on the thirty-five-hour week and on creating jobs for young workers to increase employment. Yet barriers to employment remain significant because it is both expensive to employ staff and difficult to lay them off—in other words, those in jobs do well at the expense of the unemployed. Reforms to make the labour market more flexible on the lines of the UK and USA are routinely denounced as policies to exploit workers, and change on this front can only be slow. In any case, given that France has a very good record at attracting inward investment, the impact of these barriers should not be exaggerated.

The elections of 2002

All of these problems emerged in the 2002 elections, when the debate was again dominated by the theme of insecurity. This time insecurity was taken to be caused by crime rather than by unemployment. Crime also served as a code-word for immigration, which played into the hands of Jean-Marie Le Pen, presidential candidate for the National Front. The success of Le Pen in the first round of these elections also showed the depth of the political crisis, because the majority of citizens voted neither for the head of government nor for the head of state. Political parties were marginalized in a presidential election dominated by personalities and protest votes, and became scarcely more important in the parliamentary elections, when Chirac invented a new party for the occasion and the socialist and communist parties were trounced. Though millions of people took to the streets to protest against Le Pen, political parties and trade unions were unable to harness this momentum.

As a result of Chirac's decision to call a parliamentary election in 1997, the presidential and legislative elections both took place in 2002, summoning voters to the polls four times in eight weeks. The two main candidates were Jacques Chirac and Lionel Jospin, president and prime minister respectively, and it was assumed (not least by the candidates themselves) that the pair of them would win through to the second round for a replay of the 1995 election; this led to an uninspiring campaign, and meant that people who wanted to vote against the existing authorities had to choose one of the fringe candidates in the first round. Jospin, too austere to be a natural campaigner, mounted a low-key campaign in the belief that his good record as prime minister would carry him through to the second round, when the real fight could begin against a president tarnished by allegations of corruption. Chirac campaigned energetically and acted more like an opposition leader than a president, making implausible promises about dramatic tax cuts. He focused the election campaign on insecurity in the form of crime and fear of it. This picked out a weak point in the left's platform but avoided the real issues confronting the country. As in 1995, the leading candidates discussed ways to tackle the symptoms of the crisis rather than its underlying causes, and sought to outbid each other with plans for repressive policing and sentencing. Recorded crime had increased significantly in 2001, by 7.7 per cent, with the biggest increases coming in violence against the person. Nevertheless, the official crime rate (with the reservation that recorded crime is not a certain measure) is still a long way below that of the UK: in 2001, the rate of crimes against the person in mainland France was one third that for England and Wales. The country as a whole is far from unsafe, though there are districts where crime has made life intolerable. The social deprivation at the root of much crime, often fed by long-term unemployment, was largely overlooked in the electoral debates. Most seriously, it is now widely assumed that most crime, especially violent crime, is committed by immigrants, especially from North Africa. This assumption is polarizing French society. Among the white population, it has spread xenophobia by the fear it generates; among the immigrant community, it has increased the sense of rejection.

The electorate surprised itself on 21 April by giving Chirac just 19.9

per cent of the vote, and placing Le Pen ahead of Jospin by 200,000 votes, with 16.9 per cent of the votes cast. This apparent turn to the far right was denounced by massive, spontaneous demonstrations, often led by the young, culminating in a huge demonstration in Paris on 1 May. This prepared the way for the triumphant re-election of Chirac, taking 82 per cent of the vote against 18 per cent for Le Pen, which was barely higher than his vote in the first round plus that of the other far-right candidate, Bruno Mégret. From one round of voting to another, Chirac jumped from the worst score of any incumbent president in the Fifth Republic to a majority not seen since Napoleon III. Yet the rallies held by the left did not help it in the legislative elections. Jospin vanished from the scene after his defeat and resigned after the second round of the presidential elections. His ministry was replaced by a centre-right coalition led by a little-known senator and businessman, Jean-Pierre Raffarin, who personified provincial France. Jospin's resignation was as disastrous for the socialists as a party as it was honourable for him personally. At a stroke, it deprived the party of its leader, and of the status and the practical advantages that came with government (ex-ministers' free mobile phones were swiftly cut off by their replacements). The initiative passed to the right. Chirac's concern was to avoid cohabitation again, and to this end Alain Juppé quickly assembled another new centre-right party, the Union pour la Majorité Présidentielle (UMP). This federated most of the right-wing parties into one and duly returned an absolute majority for Chirac in the legislative elections of 9 and 16 June, winning 349 seats out of 565. The National Front was largely rejected again; it only qualified for the second round of voting in the legislative elections in a few constituencies and won no seats in parliament. This meant that the right-wing vote was less split than in 1997, when the left had profited from its presence. The socialists held on to 138 seats but the PC was reduced to 21 deputies. The embarrassment of its leader, Robert Hue, who had polled just 4 per cent in the presidential election, was compounded when he lost his parliamentary seat, and the Greens won just three seats. Other notable casualties were the renegade socialist Jean-Pierre Chevènement, despite (or because of) his prominence in the first weeks of the presidential elections, and Martine Aubry, despite (or because of) her role in the creation of the thirty-five-hours law in Jospin's government. The only other winner was abstentionism, which rose to a new record of 39 per cent.

Le Pen's surprise victory in the first round of voting was thus cancelled out by the next three rounds. His early triumph was to some extent an accident. The National Front has regularly polled between 10 and 15 per cent for several years and the socialist vote had dropped below 20 per cent in the 1993 legislative elections, so the core vote for both was not dissimilar. In the first round of the presidential elections, the left was split between Jospin, a socialist-turned-nationalist (Chevènement), a communist (Hue), a Green candidate, three Trotskyists, and a pro-hunting candidate (since shooting is primarily a working-class sport in France). Opinion polls showed that the electorate flirted with other candidates before its brief fling with Le Pen: first Chevènement, then the veteran Trotskyist candidate Arlette Laguiller (but never Alain Madelin, the only full-blooded free-marketeer amongst them all). Voters thought that it was safe to play the field, since the polls also indicated that Jospin would get through the first round anyway. Le Pen was also a perverse choice for electors who demanded change, since at 73 he was the oldest of all the candidates, and for the unemployed people who voted for him, since his commitment to quit the EU would have caused more damage to the economy than the policies of any other candidate save the Trotskyists.

Yet this frivolous behaviour also reveals a deep dissatisfaction between the citizens of France and their political leaders. France remains a democracy without the people, where parties are the vehicles of the elites, where government is something done to the people, not by or for the people. More seriously still, the size of the National Front was not an accident: it has polled more than 10 per cent of the vote since 1984. The National Front is unusual among both French and European far-right parties by its sheer longevity, for other populist protest movements, such as Boulangism, Poujadism, and the leagues of the 1890s, 1920s, and 1930s, flared up quickly and died away almost as fast. Geographically, Le Pen won the departments that arc round France from the north, down the eastern border and along the Mediterranean, which defies traditional political geography. To some extent, it represents the regions of highest immigration, but this is deceptive. Many immigrants settled in these areas because they are France's border regions, and because the industries of the north and east sucked in migrant labour; their factories and mines have since closed down, and the resulting unemployment is the main reason for Le Pen's vote. The region around Paris has the greatest number of immigrants—37 per cent of the total—but it did not put Le Pen top of the poll. Rural decline has also pushed some departments to his camp, while his strongholds in the south include towns where the settlers who fled Algeria in 1962 now live, as well as North African immigrants. Sociologically, Le Pen's vote is higher among men than women, among manual workers than other occupations, and higher still among the unemployed. His supporters are likely to have been educated to 16 or 18, with relatively few passing through higher education. This profile has become more marked at each presidential election since 1988, indicating that the National Front has become an enduring part of the political landscape and not just a protest vote, while its appeal has narrowed socially. It has also displaced the socialists and communists as a working-class party: the traditional left is dead. Jospin did better among managers and professionals than among workers, largely because the thirty-five-hours law has given the former about three more weeks of holiday a year, while the latter have lost overtime. Symbolically, a vote for Le Pen was a vote on behalf of the excluded, of those who feel no connection with the Parisian elites, alienated through unemployment, fear of crime, resentment at immigration, hostility towards globalization and the European Union. Concern about immigration has real foundations because of the difficulty that many immigrants face in assimilating into French society on the one hand, and because of the difficulty that French society has in adapting to multiculturalism on the other. If these problems pushed many migrants or *Beurs* towards Islamic fundamentalism, they could scarcely avoid a collision with the secular state. Even without a religious dimension, tensions will continue between marginalized North Africans, Le Pen's constituency of the resentful, and French xenophobia. Time is more likely to exacerbate the problem than to heal it because instability and demographic pressures in the Arab world mean that the inflow of migrants will continue. The population is rising at more than 1 per cent a year in all four of the main tributaries of Muslim immigrants, Algeria, Morocco, Tunisia, and Turkey (which is relatively fast in demographic terms), and unemployment is very high in Morocco and Algeria, estimated at 23 and 30 per cent respectively for 2000. The logical solution for millions of young people is to emigrate to Europe and especially to countries where they already have relations—which for many now means France.

Chirac has at last been able to return the presidency to the status that de Gaulle intended, a dominant president with a pliant prime minister, a majority in the Senate, the National Assembly, and the regional assemblies (even de Gaulle had to accommodate a centrist Senate). Precisely because it has such a commanding grip on political power for five years, the new government has a responsibility to see through the reforms needed to restructure politics and society. Yet this grip on power may be illusory. Chirac's mandate for reform is weak because his vote in the first round of the presidential elections was low and because the electoral debates rarely discussed policies beyond the theme of security before they were overwhelmed by the campaign against Le Pen. Opposition to reform can be expected from the left, as this is the only way for it to recover lost ground, from trade unions defending their members, and from vested interests such as farmers and public-sector employees. The National Front will continue to win support among the alienated, ill-educated, and unemployed; Chirac's pre-election promises cannot all be kept; the UMP's artificial nature and the size of its majority invite internal feuding. Crucially, Chirac was in a similar position back in May 1995, when he was first elected president, only for the reforms proposed by Alain Juppé to be blocked six months later by a massive wave of strikes and protests. In the elections of April to June 2002, millions of citizens claimed that they wanted change. When they are offered it, will they accept it?

Chronology

1789	14 JULY	Storming of the Bastille
	4 AUG.	Abolition of feudal privileges and dues begun
1795	5 OCT.	Barras and Bonaparte defeat a rising by royalists
1796	2 MAR.	Bonaparte given command of the Italian army
1799	9–10 NOV.	Napoleon seizes power to become First Consul (18–19 Brumaire by the Revolutionary calendar)
1800	13 FEB.	Banque de France founded
1801	15 JULY	Concordat signed with Pope Pius VII
1802	1 MAY	Law on education and foundation of the lycées
	19 MAY	Légion d'Honneur created
1803	28 MAR.	The *franc de germinal* fixed at five grammes of silver (7 Germinal)
	1 DEC.	The *livret*, or worker's identity card, created
1804	21 MAR.	Duke of Enghien shot at Vincennes; Civil Code promulgated
	18 MAY	Bonaparte becomes 'Emperor of the French'
1805	31 DEC.	The Revolutionary calendar ends
1806	10 MAY	Foundation of the University, in charge of secondary and higher education
1807	9 AUG.	Talleyrand resigns from the ministry of foreign affairs
1808	MAY	Rebellion begins in Spain
1809	15 DEC.	Napoleon divorces Josephine
1810	2 APR.	Napoleon marries Marie-Louise, daughter of Francis II of Austria
1812	14 SEPT.	The French army enters Moscow
	19 OCT.	The French army abandons Moscow
	5 DEC.	Napoleon leaves the Grand Army
1813	MAY	French forces leave Madrid
	29 DEC.	Legislative Body votes against continuing the war
1814	6 APR.	Napoleon abdicates

	30 MAY	First Treaty of Paris; France returns to the borders of 1792
	4 JUNE	Proclamation of the Charter
1815	1 MAR.	Napoleon lands in France after his escape from Elba
	18 JUNE	Battle of Waterloo
	22 JUNE	Napoleon abdicates again
	AUG.	Legislative elections return the *chambre introuvable*
	20 NOV.	Second Treaty of Paris, France returns to the borders of 1790
1816	5 SEPT.	Dissolution of the *chambre introuvable*
1817	FEB.	Law on the electoral property qualification and conditions for eligibility
1821	15 DEC.	Villèle forms a ministry
1824	16 SEPT.	Death of Louis XVIII
1825	29 MAY	Coronation of Charles X in Reims
1827	NOV.	Legislative elections weaken Villèle's position
1828	5 JAN.	Resignation of Villèle and appointment of Martignac as head of government
1829	8 AUG.	Polignac forms a ministry
1830	18 MAR.	Vote of no confidence in the ministry organized by Royer-Collard
	16 MAY	Dissolution of the Chamber; elections in June–July won by the opposition
	5 JULY	French forces capture Algiers
	25 JULY	Charles issues ordinances that suppress freedoms, provoking the 'three glorious days' of Parisian insurrection on 27–29 July
	2 AUG.	Charles X abdicates and leaves France on 3 Aug.
	9 AUG.	Louis-Philippe becomes 'King of the French'
1831	APR.	The electorate is doubled by lowering the qualifications for voting
	DEC.	Abolition of hereditary peerage
1832	16 MAY	Casimir Perier, head of the government, dies along with 100,000 others in a cholera epidemic
	12 OCT.	Soult forms a ministry with Thiers (interior), Broglie (foreign affairs), and Guizot (public education)

1833	JUNE	Guizot's law on primary education: every commune over 500 people to have a boys' primary school
1834	9–12 APR.	Workers' insurrection in Lyon, followed by rebellion and shooting on the rue Transnonain in Paris on 13 April
	21 JUNE	Defeat of the republicans in legislative elections
1835	28 JULY	Fieschi attempts to assassinate Louis-Philippe, prompting repressive laws in Sept.
1836	30 OCT.	Attempt by Louis-Napoleon Bonaparte to raise the garrison in Strasbourg
1839	12 MAY	Attempted rebellion by the left, including Blanqui and Barbès
1840	6 AUG.	Attempted revolution by Louis-Napoleon Bonaparte at Boulogne
1847	9 JULY	Barrot leads the 'banquets' campaign
	DEC.	Surrender of Abd el-Kader gives France control over Algeria
1848	23 FEB.	Insurrection in Paris
	24 FEB.	Louis-Philippe abdicates; the Second Republic is declared at the Hôtel de Ville
	23 APR.	Election of the Constituent Assembly
	21 JUNE	Decree on closure of the national workshops, which leads to fighting in Paris on 23–26 June
	10–11 DEC.	Presidential elections; victory of Louis-Napoleon Bonaparte announced on 20 Dec.
1850	15 MAR.	Falloux's law on higher education increases Catholic church's authority over the University
1851	2 DEC.	*Coup d'état* by Louis-Napoleon Bonaparte
	21–22 DEC.	Plebiscite gives a massive victory to Louis-Napoleon Bonaparte
1852	2 DEC.	The Second Empire proclaimed
1853	1 JULY	Baron Haussmann made prefect of the Seine (he holds this post until Jan. 1870)
1854	27 MAR.	Crimean War: France and Britain declare war on Russia
1855	MAY–NOV.	Universal Exhibition in Paris
1856	18 JAN.	End of the Crimean War

1859	JUNE	War against Austria in Italy: victories of Magenta and Solferino (4 and 24 June)
1860	23 JAN.	Trade treaty with Britain
	24 MAR.	Savoy and Nice joined to France
1861	31 DEC.	Emergence of the 'liberal Empire': approval of the Legislative Body is needed to raise additional taxes or funds
1864	25 MAY	Trade unions partially legalized; the right to strike is granted
1869	16 NOV.	Opening of the Suez Canal
1870	2 JAN.	Émile Ollivier forms a ministry
	8 MAY	Referendum on the reforms of 20 April produces a massive 'yes' vote in favour of Napoleon III
	19 JULY	France declares war on Prussia
	4 SEPT.	The Third Republic is declared in Paris after French armies are defeated at Metz and Sedan
1871	28 JAN.	Armistice and surrender of Paris
	17 FEB.	Thiers is made 'chief of the executive power of the French Republic'
	18 MAR.	Troops sent by Thiers fail to take cannon from Montmartre
	28 MAR.	The Paris Commune is proclaimed
	21–28 MAY	Versailles troops take Paris
	13 NOV.	Thiers declares that the republic exists, and that it will be conservative or nothing
1872	26 SEPT.	Gambetta's speech in Grenoble
1873	24 MAY	Thiers resigns; MacMahon elected President of the Republic
1877	16 MAY	MacMahon dismisses Jules Simon, recalls Broglie to form a new ministry on 17 May
	22 JUNE	Dissolution of the Chamber
	14 OCT.	Legislative elections give victory to the republicans
1879	30 JAN.	MacMahon resigns; Jules Grévy is elected President of the Republic
1880	FEB., MAR., and JUNE	Ferry's laws on higher education passed
	21 DEC.	Law on public education and secondary education for women; the École Normale Supérieure for women at Sèvres is established by this law

1881	16 JUNE	Law on free primary education
	29 JULY	Law on freedom of public meetings and the press
1882	19 JAN.	Crash of the Union Générale des Banques
	28 and 29 MAR.	Laws passed making primary education compulsory and secular
1884	21 MAR.	Trade unions recognized by a law on workers' and employers' professional syndicates
	27 JULY	Divorce legalized (Naquet law)
1886	7 JAN.	Freycinet leads a new ministry and makes Boulanger minister of war
1887	20 APR.	Border incident between France and Germany: arrest of French police commissioner Schnæbelé
	25 OCT.	Scandal of sale of Légion d'honneur decorations by Daniel Wilson exposed
	2 DEC.	Grévy resigns as President; Sadi Carnot elected President the next day
1889	27 JAN.	Boulanger wins election in Paris but refuses to march on the Élysée Palace
1890	1 MAY	First French celebration of May Day
1891	15 MAY	Papal encyclical *Rerum novarum*
	27 AUG.	Franco-Russian alliance initiated
1892	11 JAN.	Law on protectionism
	20 FEB.	Papal encyclical *Au milieu des sollicitudes*
1894	24 JUNE	Sadi Carnot assassinated; Félix Faure elected President on 27 June
	24 SEPT.	Start of Dreyfus Affair: the *bordereau* is discovered
	22 DEC.	Dreyfus sentenced to deportation for life
1895	22 MAR.	The first film is shown in Paris, 'Workers coming out of the Lumière factory'
	SEPT.	Formation of the Confédération Générale du Travail (CGT)
1896	26 MAR.	First vote in favour of an income tax
	5 OCT.	Tsar Nicholas II visits France, sealing the Franco-Russian alliance
1897	15 NOV.	Mathieu Dreyfus denounces Esterhazy as the real traitor
1898	13 JAN.	Zola publishes his article 'J'accuse' in *L'Aurore*

	30 AUG.	Henry is arrested, commits suicide on 31 August
1899	16 FEB.	Death of Félix Faure; election of Émile Loubet as President on 18 Feb.
	23 FEB.	Failure of attempted coup by Déroulède at Faure's funeral
	22 JUNE	Waldeck-Rousseau forms a government, including Galliffet (war), Caillaux (finance), and Millerand (trade and industry)
1900	16 JULY	The first Metropolitan line opens, running between Vincennes and Porte Maillot
1902	28 MAY	Waldeck-Rousseau resigns as President of the Council of Ministers
	15 JUNE	Émile Combes forms a government
1903	JULY	First Tour de France
1904	30 JULY	Chamber votes to break diplomatic relations with the Vatican
	30 OCT.	The 'affaire des fiches' exposed in the press
1905	3 JULY	Chamber votes for the Separation of Church and State, passed by Senate on 9 Dec.
1906	25 OCT.	Clemenceau forms a government, with Caillaux (finance), Picquart (war), and Viviani (the new ministry of labour)
	12 DEC.	Separation of Church and State takes effect
1907	12 MAY	Protests by Midi wine-growers begin
1908	20 JULY	Clemenceau's ministry falls
1909	11–18 OCT.	General strike on the railways, broken by the conscription of railway workers
1911	4 NOV.	Franco-German treaty on Morocco, Congo, and Cameroon follows the second Moroccan incident of 1911
1913	17 JAN.	Poincaré elected President of the Republic
	9 AUG.	Law to extend military service to three years
1914	23 FEB.	Senate rejects income tax
	28 JUNE	Assassination of Archduke Franz Ferdinand at Sarajevo
	3 JULY	Senate votes in favour of an income tax
	20–29 JULY	Trial and acquittal of Mme Caillaux for the murder of *Le Figaro* editor Gaston Calmette
	31 JULY	Assassination of Jean Jaurès; German ultimatum to France

	3 AUG.	Germany declares war on France
	26 AUG.	Viviani forms the first *Union sacrée* ministry
	6–12 SEPT.	French victory at the battle of the Marne saves Paris
1916	21 FEB.	Start of German offensive at Verdun
1917	3 APR.	USA enters the war
	20 MAY	Beginning of mutinies in the French army
	6 NOV.	Bolshevik coup in Russia
	17 NOV.	Clemenceau becomes President of the Council of Ministers and war minister
1918	18 JULY	Second battle of the Marne begins, followed by Allied counteroffensive
	11 NOV.	Armistice signed at Rethondes
1919	28 JUNE	Treaty of Versailles signed
	16 NOV.	Legislative elections won by the National bloc
1920	5 APR.–17 MAY	French troops occupy German towns
	23 SEPT.	Alexandre Millerand elected President of the Republic
	20–26 DEC.	Congress of Tours, split of SFIO and birth of the French communist party (PC)
1921	8 MAR.	Allied troops occupy three German towns
	26 DEC.	CGTU founded
1922	7–14 AUG.	London Conference on reparations
1923	22 JAN.	General strike in the Ruhr basin and occupation by French and Belgian troops
1924	MAY	Legislative elections won by the *Cartel des gauches*
	10 JUNE	Resignation of Millerand; Gaston Doumergue elected President on 13 June
1925	16 OCT.	Locarno Pact
1926	27 JULY	Poincaré forms new National Union government
1928	25 JUNE	Law replacing the *franc de germinal* with the Poincaré franc
1929	27 JULY	Resignation of Poincaré
1931	5 JUNE	Germany announces that it cannot pay reparations any more as the Depression hits
1933	30 JAN.	Hitler becomes chancellor of Germany

1934	6 FEB.	Riot in Paris; Daladier resigns the next day
	27 JULY	Alliance of the SFIO and PC
1935	24–27 OCT.	Radicals vote to join the Popular Front with the SFIO and PC
1936	7 MAR.	Hitler reoccupies the Rhineland
	3 MAY	Electoral victory of Popular Front
	7 JUNE	Matignon Agreements
	17 JULY	Spanish Civil War begins
1937	13 FEB.	Blum announces the 'pause' in reforms
	22 JUNE	Chautemps replaces Blum in a Popular Front government led by the Radicals
1938	14 MAR.–10 APR.	Second Blum ministry
	29 SEPT.	Munich conference on Czechoslovakia (attended by Hitler, Mussolini, Daladier, and Chamberlain)
	30 NOV.	Failure of general strike by CGT
1939	23 AUG.	Nazi–Soviet non-aggression pact
	1 SEPT.	Germany invades Poland
	3 SEPT.	Britain and France declare war on Germany
1940	10 MAY	German attack on Belgium begins
	18 JUNE	De Gaulle's radio broadcast on the BBC
	22 JUNE	Franco-German armistice signed at Rethondes
	3 JULY	British sink French fleet at Mers-el-Kébir
	10 JULY	National Assembly votes full powers to Pétain
	23–24 OCT.	Laval and Pétain meet Hitler at Montoire
1941	22 JUNE	Germany invades Soviet Union
	7 DEC.	Japanese attack on Pearl Harbor
1942	16–17 JULY	The 'Vel d'Hiv' roundup of Jews
	27 NOV.	Germans occupy southern zone; French fleet sinks itself in Toulon harbour
1943	30 JAN.	Formation of the Militia
	16 FEB.	Law creating compulsory labour service (STO)
	15 MAY	Jean Moulin founds the Conseil National de la Résistance
	3 JUNE	In Algiers, de Gaulle and Giraud form the Comité Français de la Libération Nationale
	8 JULY	Probable date of Jean Moulin's death
1944	6 JUNE	Allied landings in Normandy
	25 AUG.	De Gaulle arrives in Paris
1945	8 MAY	Capitulation of Germany; rioting in Sétif (Algeria)

	5–12 JUNE	Yalta conference
	21 OCT.	Referendum and election of the Constituent National Assembly
1946	20 JAN.	Resignation of de Gaulle as head of the French government
	2 JUNE	Election of second Constituent Assembly
		Constitution of Fourth Republic declares equality of men and women in all spheres
1949	27 JULY	Ratification of the Atlantic Pact (establishes NATO)
1954	7 MAY	Fall of Dien Bien Phu
	1 NOV.	Uprising in Algeria begins
1956	5–6 NOV.	Suez expedition by France and Britain
1957	25 MAR.	Treaty of Rome creating the EEC
1958	13 MAY	Government headquarters in Algiers seized by the Committee of Public Safety
	1 JUNE	De Gaulle approved as head of government
	28 OCT.	Referendum in favour of new constitution
	21 DEC.	De Gaulle elected President of the Republic
1960	24 JAN.–1 FEB.	Week of the barricades in Algiers
1961	FEB.	Organisation Armée Secrète (OAS) formed
	22–25 APRIL	Attempted coup by generals in Algiers; de Gaulle takes emergency powers
	17 OCT.	Algerians demonstrate against a curfew in Paris
1962	18 MAR.	Évian Accords on independence for Algeria signed
	3 JULY	Independence for Algeria
1963	22 JAN.	Élysée Treaty signed between France and Germany
1965	19 DEC.	De Gaulle re-elected President of the Republic, by direct vote
1966	4 MAR.	France leaves integrated NATO command
1968	3 MAY	Occupation of the Sorbonne and first barricades
	22 MAY	General strike in France: seven million workers on strike
	30 MAY	De Gaulle dissolves National Assembly
1969	28 APR.	Resignation of de Gaulle after the defeat of referendum on reforms to the regions and the Senate on 27 Apr.

	15 JUNE	Election of Georges Pompidou as President of the Republic
1970	AUG.	Demonstration by the Women's Liberation Movement
1971	21 JUNE	Mitterrand's party joins the Parti Socialiste (PS) and he becomes its first secretary
1973	OCT.	Yom Kippur War and first oil shock: price of a barrel of oil quadruples
1974	2 APR.	Death of Pompidou
	19 MAY	Giscard d'Estaing elected President of the Republic
1975	17 JAN.	Veil law on abortion passed
	11 JULY	Law on reform of divorce passed
1976		Number of unemployed reaches one million
1977	25 MAR.	Jacques Chirac elected mayor of Paris
1979		Second oil shock: price of a barrel doubles
1981	10 MAY	Mitterrand elected President of the Republic
	21 JUNE	Second round of legislative elections gives the socialist party an absolute majority of seats
	18 DEC.	Law on nationalization passed
1982	28 JAN./26 MAR.	Laws on decentralization passed
1983	MAR.	PS loses local elections and abandons socialist economics
1984	JUNE	European elections; collapse of PS to 20 per cent of the vote and breakthrough of National Front to 11 per cent
1985	10 JULY	Sinking of the *Rainbow Warrior*
1986	20 MAR.	First cohabitation begins: Chirac appointed as prime minister after the right wins the legislative elections
1988	8 MAY	Mitterrand re-elected President
1989	4 OCT.	Beginning of the affair concerning Muslim girls wearing headscarves in schools
1991	JAN.–FEB.	French forces participate in the Gulf War
1992	7 FEB.	Maastricht Treaty on further European integration signed

1993		Number of unemployed exceeds three million, 10 per cent of the workforce
	MAR.	Legislative elections and second cohabitation begins; Balladur appointed prime minister
1995	7 MAY	Chirac elected President of the Republic; Le Pen scores 15.7 per cent of the vote in first round of the election
	24 NOV.	Beginning of strikes and protests against Juppé government
1997	MAY/JUNE	Legislative elections won by left-wing coalition; Lionel Jospin becomes prime minister on 2 June
1998	13 JUNE	First law to prepare for the thirty-five-hour week; this is confirmed by further legislation on 19 Jan. 2000
1999	16 NOV.	Law creating the Pacte Civil de Solidarité (PACS) passed
2001	11 SEPT.	Attack on World Trade Center and Pentagon by al-Qaeda terrorists
2002	1 JAN.	Euro comes into circulation as a hard currency; franc withdrawn in February
	21 APR.	First round of presidential elections: Chirac and Le Pen top the poll with 20 and 17 per cent of the vote respectively
	5 MAY	Second round of presidential elections: Chirac crushes Le Pen by 82 per cent to 18 per cent
	16 JUNE	Second round of legislative elections gives an absolute majority to Chirac's Union pour la Majorité Présidentielle

Guide to further reading

A complete bibliography of the past 200 years of French history would be far longer than the rest of this book. This guide to further reading lists some of the more useful overviews in English, and details some of the monographs in English and French that have had most influence on this book.

The best thematic introductions to the whole of the nineteenth and twentieth centuries are provided by collective works, notably the three massive volumes edited by Yves Lequin, *Histoire des français, XIXe–XXe siècles* (Paris, 1984) and a more accessible single volume of essays in English edited by Martin S. Alexander, *French History since Napoleon* (London, 1999). The seven volumes of *Les Lieux de mémoire* (Paris, 1984–92), edited by Pierre Nora, are organized under Lavisse's three headings of state, nation, and republic. They include a number of chapters on the last two centuries, notably Antoine Prost's contribution on war memorials, 'Les monuments aux morts'. These volumes have been translated into English in three reduced and reordered volumes as *Realms of Memory* (New York, 1996–8), ed. Lawrence D. Kritzman.

The nineteenth century is well served by two recent general histories: François Furet, *Revolutionary France 1770–1880* (Oxford, 1992; 1st edn. Paris, 1988), and Robert Tombs, *France 1814–1914* (London, 1996). The twentieth century has been covered as a whole and for diverse periods by Robert Gildea, *France since 1945* (Oxford, 1996), Maurice Larkin, *France since the Popular Front 1936–1986* (Oxford, 1988, 1997), James F. McMillan, *Twentieth-Century France: Politics and Society 1898–1991* (London, 1992), and Richard Vinen, *France 1934–1970* (Basingstoke, 1996). Maurice Agulhon's *The French Republic 1879–1992* (Oxford, 1993; 1st edn. Paris 1990) is in the same series as Furet's volume on *Revolutionary France*; Serge Berstein and Pierre Milza's five-volume *Histoire de la France au XXe siècle* (Brussels, 1991) has not yet been translated into English.

Different perspectives on the past two centuries are provided by the political scientist Maurice Duverger in *La Démocratie sans le peuple* (Paris, 1967), by the anthropologists Hervé Le Bras and Emmanuel Todd in *L'Invention de la France* (Paris, 1981), and by Le Bras in *Les Trois France* (Paris, 1986). Theodore Zeldin broke new ground for the historian with his two-volume history *France 1848–1945* (Oxford, 1973), since republished as *A History of French Passions 1848–1945* in two hardback and five paperback volumes. Other thematic studies to note came from René Rémond, *The Right-wing in France*, 2nd edn. (Philadelphia, 1969), and Robert Gildea,

The Past in French History (New Haven, Conn., 1994). Stanley Hoffmann's long essay 'Paradoxes of the French political community' explored many of the themes also taken up by Duverger (pp. 1–117 in Hoffmann et al., *France: Change and Tradition*, London, 1963).

Apart from the mass of biographies written about personalities of this period, from Cora Pearl to Pierre Laval, two towering figures command attention, Napoleon and de Gaulle. Hundreds of volumes have been written on Napoleon alone, and the recommended starting point for further research is Geoffrey Ellis, *Napoleon* (London, 1997). The leading biography of de Gaulle is by Jean Lacouture. It is published in English in two large volumes (down from three in French), as *De Gaulle: The Rebel, 1890–1944* and *The Ruler, 1945–1970* (London, 1990 and 1991). Brief introductions have been written by Julian Jackson (*Charles de Gaulle*, London, 1990) and by Andrew Shennan (*De Gaulle*, London, 1993). These volumes deal to some extent with military history, though that is not their primary focus. *The Napoleonic Wars* by David Gates (London, 1997) provides a good textbook introduction for the former, while a more colourful view is available from the recently translated memoirs of Baron de Marbot, a Napoleonic officer and inspiration for Arthur Conan Doyle's Brigadier Gerard: Jean-Baptiste Marbot, *The Exploits of Baron de Marbot*, ed. C. J. Summerville (London, 2000). On the period of de Gaulle, Alastair Horne's books *To Lose a Battle: France 1940* and *A Savage War of Peace: Algeria 1954–1962* (London, both republished numerous times) are both immensely readable and erudite. One outstanding film must also be mentioned, *The Battle of Algiers* (Italy, 1965), co-produced by Gillo Pontecorvo and Saadi Yacef, a leader of the FLN, who played himself in the film.

The French countryside and rural life have been portrayed in numerous ways. Classic portraits of rural France of the late nineteenth and mid-twentieth centuries are the life of Ephraïm Grenadou, written with Alain Prévost, *Grenadou, paysan français* (Paris, 1966), and the sociologically minded accounts of Roger Thabault, *Mon village: ascension d'un peuple* and Laurence Wylie's *Village in the Vaucluse* (3rd edn. Cambridge, MA, 1974). Important academic works are by Xavier de Planhol and Paul Claval, *An Historical Geography of France* (Cambridge, 1994, 1st edn. Paris, 1988), Annie Moulin, *Peasantry and Society in France since 1789* (Cambridge, 1991; 1st edn. Paris, 1988), and Eugen Weber, *Peasants into Frenchmen* (London, 1979).

Introductions to the long debates about the performance of the French economy can be found in essays by Roger Magraw and Kenneth Mouré in Alexander, *French History since Napoleon*, cited above. For the nineteenth century, the best starting point is the concise survey by Colin Heywood, *The Development of the French Economy, 1750–1914*, 2nd edn. (Cambridge, 1995). Other books in English include Maurice Lévy-Leboyer and François

Bourguignon, *The French Economy in the Nineteenth Century* (Cambridge, 1990), while Clive Trebilcock put France into a European context with *The Industrialization of the Continental Powers 1780–1914* (London, 1981).

Turning to social history, two essays should be noted first. The definition of social classes used here comes from Jürgen Kocka in his article 'The study of social mobility and the formation of the working class in the nineteenth century', *Mouvement Social*, 111 (1980), pp. 97–117. The paradox of high worker militancy with low union membership is examined by Alain Cottereau in 'The distinctiveness of working-class cultures in France, 1848–1900', pp. 111–54 in Ira Katznelson and Aristide R. Zolberg, eds., *Working-Class Formation: Nineteenth Century Patterns in Western Europe and the United States* (Princeton, NJ, 1986). On the family, see especially Martine Segalen, *Historical Anthropology of the Family* (Cambridge, 1986), and Louise A. Tilly and Joan W. Scott, *Women, Work and Family* (New York, 1978). Other important works include Christophe Charle, *A Social History of France in the 19th Century* (Oxford, 1994; 1st edn. Paris, 1991), Gérard Noiriel, *Workers in French Society in the 19th and 20th Centuries* (Oxford, 1990; 1st edn. Paris, 1986), Jean-Pierre Chaline, *Les Bourgeois de Rouen* (Paris, 1982), and the autobiography of Martin Nadaud, *Mémoires de Léonard, ancien garçon maçon* (Paris, 1976 edn.). Two further books cover what their titles indicate: Ralph Gibson, *A Social History of French Catholicism, 1789–1914* (London, 1989), and James F. McMillan, *Housewife or Harlot? The Place of Women in French Society 1870–1940* (Brighton, 1981).

Finally, the following works deal with specific themes or periods. Isser Woloch's *The New Regime* (New York, 1994) has been crucial to Chapter 1 of this book. Ernest Renan's lecture of 1882 still makes good reading: 'Qu'est-ce qu'une nation?', *Œuvres Complètes*, I (Paris, 1947). The main work used here on the economics of empire is Jacques Marseille, *Empire colonial et capitalisme français: histoire d'un divorce* (Paris, 1984). It is summarized in an article in English, 'The phases of French colonial imperialism', *Journal of Imperial and Commonwealth History*, XIII (1985), 3. In addition, two useful introductory books on the conquest and loss of empire respectively are Robert Aldrich, *Greater France: A History of French Overseas Expansion* (Basingstoke, 1996), and Antony Clayton, *The Wars of French Decolonization* (London, 1994). The best short account of the Dreyfus Affair is Eric Cahm, *The Dreyfus Affair* (London, 1996, 1st edn. Paris 1994), while Julian Jackson's account of *The Popular Front in France* (Cambridge, 1988) is an excellent interpretation of another complex event. Zeev Sternhell's work on Fascism is more contentious, at least in France, but should not be ignored. His main works on this are *La Droite révolutionnaire, 1885–1914: les origines françaises du fascisme* (Paris, 1978) and *Neither Right nor Left: Fascist Ideology in France* (Princeton, NJ, 1986). Pierre Birnbaum, *Antisemitism in France* (Oxford, 1992, 1st edn.

Paris 1988), and Michel Winock, *Nationalisme, antisémitisme et fascisme en France* (Paris, 1990) make further contributions to the debate on Fascism and anti-Semitism in France. Françoise Gaspard's *A Small City in France* (Cambridge, MA., 1995; 1st edn. Paris, 1990) is an account of the electoral breakthrough of the National Front in her home town of Dreux in 1989.

Important works in French on the period from the Great War to the Liberation are Jean-Jacques Becker, *1914: comment les Français sont entrés dans la guerre* (Paris, 1977), Yves Durand, *La France dans la seconde guerre mondiale* (Paris, 1989), Pierre Laborie, *L'Opinion française sous Vichy* (Paris, 1990), Guy Pedroncini, *Les Mutineries de 1917* (Paris, 1967), and Nicolas Rousselier, *Le Parlement de l'éloquence* (Paris, 1997). In English, see Jean-Pierre Azéma, *From Munich to the Liberation 1938–1944* (Cambridge, 1984, 1st edn. Paris, 1979) and Robert O. Paxton, *Vichy France: Old Guard and New Order, 1940–44* (New York, 1972). For Vichy France, another film must be mentioned, *Le Chagrin et la pitié* by Marcel Ophuls (1971).

Index

Note: page numbers in *italic* refer to illustrations; 'n' indicates a footnote on that page.

11 Sept 2001: 243, 253

abortion 28, 142, 177, 214, 236
Action Française 96, 118, 119, 120, 160, 161, 162
Adenauer, Konrad 240
African colonies 65, 86, 87, 88, 198, 241, 244–5
agricultural industry 2–3, 43–5, 59, 125, 147, 156, 166–7, 250
    Fifth Republic 224–5, 226–7
    and Great Depression (1873–96) 49, 82–3
    wine-growers' strike 104–5
Alain (Émile Chartier) 143
Algeria 28, 65, 86, 89, 93, 249, 260
    war in 192, 193, 198–200, 204–6
Alibert, Raphaël 175, 180
Allègre, Claude 225
Alliance Démocratique 80, 129–30, 131
Alliance Libérale Populaire 80
Alsace 49, 69, 76, 120, 146, 154, 173
Alsace-Lorraine 12, 85, 129, 138
André, Louis 102
anti-Americanism 238–45
anti-Bolshevism 130
anticlericalism 70, 76, 78, 90, 97, 101, 131, 133
anti-communism 167
anti-Fascism 163, 168
anti-globalization 225
anti-Semitism 167, 170–1, 192
    Third Republic 83, 85, 92, 94
    Vichy regime 176, 178, 190–1
Arab world 241, 244, 253
ARAC (Association Républicaine des Anciens Combattants) 143
Asian colonies 86, 87, 88
Atlantic Alliance 190

Aubry, Martine 258
Auclert, Hubertine 107
Auriol, Vincent 169, 191
automobile industry 111, 145, 156, 186, 226
aviation industry 156, 166, 186

Badinter, Raymond 217
bagnes (penal colonies) 97–8
Balkans 114, 242
Balladur, Édouard 222
banking industry 50, 83, 186
Banque de France 14, 31, 122, 138–9, 154–5, 164, 166, 186
Barbès, Armand 58, 60
Barbusse, Henri: *Le Feu* 119
Barre, Raymond 214, 216, 220
Barrès, Maurice 85, 94, 96, 98
Barrot, Odilon 55, 56, 59, 62
Barthou, Louis 131, 194
Beauharnais, Joséphine de 8, 9, 21
Beauvoir, Simone de 147–8
Becker, Jean-Jacques 117
Benda, Julien 95
Bérégovoy, Pierre 221–2
Berstein, Serge 167
Beuve-Méry, Hubert 178
Bidault, Georges 188, 189, 209–10
biens nationaux 12, 15, 17, 25, 30
Birnbaum, Pierre 94
birth control 28, 30, 108–9, 142, 236
birth rates 28, 29, 30, 111, 141–2, 228, 248
births, registration of 14, 15
Bismarck, Otto von 66–7, 69, 71
Blanqui, Auguste 58, 60, 67, 68, 70
Blum, Léon 136, 164, 165, 168–9, 188, 195
Bolshevism 163, 180
Bonaparte family 8, 9–10, 21, 68

Bonaparte, Louis-Napoleon 24, 34, 54, 56, 58, 61–4, 97
  see also Napoleon III
Bonaparte, Napoleon *see* Napoleon I
Bonnet, Georges 169
Boulanger, Georges 9, 85–6
Bourbon dynasty 26, 31–2, 50
  see also Louis XV; Louis XVI; Louis XVIII
Bourbon Restoration 10, 24–7, 32
bourgeoisie 30–1, 38, 39–40, 41, 77–8, 234
Bourguignon, François 49
Boussac, Marcel 125, 148–9
Bouvier, Jeanne 107
Bové, José 2, 3, 225
Brandt, Willy 240
Briand, Aristide 102, 104, 118–19, 120, 133, 134, 194
Broglie, Albert de 71, 72
Broglie, Victor de 58, 62, 67
Bugeaud, Thomas-Robert 59
Bush, George W. 253

Cagoule movement 167
Caillaux, Joseph 115, 120, 133, 138, 139
  finance minister 80, 98, 99, 102
Cambacérès, Jean-Jacques-Régis de 14–15
Canard enchaîné, Le 119, 121
CAP (Common Agricultural Policy) 3, 224, 227, 241, 250
Carlyle, Thomas 8
Carnet B 118, 120
Carnot, Sadi 85, 92
Cartel des gauches 137–9
Catholic church 5, 11, 32–3, 55, 58–9, 78, 109–10, 177
  Concordat 12–13, 17, 25, 138
  and education 61–2, 99–100
  separation from state 4, 96, 99–101, 249
Cavaignac, Louis-Eugène 61
censorship 17–18, 82, 119, 121, 122, 129
Centre Démocrate (formerly MRP) 210

Centre National de la Recherche Scientifique 167
CFDT (Confédération Française Démocratique du Travail) 209, 231
CFLN (Comité Français de Libération Nationale) 183–4
CFTC (Confédération Française des Travailleurs Chrétiens) 151, 158, 187
  see also CFDT
CGPF (Confédération Générale de la Production Française) 145, 165, 168
CGT (Confédération Générale du Travail) 83, 124, 127, 151, 158, 163, 165
  Congress of Lyon (1919) 149–50
  during First World War 117, 118, 124, 127, 128
  under Fourth Republic 185, 187
  May '68: 233
  and strikes 127, 150, 187, 231
CGT Force Ouvrière 187
CGTU (Confédération Générale du Travail Unitaire) 150–1, 158, 163, 165
Chaban-Delmas, Jacques 207, 212, 213
Chaline, Jean-Pierre 40
Changarnier, Nicolas 61
Charles X 5, 27, 32, 34, 52–5, 64–5
Chartier, Émile *see* Alain
Chateaubriand, François René, viscount of 8, 19, 23–4, 27
chemical industries 31, 146, 156, 226
Chevaliers de la Foi 22, 54
Chevènement, Jean-Pierre 212, 258, 259
children, employment of 35–6, 42
Chirac, Jacques 2, 3, 76–7, 213, 214, 216, 248, 253
  assessment of 261
  and cohabitation 219–20, 222–5
  and EU 242–3
  presidential elections (2002) 256, 257, 258
Churchill, Winston 182, 196

citizenship 4, 27, 112, 179–80
Citroën, André-Gustave 125, 148–9
Civil Code 14–16, 25, 31, 74
civil servants 10, 38–9, 59
class formation 35–44
classes moyennes 40
Clemenceau, Georges 75, 129, 130, 134
   in power 102, 104, 105, 123, 128–9,
      131–2, 149
   and press 95, 119, 120, 121
Clémentel, Étienne 124, 145
Clinton, Bill 253
CNPF (Conseil National du Patronat
      Français) 187
CNR (Conseil National de la
      Résistance) 183, 184, 186, 188
coal industry 41, 46, 47, 83
Code de l'Indigénat 89
Code Napoléon 14
Code of Civil Procedure 15
Code of Criminal Procedure 15
cohabitation 202, 219–20, 222–5, 247
Cold War 189–90, 198, 243–4
collaboration 173–4, 178–9, 196
collective factory system 41, 50
Colonial Exposition 197
colonies 33, 88, 198
   Fourth Republic 191, 192
   Third Republic 86–9
colons see *pieds noirs*
Combes, Émile 99, 102
Comintern 161, 163
Comité de Secours National 118
Comité des Forges 124
Comité National Français 183
Comités de Défense Paysanne 160
Commercial Code 15, 31
Commissariat Général aux Questions
      Juives 180
Common Market 197
Commune 24, 69–70, 98
communications 44, 77, 79
   see also railways
communism 130, 154, 158
Communist International
      (Comintern) 161, 163

Communist party 209
   Fourth Republic 185, 187, 188, 189
   Third Republic 159, 163, 164, 171
   under Vichy 178, 181, 182
Concordat 12–13, 17, 25, 96, 99, 138
Confédération de la France Meurtrie
      143
Confédération Générale Agricole 187
Confédération Générale des Cadres 187
Confédération Paysanne 2, 225, 235
Conference on Security and
      Cooperation in Europe 243
Congress of Lyon 149–50
Congress of Paris 65
Congress of Tours 136
conscription 10, 13, 14, 16, 76–7, 103–4
Conseil de Défense de l'Empire 183
Conseil National des Femmes
      Françaises 109
construction industry 41, 226
Convention 13, 16, 18, 25
corruption 79, 84, 92
Corsica 7, 8, 33, 200, 255
Cottereau, Alain 42–3
Courbet, Gustave 24
Couve de Murville, Maurice 210
craftsmen 112, 146–7
Crédit Agricole 227
Crédit Mobilier 50
Cresson, Edith 221
crime 256, 257
Criminal Code 14, 15
Croix de Feu 160
currency:
   assignats 13–14, 30
   euro 242, 251
   European monetary snake 216, 241
   franc, introduction of new 225–6
   franc crises 133–4, 135, 138–9, 144–5
   franc de germinal 14, 154
   gold standard, return to 6, 153–4
cycling 110
Czechoslovakia 195, 197

Daladier, Édouard 159–60, 162, 164,
      169–70, 171, 195

Darlan, François 175, 178
Darquier de Pellepoix, Louis 180
DATAR (Délégation à l'Aménagement
    du Territoire) 228
Daudet, Léon 120, 131
Dawes Commission 134, 135
de Gaulle, Charles 9, 45–6, 96–7, 188–9,
    227
    and Algerian crisis 200, 204–6
    and anti-Americanism 238–9, 243
    and eastern bloc 239–40
    and Fifth Republic 203–4
    foreign policy 196, 238–41
    and Free French 182–3
    liberation 184–5
    May '68: 210, 233
    'monarchy' 207–11
    provisional government 184, 199
    and Resistance 181–2
de La Rocque, François 160, 178
de Lesseps, Ferdinand 91–2
de Mun, Albert 90
death rates 29, 140, 228
deaths, registration of 14, 15
Debré, Michel 203, 204, 207, 227
Declaration of the Rights of Man and
    of the Citizen 19
Defferre, Gaston 209, 212
Delcassé, Théophile 80, 91, 118
Delors, Jacques 222, 242
democracy, assessment of 246–7
d'Enghien, Louis-Antoine-Henri de
    Bourbon-Condé, duke 18
Déroulède, Paul 9, 85, 96, 99, 161
Deschanel, Paul 131–2, 133
Directory 8, 16, 18, 25
divorce 14, 15, 25, 76, 109, 177, 214, 236,
    248
Doriot, Jacques 160, 178
Doumergue, Gaston 137, 162–3
Dreyfus, Alfred 94–5, 96
Dreyfus, Mathieu 95
Dreyfus Affair 92–8
Drumont, Édouard 92, 96
Dunoyer de Segonzac, Captain
    178

Durand, Yves 178
Duverger, Maurice 9, 80, 208, 247

École de Sèvres 75
École Libre des Sciences Politiques
    (Sciences-Po) 39
economy 31, 35, 44–51, 60, 77, 122, 123
    assessment of 250–1
    budget deficits 155, 156, 157
    and colonies 86–7
    deflation 135, 156, 157, 169
    devaluation 133–4, 155, 156, 168, 169,
        186, 218
    First World War 122–5
    franc, defence of 155–6
    Great Depression (1873–96) 82–3
    growth of 47, 48, 59, 144–6, 233–4
    income tax 14, 99, 102–4, 123
    inflation 123, 145, 186, 215, 216, 218,
        227
    modernization 192, 201
    national market, development of 35,
        44–6
    population growth, effect of 46, 49
    second industrial revolution 110–11
    state intervention in 157, 250–1
EDC (European Defence Community)
    190, 192, 197
education 26, 147, 228–9
    Catholic church and 61–2, 99–100
    Fifth Republic 214, 217, 218–19
    for girls 13, 35, 76
    lycées 13, 35
    primary schools 13, 25, 35, 154
    reforms 13, 154, 167
    Second Republic 61–2
    student unrest 232
    teacher training colleges 35, 75
    Third Republic 75–6
    universities 13, 26, 35
    Vichy regime 177–8
    for women 75, 76, 99, 101, 108
EEC (European Economic
    Community) 193, 212, 226, 227,
    240, 241–2
Eiffel, Gustave 91–2

Eiffel Tower 89
Einaudi, J.-L. 206n
electrical industry 146, 156, 186
Élysée Treaty 240
EMS (European Monetary System) 216, 218, 242
Entente cordiale 114
Entente Républicaine 131, 132
ERM (Exchange Rate Mechanism) crisis 222
Esterhazy, Ferdinand (Walsin-) 95
Étienne, Eugène 87, 88, 89
EU (European Union) 2, 3, 242–3, 252
European Central Bank 252
European Coal and Steel Community (Monnet-Schumann plan) 190
European monetary snake 216, 241
European Parliament, direct elections to 215
Évian Accords 206
Express, L' 191–2, 209

Fabius, Laurent 219
family life 37, 236, 248
Fascism 160, 161, 163
fashion industry 127, 148
Faure, Edgar 193, 198
Fédération de la Gauche Démocrate et Socialiste 209
Fédération Nationale Catholique 138
Fédération Républicaine 80
fellaghas (nationalist fighters) 205
feminism 106–10, 235–6
Ferry, Jules 74, 75, 80, 87
Fifth Republic:
    agriculture 224–5, 226–7
    Algeria, independence of 204–6
    anti-Americanism 238–45
    assessment of 253–5
    cohabitation 202, 219–20
    constitution 203–4
    diarchy 211–16
    economic policies 217, 225–6
    education 214, 217, 218–19
    foreign policy 238–41
    Gaullist 'monarchy' 207–11

internal problems 254–5
    May '68: 232–3
    monetary policies 216, 218, 225–6
    politics, alternation in 217–19, 221–2
    presidential elections (2002) 255, 256–61
    social changes 230–5
    social crisis 254–5, 256
    social geography 229
    social policies 217–18
    social revolution 235–8
    social transformation 225–32
    strikes 3, 223, 231
    unemployment 236–7, 255–6
film industry 110, 167, 251–2
First World War 140
    economy 122–5
    effect on demography 141–2
    effects on society 6, 147–9
    morale during 121–2, 125–8
    mutinies 126–7
    outbreak of 113–15
    pacifism 117, 118, 120, 121
    veterans 142–4
FLN (Front de Libération Nationale) 199, 204–5, 206, 206n
Foccart, Jacques 241
foreign policy 60, 61, 64–6, 68, 137, 238–41
    assessment of 252–3
Forest Code 25, 54
Fouché, Joseph 18–19, 24, 26
Fouillée, Alfred 11–12
Fourastié, Jean 185
Fourcroy, Antoine 13
Fourth Republic:
    communist party 185, 187, 188, 189
    economic policies 186, 201
    modernization 185–6, 187
    parliamentary institutions 188, 189–90
    political parties 187–8
    social policies 187, 193
    trade union movement 185, 187
    tripartism 188, 189
Francis of Austria 21

Francisme 160
Franco-Prussian war 49, 67, 68–9
Free French 182–3
freemasonry 78, 102, 178, 180
French Guiana 86, 98
French Revolution 7–8, 25
French Union 198
Freycinet, Charles de 35, 74, 75, 77, 87
Furet, François 34, 73

Galliffet, Gaston-Alexandre-Auguste, marquis of 98–9
Gambetta, Léon 69, 72, 74–5, 77, 140
Garde Mobile 61
Gaullism 208–9
Geneva Protocol 138
Geyl, Pieter 23
Giraud, Henri 183
Giscard d'Estaing, Valéry 209, 210–11, 216, 242, 243
    diarchy with Pompidou 211–16
    economic policies 215, 227
    political reforms 214–15
    presidential elections (1974) 213
    and USSR 243–4
GM crops 2, 3
Goethe: on Napoleon I 7
Gravier, Jean-François 201
Great Depression (1873–96) 49, 82–3
Great Depression (1930s) 153, 154–9
Great War *see* First World War
Green movement 254, 258, 259
Grévy, Jules 84
guerre des Demoiselles 54
Guesde, Jules 105, 118
Guillot, Marie 108
Guizot, François 35, 57–8, 59, 65
Gulf War 241, 243, 244, 252

harkis (Algerians loyal to France) 206
Haussmann, Georges-Eugène, Baron 50–1
Hautpoul, General 62
Henri, comte de Chambord 71
Henry, Hubert Joseph 95, 96, 97

Herriot, Édouard 130, 136–8, 151, 154, 159, 162
    and *Cartel des gauches* 137–9
Hitler, Adolf 171, 172, 195
Homme enchaîné, L' 119, 120
Homme libre, L' 119
housing 154, 230, 235
Hue, Robert 258, 259
Hugo, Victor 54, 82
Hundred Days 24
hunting 224, 259

immigration 141, 142, 228, 237, 248–50, 259–60
    and citizenship 112
    and crime 257
    French attitudes to 4–5
    and unemployment 5, 157
Independent Republican party 208–9
Indochina 87, 88, 191, 192, 198
industry 47, 48–9, 166, 169
    assessment of 250, *251*
    children in 35–6, 42
    crises in 59, 156
    during First World War 123–4, 127–8
    growth of 31, 145
    modernization 144, 145, 185–6, 187
    women in 41, 42
infant mortality 28
infanticide 28
inflation 123, 145, 186, 215, 216, 218, 227
insurance industry 154, 186
International Working Men's Association 67
iron and steel industries 31, 46, 47, 146, 156
Islam *see* Muslims
Israel 213, 215, 241, 244

Jacobins 10, 11
    Terror 16, 18, 25, 55
Jaurès, Jean 95, 96, 97, 105, 115, 116, 118, 138, 217
Jeunesse Agricole Chrétienne 227
Jeunesses Patriotes 160, 162

Jews 4, 10, 12, 78, 93, 94
    see also anti-Semitism
Jospin, Lionel 222, 223, 224, 256
    presidential elections (2002) 257,
        258, 259, 260
Jouhaux, Léon 117, 124, 187
Jourdan's law (1798) 16
Jouvenel, Robert de 81
July Monarchy 34, 39, 56–9, 65
Juppé, Alain 222, 223, 258, 261
Jurgan, Jeanne 36

Kennan, George 116
Keynes, John Maynard 129, 169
Kocka, Jürgen 38
Kohl, Helmut 242

Laborie, Pierre 179
Labour Charter 177
Lafayette, marquis of 53, 55
Laffitte, Jacques 55–6
Lamartine, Alphonse de 60, 61
Latin America 244
Laval, Pierre 157, 174, 178, 180, 181, 184,
    195
Lavisse, Ernest 73, 75
Le Bras, Hervé 30, 41, 105–6
Le Chapelier, Jean 15–16
Le Pen, Jean-Marie 220, 222, 237
    elections (2002) 256, 258, 259–60
Le Play, Frédéric 50
League of Nations 137, 138, 194
Lebrun, Albert 162
Lecanuet, Jean 210
Leclerc, Jacques-Philippe 184, 198
Ledru-Rollin, Alexandre 60, 61
legal codes 10, 14, 25
Légion Française des Combattants 176
Legion of Honour 14
Legitimists 56
Legrange, Léo 165
Lenin, V. I. 135
Leo XIII, pope 89–90
Lévy-Leboyer, Maurice 49
Libre Parole, La 92, 94
Ligue des Femmes Françaises 109

Ligue des Patriotes 85
Ligue Patriotique des Dames
    Françaises 109
livret (workers' identity card) 16, 50,
    91
Londres, Albert 98
Lorraine 49, 69, 76, 120, 146, 173
    see also Alsace-Lorraine
Loucheur, Louis 125
Louis XV 7
Louis XVI 13, 18
Louis XVIII 5, 16, 18, 22, 24–6, 27, 52,
    64
Louisiana Purchase 33
Louis-Napoleon see Bonaparte, Louis-
    Napoleon and Napoleon III
Louis-Philippe d'Orléans 24, 34, 50, 53,
    54, 65
    assessment of 55–9

Maastricht Treaty (1992) 221, 242
McDonald's controversy 2, 3, 225
MacMahon, Patrice de 5, 34, 68, 71, 72,
    80
Malvy, Louis 120, 138
Marinoni, Hippolyte 81
marriage 14, 15, 28, 141–2, 236
Marshall Plan 186, 187, 190, 197
Martignac, Jean-Baptiste-Sylvère-Gay,
    viscount of 53
Marty, André 149
Marx, Karl 27, 63, 67
Marseille, Jacques 87
Massu, General 200, 205
Matignon Agreement 165
Mauroy, Pierre 212, 217
Maurras, Charles 96, 160
May '68: 210, 232–3
Méline, Jules 80, 87, 90, 91, 97, 155–6
Mendès France, Pierre (PMF) 169,
    191–3, 198, 204, 209
Mendras, H. 227, 228
Mercier, Auguste 94, 96
Mercier, Ernest 159
Merrheim, Alphonse 128
Messier, Jean-Marie 251, 252

military service:
  conscription 10, 13, 16, 76–7, 103–4
  under Third Republic 76, 102,
    114
Millerand, Alexandre 98, 106, 118, 130,
    132–4, 137
mining industry 83, 104, 156
Mitterrand, François 193, 199, 204, 209,
    210, 212, 220
  economic policies 251
  elected president 216
  and EMS 242
  presidential elections (1974) 213
  and USSR 244
mobilization 67, 119, 122, 123
Mohammed Ali, pasha of Egypt 58
Molé, Louis Mathieu 58
Mollet, Guy 193, 199–200, 209, 212
monetary policies 252
  deflation 135, 156, 157, 169
  devaluation 133–4, 156, 168, 169, 186,
    218
  Fifth Republic 216, 218, 225–6
  gold standard, return to 6, 153–4
  new franc, introduction of
    225–6
Monnet, Jean 186
Monnet-Schumann plan 190, 197
Moral Order 72
Morgan Bank 135
Morny, Auguste de 64, 67
Morocco 193, 198, 249, 260
Moulin, Annie 43
Moulin, Jean 183, 217
Mounier, Emmanuel 161
MRP (Mouvement Républicain
    Populaire) 187, 188, 189, 190, 192,
    200, 209, 210
multiculturalism 4–5
multiple employment 49–50, 104, 158,
    250
Munich Agreement 169–70
Muslims 88
  in Algeria 89, 198–9
  in France 4–5, 249–50
Mussolini, Benito 195

Nadaud, Martin 42, 62, 98
Napoleon I 5, 32, 55
  assessment of 23–4
  conquest of Europe 19–21
  Continental system 31, 32
  Elba, escape from 22–3
  exile 22
  monetary policies 13–14
  Napoleonic regime 9–19
  rise to power 7–8
Napoleon III 9, 49, 50
  see also Bonaparte, Louis Napoleon
National bloc 136
  election of 129–32
  rule of 132–5
National Front 218, 237–8, 258, 259, 260
  261
National Guard 52, 55, 56, 61
national identity 27–8
nationalism 96–7, 179–80
nationality, definition of 93–4
NATO (North Atlantic Treaty
    Organization) 190, 197, 212, 239,
    243, 253
Nazi-Soviet non-aggression pact 170,
    171, 195
New Caledonia 86, 98, 219, 220, 221
Ney, Michel, Marshal 20, 25
Nicholas II, Tsar 91, 114
Nivelle, Robert-Georges 126, 127
Noiriel, Gérard 111
Nouvel Observateur, Le 209

OAS (Organisation Armée Secrète)
    205, 206
Oberg-Bousquet accords 181
OECE (now OECD) 226
Ollivier, Émile 68
Orléanists 69, 71
Ottoman empire 58, 65, 88, 114,
    149

Pacific colonies 86, 98, 219, 220, 221
pacifism 141, 171
  First World War 117, 118, 120, 121
  veterans' 143–4

PACS (Pacte Civil de Solidarité) 224, 248
Painlevé, Paul 120, 137
Palestinian state 244
Panama affair 91–2
Papon, Maurice 206n
Parti Populaire Français 160
PC (Parti Communiste) 136, 150–1, 204, 212, 215, 216, 217, 258
Péchiney, A. R. 145
Pedroncini, Guy 126–7
Pelletier, Madeleine 107–8
Penal Code 15–16
Peninsular war 20
Perier, Casimir 55, 56
Pétain, Philippe 9, 126, 127, 172, 173, 184, 196
    Jews, attitude to 180
    National Revolution 176–7
    Vichy regime 174–5
Pétainism 176, 178
Petit Journal, Le 67, 81–2
Petit Parisien, Le 81–2
Petites Sœurs des Pauvres 36
Peugeot brothers 111
Pfimlin, Pierre 200
Picquart, Georges 95, 96, 102
pieds noirs 199, 205, 206, 228, 230
Pinay, Antoine 191, 207
Pinay-Rueff plan 225, 227
Pinot, Robert 124
Piou, Jacques 80, 90
Pius VII, pope 12–13
Pius X, pope 99, 101
Planhol, Xavier de 113
Pléven plan 190, 192, 197
Poincaré, Raymond 115, 117, 120, 121, 133, 134, 154
    budgets 135, 153
    and devaluation 155
    return as premier 151, 160, 194
Poland 171, 195, 196
Pompidou, Georges 203, 207, 208, 210, 213, 233, 243
    diarchy with Giscard 211–16
    and EEC 241–2

Popular Front 159, 161, 163–71, 176
population growth 28, 29, 46, 49, 111, 141, 228
Poujade, Pierre 193
poujadisme 193, 228
prefectoral system 11, 17, 25, 63–4, 78
press 59, 161, 209
    censorship 17–18, 53, 82, 119, 122
    freedom 76
    mass circulation 67, 81–2
prison system 97–8
proportional representation 190, 219
Prost, Antoine 140, 141
prostitution 28, 36, 109
Protestants 4, 10, 12, 24, 78
Proudhon, Pierre-Joseph 67–8
Proudhonists 70
PS (Parti Socialiste) 167, 218, 219, 220, 221, 224
    under Mitterrand 193, 212, 217
    and PC 212, 216
PSF (Parti Social Français) 160
PSU (Parti Socialiste Unifié) 209

Quadruple Alliance 65

Radicals 78, 80, 130, 131, 146, 161, 190
    and government 136–7
    and Popular Front 159, 163, 164
Raffarin, Jean-Pierre 258
railways 35, 47, 49, 50, 59, 77, 79
    in Franco-Prussian war 68
    nationalization of 166
    strikes on 150
Rainbow Warrior affair 219
Ralliement 89–92
Ramadier, Paul 190
Raspail, François 60
Reinach, Joseph 95, 98
Rémond, René 9, 208
Renan, Ernest 93
Renault, Louis 158
Renault family 111, 125
reparations 132, 134, 135
Resistance movement 179, 181–2, 183, 184

Reynaud, Paul 170, 171
Rocard, Michel 209, 220–1
Rochefort, Christiane: *Les Petits
    Enfants du Siècle* 230
Rousselier, Nicolas 129
RPF (Rassemblement du Peuple
    Français) 189
RPR (Rassemblement pour la
    République) 214, 215, 216, 219,
    221
Ruhr, invasion of 134, 135
Rural Code 15
rural France 2, 15, 112–13, 146–7
Russia 91–2
    see also USSR
Rwanda 245, 253

Saint-Arnaud, Armand-Jacques Leroy
    de 62
Salengro, Roger 167
Sarraut, Albert 154
Schmidt, Helmut 242
Schnæbelé affair 85
Scott, Joan 37
Second Empire 50, 63–9
Second International 135
Second Republic 60–3
Second World War 170, 171–4, *175*,
    183–5
    see also Vichy regime
Segalen, Martine 37
Sembat, Marcel 118
Service d'Ordre Légionnaire 176
service industries 227, 250
Sewell, William 43
SFIO (Parti Socialiste, Section
    Française de l'Internationale
    Ouvrière) 188, 189, 190, 209,
    212
    rise of 105–6, 132
    split in 135–6
Sillon movement 161
Single European Act 242
slavery 16, 60
SNCF (Société Nationale des Chemins
    de Fer Français) 166

social unrest 161, 162, 163, 227–8
    see also strikes
socialist parties 80, 103–4, 130, 159, 161
    see also PS
Society of the Rights of Man 56
Solidarité Française 160
Soult, Nicolas-Jean de Dieu 55, 58
Soult–Guizot ministry 58–9
Soustelle, Jacques 199, 209–10
Spanish Civil War 163, 168, 195
Stalin, Joseph 171, 195–6
Stavisky Affair 162
Sternhell, Zeev 96, 161
strikes 150, 187
    Fifth Republic 3, 223, 231
    First World War 127–8
    in support of students 232–3
    Third Republic 83, 104–5, 127–8,
        164–6, 170
Suez canal 50, 88
suffrage 17, 54, 56, 59, 60, 62, 101, 188

Talleyrand-Périgord, Charles Maurice
    de 18–19, 22, 24, 26, 53, 55
Tardieu, André 129, 156–7, 162
tax system 25, 60, 99
    income tax 14, 99, 102–4, 123
technology 81, 110, 111
teenagers 229–30
telegraph system 79, 81
television: in elections 210
textile industry 36, 41, 108, 156, 226
    cotton 31, 46, 47, 48, 49
    silk 46, 47–8, 49, 56
Thabault, Roger 112
Thiers, Adolphe 55, 57, 58, 62, 67, 69, 71
    laws 44, 76
Third International 135–6
Third Republic 24, 68, 71–2, 84, 101, 108
    alliance with Russia 91–2
    anticlericalism 76, 78, 90, 101
    anti-Semitism 83, 85, 92, 94
    Chamber of Deputies 71–2, 79, 80,
        92, 103, 129–32
    civil war 69–70
    Colonial Army 88, 89

Commune 69–70
conscription 103–4
Dreyfus Affair 92–8
economy 50, 77, 82–3, 166
education 75–6
empire, expansion of 86–9
foreign policy 85–9
instability of governments 79–82
military service 76, 102, 114
politics of 76–7, 78, 79–82, 83–4,
    85–6, 159–63, 170–1
protectionism 90–1
Ralliement 89–92
reforms 74–6, 102
royalism 71–2
social changes 77–8, 102
strikes 83, 104–5, 127–8, 164–6,
    170
trade unions 76, 83–4, 102
triumph of (1879–85) 74–9
Thomas, Albert 124, 127, 128
Thorez, Maurice 163–4, 165, 184
Tilly, Louise 37
Tocqueville, Alexis de 27, 55, 60, 62
Todd, Olivier 105–6
Tombs, Robert 57
trade union movement 42–3, 76,
    83–4, 102, 234, 255
    see also CGT; CGTU
Treaty of Locarno 138
Treaty of London 58
Treaty of Paris (1st and 2nd) 33
Treaty of Rapallo 134
Treaty of Rome 193
Treaty of Versailles 129, 146
tripartism 188–9
Tunisia 192, 193, 198, 200, 249, 260
Turé, Samori 88
Turkey 249, 260

UDF (Union pour la Démocratie
    Française) 214–15, 216, 219, 247
UDR (Union des Démocrates pour la
    Ve République) 214
UDSR (Union Démocratique et
    Socialiste de la Résistance) 188

UMP (Union pour la Majorité
    Présidentielle) 247, 258, 261
UNEF (Union Nationale des Étudiants
    de France) 209
unemployment 5, 157–8, 236–7, 255–6,
    259
Union des Forces Démocratiques
    204
Union des Intérêts Économiques 130
Union Fédérale 143
Union Générale des Banques 49, 83
Union Nationale des Combattants
    143
Union sacrée 116–19, 120–1, 128–32, 136,
    140–1
United Nations Security Council 196
UNR (Union pour la Nouvelle
    République) 204, 207, 208, 214
urbanization 230
USA 2, 3, 242
    see also anti-Americanism
USSR 243, 244

Vallat, Xavier 180–1
Veil, Simone 214
veterans 142–4, 176
Vianney, Jean-Marie 32
Vichy regime 173–85
Vietnam 198
Villèle, Joseph, count of 26–7, 52, 64
Villermé, Louis 36
Vivendi 251–2
Viviani, René 102, 115, 118, 123

Waldeck-Rousseau, René 76, 98, 99
Wall Street crash 155
Weber, Eugen 73, 112–13
Weil, Simone 166
Weygand, Maxime 172, 175
White Terror 24–5
Wilson, Daniel 84
Wilson, Woodrow 129
Woloch, Isser 10
women 15, 78, 107, 164
    and Catholic church 32–3, 36,
    109–10

women (*cont.*):
    education 75, 76, 99, 101, 108
    and feminism 106–10, 235–6
    prostitution 28, 36, 109
    role in class formation 37–8
    sexual rights 108–9
    suffrage 101, 188
    and unemployment 157–8
    work 36, 37, 41, 42, 108

xenophobia 248–50, 257

Yom Kippur War 213, 215, 244

Zay, Jean 164, 167, 179
Zola, Émile 45–6, 83, 95, 96–7